52 Weekends
by the Sea

52 weekends
by the Sea

Brigid Benson & Craig Easton

Virgin BOOKS

Published by Virgin Books 2010

2 4 6 8 10 9 7 5 3 1

Designed by David Rowley

Maps copyright © Michael Hill 2010

First published in Great Britain in 2010 by
Virgin Books
Random House, 20 Vauxhall Bridge Road,
London SW1V 2SA

www.virginbooks.com
www.rbooks.co.uk

Addresses for companies within The Random House Group Limited can be found at:
www.randomhouse.co.uk/offices.htm

The Random House Group Limited Reg. No. 954009

A CIP catalogue record for this book is available from the British Library

ISBN 9780753519325

The Random House Group Limited supports The Forest Stewardship Council (FSC), the leading international forest certification organisation. All our titles that are printed on Greenpeace approved FSC certified paper carry the FSC logo.
Our paper procurement policy can be found at www.rbooks.co.uk/environment

Printed and bound in C&C Offset Printing Co., Ltd

To Ella and Felix, Muriel and Michael with love

Contents

Foreword by Rick Stein

Yesterday I carried out a once-yearly journey through all the forty guest bedrooms that make up The Seafood Restaurant to decide where to refurbish. They are not all actually at the restaurant but are a stone's throw away in some attractive houses nearby. In spite of the really quite comfortable interiors I was struck by the photography of Craig Easton, whether it was a couple of Padstow lobster fishermen mending their pots; a proud-looking Matthew Stevens, our fishmonger, holding a fish aloft; a tumble of rounded rocks on a beach near Padstow looking like a seal colony; or a mysterious circular crop of trees in the snow on a hilltop on the Cornwall/Devon border; or even a gaunt granite cross in the foreground with the crooked spire of St Enedoc Church and Stepper Point at the mouth of the Camel Estuary beyond. They all impose themselves in those rooms.

Craig's work seems to me to constitute one of the finest collections of photography as art; all his pictures have a sort of mesmerising quality, which in the case of our pictures of the people and scenes of Padstow creates an unforgettable atmosphere of our lovely part of the country. His photographs in 52 *Weekends by the Sea* do the same thing for some of the most beautiful and interesting parts of coastal Britain.

Brigid writes with warmth and appreciation of communities that she knows and loves, and she inspires us to explore them. The past is revisited and she introduces us to some of today's characters like 'Aunty Vi' in her teashop in South Wales and the extraordinary alchemist Lotte Glob on her sculpture croft in Scotland – the people that make our coast so diverse, fascinating and unique.

Whether it's the long walk to Cape Wrath, the most north-westerly tip of the mainland or the myriad of seabirds perched on the high cliffs of Flamborough Head, the dreamy Celtic quality of the Llŷn peninsular in West Wales and Pembrokeshire, or the art deco splendour of the heated, salt-water swimming pool at Stonehaven close to Aberdeen, Brigid and Craig's book is a delightful enticement to get in the car or on the train and leave our daily routine behind for a while.

Rick Stein

Introduction

Keep close to Nature's heart, yourself; and break clear away, once in awhile

John Muir

Sometimes you find yourself with a wealth of information that comes in useful. That's what happened with 52 *Weekends by the Sea*.

Curiosity and my work as a writer have taken me up, down and around Britain. When friends and family were looking to escape for a weekend in special places, they would ask for suggestions and it felt great to put together a capsule of inspirational ideas and tips to help them avoid wasting precious time in, for example, the café on the high street with sloppy service and a miserable manager when there was a hidden gem offering a friendly welcome, good food and quirky design just around the corner. For Craig, as a photographer, it was much the same; he'd send friends with cameras to locations that truly capture the drama, mystery and character of a landscape.

And so we realised that, between us, there was enough information to create a collection of inspirational weekends, not just for friends and family, but for anyone keen to make the most of their free time in special places around Britain.

The idea is simple: we've created fifty-two weekends that deliver a flavour of our shores. Along with great adventures and people to meet, we've included special places to eat, drink and sleep too, all carefully handpicked from our own experience.

Most importantly, nobody has paid to be included. It's who they are, what they are, and where they are that makes them all special. Some are simple affairs in extraordinary locations; others are offbeat, quirky and imaginative. Some are cheap and cheerful; others are treats well worth saving up for. Because these communities depend hugely on income from visitors, we urge you to shop locally and keep these characterful places alive.

Our words and pictures are accompanied by lovely maps, which provide a sketch of each area. We hope the combination will inspire you to pack your bags and maps to make your own discoveries and magic memories.

We'd love to hear how you get on, so please join us for more information, pictures and updates at www.52hq.co.uk.

brigid benson   Craig Easton

Places to Remember

John Lennon's holidays A lighthouse expedition Volcanic ceramics

Designed by Robert Stevenson, Cape Wrath lighthouse is a mammoth feat of engineering. The twenty-metre tower stands in splendid isolation, protecting shipping from danger around Britain's highest sea cliffs at Clo Mor.

In the top left corner of a map of the British Isles you'll find the most north-westerly community in mainland Britain at Cape Wrath and Durness. A few hundred souls inhabit an untamed territory in which it's easy to lose yourself, whether you want to or not.

This is a magnificent, mean and moody place where old tin sheds are kept on this earth by lumps of rock. There are 200 days of rainfall every year, much of it horizontal, yet the climate is unpredictable: one day, sea fog; the next, clear skies. Four seasons in one day is not unusual. Even in July there's a distinct waft of peat fires in the air.

There's primitive magic in twenty hours of daylight in June and just six in January. This is nature at large in the wild and wonderful outpost that was, for many years, the summer holiday playground of John Lennon.

While other kids hopped from Liverpool to North Wales, nine-year-old John boarded a bus to the top of Scotland. He'd stay with cousins in the family's whitewashed croft house at Sangomore, near spectacular Sango beach.

Surrounded by moorland hills, racing mountain streams, peat bogs and sandy coves, John's days in the wilderness were full of simple pleasures; walking, fishing, sketching and writing poetry. He loved it.

The croft is still there, just below the radio transmitter on the hill. A little further along the road, local people created the windswept John Lennon memorial garden in celebration of those boyhood days. Standing stones are inscribed with the lyrics of the Beatles' nostalgic song 'In My Life' and primary-school children have created a bright courtyard haven of sculptured tiles. You get the feeling John would approve.

You have to be determined to visit Cape Wrath lighthouse. It's a long way from anywhere but there are two routes. The first is a challenging slog on foot, from Sandwood Bay to the south, but this route is dangerous. The second is by ferry from Keoldale, just outside Durness.

The ferry operates only in summer, weather permitting. Fares and schedules are posted on the ferryman's board at the slipway; it pays to check them out in advance of your journey and to establish your place in the merry band of walkers, cyclists, children and dogs queuing for the Cape.

The little boat bobs across the Kyle of Durness where you disembark for a 12-mile rock and roll minibus ride along a single-track road in need of constant repair. The bus lumbers past an abandoned school and

farmsteads, the hut of a military checkpoint and straight through the largest RAF and NATO ship to shore bombing range in Europe.

Between May and September, military activity gives way to breeding seabirds and lambing. It's a good time to visit, although the short ferry-boat crossing is still dependent on the state of the sea, weather and tide.

In this wilderness, weather conditions change quickly and suitable clothing is essential. Take maps, food and drink (there are limited facilities at the lighthouse), cash for the ferry and minibus fares and binoculars: you could spot anything from red deer to killer whales. Allow around three hours for the round trip.

Designed by Robert Stevenson, Cape Wrath lighthouse is a mammoth feat of engineering. The twenty-metre tower stands in splendid isolation, protecting shipping from danger around Britain's highest sea cliffs at Clo Mor. The wild atmosphere of this remote landscape is haunting and the minibus ticket is a souvenir to treasure.

...tired?

The sea air is going to knock you out, so snuggle down in Durness by the coal-burning stove of the youth hostel or in luxury at Mackay's, restaurant with rooms.

Fall asleep to the sound of the surf at Sango Sands Caravan and Camping site.

SPECIAL PLACES

Smoo Cave

The gaping monkfish mouth of Smoo Cave is an intimidating sight. Over 15 metres high, it's the largest entrance of any sea cave in the British Isles. There are three floodlit chambers, a noisy waterfall, stalactites (going down) and stalagmites (going up) and tales of smugglers and ghosts. The sea has done its work at Smoo, having created the cavern; now only the highest tides return to visit.

Balnakeil Bay and Faraid Head

Facing west with clean rolling surf from the Atlantic, Balnakeil beach is far from the madding crowd. In August the average sea temperature is a cool 13° C but then what do you expect from a beach nearer the Arctic Circle than the south of England? Hire wetsuits in Durness village.

Sunsets are sublime and Balnakeil appears idyllic but it's been keeping dark secrets. In 1991, the shifting sands revealed a shallow grave and the skeleton of a young Viking warrior, around twelve years old, with his weapons, shield and grave goods.

From the beach it's a 2.5 mile walk to Faraid Head, a narrow peninsula of dunes and steep cliffs with stupendous views towards Loch Eriboll in the east and Cape Wrath in the west. Seabirds nest on terraced sandstone cliffs and pods of whales often pass by.

Loch Eriboll Sculpture Croft

On the shores of Britain's deepest sea loch lives Lotte Glob, a ceramic artist and alchemist whose raw materials are the rock and sediment around her. Firing these unrefined ingredients to white heat at 13,000 degrees, Lotte recreates the origins of the volcanic landscape beyond her ceramics studio. Metamorphosis begins and from the molten rock Lotte moulds fantastic creations.

On occasion, Lotte welcomes visitors to her intriguing sculpture croft where weird and wonderful creations lurk in bushes, stand proud on the hillside and wobble in the wind.

The Necessity of Wilderness

Distant shores   Pioneer John Muir   Low-impact camping

Sea breezes tug at the tent and it seems impossible to sleep but, eventually, salty

air and the hypnotic sound of the waves induce drowsiness,

transporting happy campers to the Land of Nod.

emote Sandwood Estate in the highlands of Sutherland boasts undeveloped countryside and two of Britain's best beaches: the golden sands of Oldshoremore, reached easily from a single-track road, and the distant arc of Sandwood Bay over a mile long.

Accessible only on foot, rugged Sandwood Bay is the perfect place to experience the natural high of wild camping, just you, your tent and the elements.

The rough track from Blairmore to the beach begins just under 4 miles beyond Kinlochbervie, a fishing community surrounded by the scenic peaks of Arkle, Foinaven and Ben Stack – names that inspired winning racehorses.

Given the increasing popularity of the remote beach, there's now a car park with toilets at Blairmore. From here, Sandwood Bay is around 4 miles away over the old peat path through barren moorland and lonely hills. The path can be wet at times, so take your walking boots.

While there's no view of the beach until the final stages, clifftop Cape Wrath lighthouse appears like a white thimble in the distance. The sound of Atlantic rollers crashing on the shore carries on the wind and the heart beats a little faster as the track rises over the last hill.

Roofless Sandwood Cottage is said to be haunted, but that doesn't deter wild campers from pitching their tents in the walled garden close to Sandwood Loch. Fishing for brown trout is good here; permits can be bought from the hotels in Kinlochbervie and Rhiconich.

Soft green machair separates the loch from the shore; studded with wild flowers in spring, it is a welcome contrast to the earth tones of the walk thus far. When at last the exposed beach comes into view, the scale is breathtaking; low tide reveals sand, sand and more sand. To the left is one of the most stunning sea stacks in Britain, Am Buchaille, 'the herdsman,' a Jenga-like tower of Torridon sandstone. To the right loom the dramatic cliffs of Lewisian Gneiss and Cape Wrath, the most northwesterly point of the mainland.

Spring and summer nights fall slowly in the far north of Scotland. There's plenty of time to savour the isolated splendour of the beach before crawling under canvas and zipping up the door to the outside world and the ghost of the bearded sailor that patrols Sandwood's shore.

Sea breezes tug at the tent and it seems impossible to sleep but, eventually, salty air and the hypnotic sound of the waves induce drowsiness, transporting happy campers to the Land of Nod. With morning comes the thrill of breakfast on the beach and, perhaps, the whole place to yourself before the first pilgrims of the day arrive.

Roofless Sandwood Cottage is said to be haunted, but that doesn't deter wild campers from pitching their tents in the walled garden close to Sandwood Loch.

KEEP IT LOCAL

There are few facilities in these wild places; that's all part of the attraction.

However, local business needs the support of visitors, so do your shopping at the London Stores in Badcall Inchard and the Spar in Kinlochbervie, open seven days. Both have cash machines.

Spoil yourself with langoustines and spectacular views at the Old School Restaurant with rooms at Inshegra.

JOHN MUIR AND THE SANDWOOD ESTATE

The wild land of Sandwood is protected thanks to John Muir (1838–1914), the Scottish-born conservation pioneer whose writings and passion for the wilderness influenced American Congressmen and Presidents.

Muir understood the need to escape to the wilderness once in a while. He was the son of a fanatically religious father who imposed his pious and spartan lifestyle on the boy. John escaped tyranny at home, finding freedom in nature. Recalling his childhood he wrote, *'Like devout martyrs of wilderness, we stole away to the seashore with religious regularity.'*

In the early 1900s, inspired by a four-day wild camping trip with Muir in Yosemite, President Roosevelt created five new National Parks and 150 forests. The John Muir Trust acquired Sandwood Estate in 1993.

TAKE ONLY PHOTOS LEAVE ONLY FOOTPRINTS

Wild camping is legal in Scotland, with certain restrictions. It is *not* legal in England and Wales where the landowner must give permission to camp. Considerate campers keep a low profile. Among the golden rules of low-impact wild camping are:

- keep groups small
- stay away from roads and out of sight of homes and farms
- pitch late, leave early
- don't light fires
- carry out what you carry in – leave no trace
- make a plan and let someone know where you are going.

Highland Fling

Scattered crofts Heavenly islands Good living

Beyond Ullapool on the north-west coast of Scotland there's a string of small settlements dotted around the beautiful Coigach peninsula. The scenery is breathtaking and people are few – it's an irresistible combination.

This most sparsely populated corner of Scotland is one of the oldest landscapes in Europe and part of the North West Highland Geopark that extends from the Summer Isles in Wester Ross through west Sutherland to the north coast.

A single-track road off the A835 squeezes between Loch Lurgainn and one of Scotland's best-loved hills, Stac Pollaidh (aka Stac Polly), a magnet for walkers and climbers. There's a popular direct route up the hill from the car park on the shore of the loch. It's a moderate walk of 2.75 miles, with a short but strenuous climb at the start and later an optional ascent to the ridge, which can be dangerous and requires scrambling expertise. If you like to be alone with the views, set out at first light.

Summer is a lovely time to be in Coigach. Freshly shorn sheep, like roughly peeled potatoes, totter along single-track roads, the days are long and the night skies star-spangled. Sandy beaches are clean and uncrowded; you'll probably get one to yourself. At beautiful Achnahaird Bay, there's a vast expanse of golden sand with safe swimming and heavenly picnic spots.

THE GATHERING

The traditional Coigach Gathering takes place in early July at Bardentarbet. The event starts at a reasonable hour on Saturday after a ceilidh and serious preparation in the bar on the Friday.

Rural entertainment includes fly-casting, net-mending and a hard-fought hill race. Talented pipers, accordion players and highland dancers compete for prizes in the faing (sheepfold) alongside displays of pedigree livestock.

Stop at the 'phew point' on the road to Altandhu. Climb the small hill for panoramic highland and island views of the dramatic peaks of Ben More Coigach, Cul Beag, Stac Pollaidh and Cul Mor, backed by the mountains of Sutherland, the Summer Isles archipelago at the mouth of Loch Broom and the Torridons in the distance.

Head north-west from Altandhu to the road end and sandy beach at

Reiff. From here there are views to the mountains of the Hebrides and wilderness walks to Rhu Coigach, the Cape of Coigach. A 5-mile stretch of spectacular sandstone cliffs attracts rock climbers and bird watchers.

Double back to the junction and follow the road to Old Dornie, a sheltered anchorage protected by the low-lying wildlife reserve of Isle Ristol.

One of the best ways to discover the sheltered bays, sea caves and sunbathing seals of the Summer Isles is to take a trip aboard the MV *Hectoria* commanded by Iain McLeod. The little boat sails in summer from Bardentarbet pier.

Some sailings land at Tanera Mor, the largest of the Summer Isles, at about 1.5 square miles, and the only inhabited island – many others are just tiny skerries and some are exposed only at low tide.

In the eighteenth century, Tanera Mor was a busy fishing station, exporting herring to Russia, Holland and Mediterranean ports. Now there are few permanent residents and Tanera Mor's main businesses are a fish farm, a sailing school and a residential art school. Buy Tanera Mor island stamps, issued since 1970, and homemade ice cream from the village hall.

Achiltibuie is the largest of Coigach settlements and the hub of local services. Residents are justly proud of their award-winning community hall and performance venue; facilities include a library, snooker table, showers and a pretty community garden. There's a doctor's surgery once a week and hairdressing once a month.

The single-track road continues along the coast, past scattered crofts and the rustic youth hostel at Achininver before terminating at Cul Na Craig. From here the only way through Ben Mor Coigach Nature Reserve is on foot.

Simple slate way-markers indicate the 'Postman's Path', a demanding walk of about 7 miles that must have kept the postie super-fit as he scrambled over rough and steep terrain to collect the mail from Ullapool.

Around these magical islands, there's a feeling that anything might happen. As I returned from a recent trip to Tanera Mor, I spied Gary the fisherman and his horses. He rode Polly Beag bareback with Tosca on a short rope alongside. Taking them across the shingle beach, he whispered their names and coaxed both creatures deeper and deeper into the glassy sea. Suddenly, with loud snorts and a wild tossing of manes, the pair became sea horses, swimming in tandem across the bay with King Neptune astride.

...hungry?

While Coigach is remote, essentials and luxuries are to hand.

In Polbain
Visit the Summer Isles Smokehouse for delicious, naturally smoked fish, meat and cheese. Take tea in the garden of the Coigach craft and gift shop: there's a magnificent view of the Summer Isles archipelago from here.
Don't miss the legendary Polbain Stores, selling just about everything from champagne to sheet music with thirty different whiskies, tent pegs and more in between.

In Achiltibuie
Stock up with fresh fruit and vegetables from the Achiltibuie Garden; and groceries, petrol, diesel and calor gas at the Stores.
Enjoy hearty Scottish breakfasts and light snacks at the Piping School café, surrounded by great photos of famous pipers.

...thirsty?

The rich Gaelic place names of Coigach provide clues to their geography and history. Even 'Am Fuaran' Bar at Altandhu translates as 'at the well'! The friendly welcome and local seafood make it an essential part of the Coigach experience.

The cosy crofters' bar of the comfortable Summer Isles Hotel serves food and drink throughout the day. The hotel restaurant has an award-winning chef and Michelin star.

Local people say the mountain makes its own weather and condition

about getting out of your vehicle. People have

Take the High Road

Dramatic mountain pass Highland scenery Super seafood

ere change very quickly. In swirling wind or fog, don't even think

allen from the hill that way.

If you're looking for a white-knuckle drive with jaw-dropping views, head for the Bealach nam Bò, or 'Pass of the Cattle', in the spectacular Highland scenery of Wester Ross, Scotland. From Kishorn to Applecross, the single-track mountain road is bleak, dangerous and not for the faint-hearted.

Starting at Kishorn, the road bristles with warning signs and a low-level alternative is suggested for learner drivers, large vehicles and scaredy-cats. So who is going to drive? Passengers have permission to gasp at the views; drivers must have eyes only for the snaking road ahead. Otherwise it's curtains.

The Pass opened in 1822 for use by stalkers on the flourishing Applecross estate. Traditional stalking still takes place with the aim of maintaining a healthy herd of red deer in balance with their environment. Stags are shot between August and October; hinds are shot from the close of the stag-hunting season in October to February. Signposts urge caution to walkers in the stalking season while recognising the tradition of free access to the hill.

From a fairly level start, steep inclines loom quickly into view. It's hard to see where the road is heading as it twists and turns away over beautifully constructed bridges across torrents of water cascading down the hillside. The drystone masonry and culverts are testimony to the skills of the workers who built this extraordinary pass in just four years.

The road rises steeply, passing places become more regular and the panoramic view over Loch Kishorn and Loch Carron is spectacular – but there's no time to take it all in as the road climbs steadily on through the heather.

Swerving hairpin bends become tighter and steeper and negotiating passing places on the mountain ledge can be tricky when the oncoming downhill driver is paralysed by fear. There may be times when your passengers simply cover their eyes in terror. I did!

This is the longest steep hill of any classified road in the UK and

So who is going to drive? Passengers have permission to gasp at the views; drivers must have eyes only for the snaking road ahead. Otherwise it's curtains.

after an immense climb to 626 metres, the pass levels out at an AA triangulation point.

Before getting out of the car to admire the view, you'll need an extra layer, even on a sunny day. Local people say the mountain makes its own weather, and conditions here change very quickly. In swirling wind or fog, don't even think about getting out of your vehicle. People have fallen from the hill that way.

If you're lucky and it's a clear day, the views are staggering. From here you can see the Outer Hebrides, the Kintail Mountains, Ben Nevis and the Cairngorms, the Cuillin Hills of Skye, the Kyle of Lochalsh, the Crowlin Islands and the isles of Raasay and Scalpay. It's like being on top of the world.

From the rocky summit, where it's too wet for heather to survive through winter, the road descends, past lone trees tortured by the wind, to the peaceful village of Applecross, known in Gaelic as *A' Chomraich*, the sanctuary. Here you'll find comfortable rooms at the Applecross Inn.

...thirsty?

Raise a glass to the Pass at the Applecross Inn; idyllic views and good food available all day.

Simple pleasures at Shieldaig Bar & Coastal Kitchen: local seafood in a stunning lochside location.

...hungry?

There's good food all the way this weekend – from garlic scallops with croissants in the log cabin at Kishorn Seafood Bar to pizzas and great coffee in the Broch Bar and polytunnel at the campsite in Applecross.

Don't miss the Potting Shed Café in the walled garden of Applecross House. When I first visited, the café was open but the garden was derelict. Now it's all flourishing. The restaurant funds the garden and, in turn, the produce feeds the guests. Perfect.

The sheltered village overlooks the Inner Sound of Raasay. In the seventh century, St Maelrubha sailed his curragh from Northern Ireland to Applecross and established an important monastery, second only to Iona. The holy site was a sanctuary for all, hence the Gaelic name. Norsemen destroyed it in the late eighth century. Learn more at the lovely Applecross Heritage Centre. From May to October, the Applecross estate organises accompanied low-level walks to discover local flora and fauna.

The Bealach nam Bò was the only road in and out of Applecross until the road to Shieldaig was opened in 1975. Take this route to visit the weaver's croft at Cuaig where Thomas and Lesley Kilbride's flock of grey Gotland sheep feed on heather and seaweed.

From the headland at Fearnmore, the road runs alongside Loch Torridon towards Shieldaig village, created in the 1800s to attract seamen, herring fishermen and boat builders to the area in preparation for the Napoleonic war.

Bristling with towering Scots pines, Shieldaig Island is a mystery – no one knows why the trees were planted. Were they intended for use in shipbuilding or as drying poles for fishing nets? Whatever their original purpose, gazing at them from the shore, with a glass of wine and fresh seafood platter, provides the perfect contrast to the high drama of the Bealach nam Bò.

GOOD TO KNOW

Close to the shore of Loch Carron there's a nine-hole golf course; visitors are welcome to hire clubs and play or simply sit and admire the scenery with a cup of tea on the terrace. When the clubhouse is closed, there's an honesty box for anyone keen to get a round in.

CROFT
WOOLS
AND
WEAVERS

5

Between Heaven and Hell

Highland bothy. Isolated village. Far-flung pub.

Some of Britain's highest mountains rise in Knoydart, an untamed peninsula on the north-west coast of Scotland. Wedged between the sea lochs of Nevis and Hourn – known as the lochs of heaven and hell – the magnificent 'Rough Bounds' of Knoydart feel like an escape to another world.

A cluster of shoreline cottages at Inverie is at the heart of a pioneering community that owns much of the land after a buyout in 1999. Self-sufficient in hydroelectric power, it is also the largest settlement in mainland Scotland without direct links to the road network, although you can reach this far-flung place by public transport. Trains to Mallaig connect with the TSMV Western Isles passenger ferry. From the port, the wild land across Loch Nevis is just forty-five minutes away.

Crossing on a quiet, damp day in July there were just eight of us aboard the small boat, including a Danish couple who were enjoying the Scottish experience, wearing all the wet-weather gear they could muster, on loan from their bed-and-breakfast landlady: this is the wettest part of the Highlands.

The mountain scenery around the sea loch is exhilarating with views to the Isles of Rum and Skye. A shout goes up when the skipper or crew spot leaping dolphins or diving porpoise. Remote 'plastic Mary', an incongruous shiny white Madonna on dark Rubha Raonuill rocks, intrigues passengers who spy her from afar.

On approaching Inverie, the looming mass of Sgurr Coire Choinnichean dwarfs the whitewashed specks of cottages on the shore. A friendly welcoming committee gathers at the stone pier to fetch parcels and passengers from the ferry and many make a beeline for the most remote pub on the British mainland, just a moment's walk from the quayside.

...tired?

There's a wide choice of accommodation, from the Knoydart Foundation Bunkhouse to rudimentary mountain bothies, a luxury farmhouse on the Kilchoan estate, cosy bed-and-breakfast lodgings and Long Beach campsite with compost loo and sunset view.

Bed down in a communal bothy and you can be on the hills at first light, before anyone else has even thought about a full Scottish breakfast. Carry all essentials in with you, including cooker, firewood and trowel, and you'll need to check in advance whether there's a stream for water.

...hungry?

There's a delicious smell of home baking at the Knoydart pottery and tearoom, run by sisters Rhona and Isla. After an energetic walk, settle into deep sofas by the wood-burning stove or by the big picture window and allow your thoughts to wander.

Guests staying at Doune are treated to award-winning three-course meals in the cosy, remote dining room. They cater for non-residents too but booking is essential.

The Old Forge is well used to folk getting away from everything but beer, whisky, fine wine, good food and banter. A sign in the lively bar reads 'Fancy a tune? We've got guitars, fiddle, bodhran, cellos, bongo and percussion for your use.' From a rack on the ceiling wet clothes are hung to dry over the open fire and mucky campers enjoy the benefits of the pub's hot showers and a pint.

For an easy-going weekend, you could simply mooch around Inverie shore, visit the pottery, wander in the woods or perhaps join the Knoydart Foundation rangers on a free, guided walk. There's good fishing in the shady pools of the Inverie river on the Kilchoan estate and deer stalking on the hill between September and February.

Alternatively, you could rise to the challenge of climbing a Munro, a Scottish mountain over 3,000 feet high, to experience wild Highland scenery in the company of red deer and golden eagles.

Whatever your intentions, Knoydart expeditions must be planned with care. Consult Tommy and Jim at the rangers' office in Inverie for the latest updates on the weather, rivers in spate and deer stalking, and don't forget to record your sightings in the fascinating wildlife log.

...thirsty?

From ceilidhs to wildlife, expect the unexpected at the Old Forge pub in Inverie. One evening I was there, a family of dolphins came closer to shore than anyone could remember. Dolphin playtime, right outside the door, left everyone in awe.

There's a surge of excitement as the Caledonian Sleeper from London arrives at the next platform. Bleary-eyed travellers spill out, and many cross directly to the Jacobite. At last we're ready to go: a whistle, squeals of delight and chuff chuff chuff, we're away.

Arriving at Platform 9¾

Hogwarts Express   A world-class train journey   Silver sands

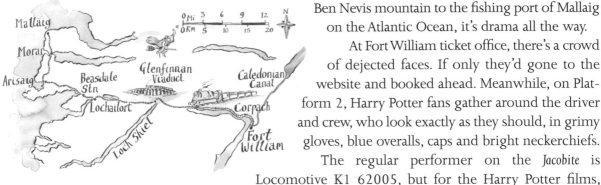

It's not often you arrive at the station to be greeted by a chalk board declaring all 400 train tickets are 'Sold Out', but that's what happens at Fort William when the train in steam is the magical *Hogwarts Express*. In the Harry Potter films, the *Hogwarts Express* leaves London's King's Cross Station from Platform 9¾ and races through dramatic scenery along 'the Road to the Isles', the route of the West Coast Railways' *Jacobite* steam train.

For two hours, from Fort William at the foot of Ben Nevis mountain to the fishing port of Mallaig on the Atlantic Ocean, it's drama all the way.

At Fort William ticket office, there's a crowd of dejected faces. If only they'd gone to the website and booked ahead. Meanwhile, on Platform 2, Harry Potter fans gather around the driver and crew, who look exactly as they should, in grimy gloves, blue overalls, caps and bright neckerchiefs.

The regular performer on the *Jacobite* is Locomotive K1 62005, but for the Harry Potter films, Locomotive 5972, *Olton Hall*, was plucked from the casting couch, given a coat of red and black paint, renamed *Hogwarts Castle* and never looked back.

Passengers wander down the train in search of their seats. The first-class carriage has fresh flowers at every table and tea is served in china

The *Jacobite* rattles along, exhaling steamy clouds of magic into the air.

cups, with jam scones. There's a wonderfully compact souvenir stall in the luggage van, run by a knowledgeable chap who fields questions from young Americans on a once-in-a-lifetime whistle-stop tour of Harry Potter film locations.

There's a surge of excitement as the Caledonian sleeper from London arrives at the next platform. Bleary-eyed travellers spill out, and many cross directly to the *Jacobite*. At last we're ready to go: a whistle, squeals of delight and chuff chuff chuff, we're away.

Well-wishers wave at the train from bedroom windows, back gardens, bridges and boats. We steam past Neptune's Staircase, Thomas Telford's flight of eight locks on the Caledonian Canal, past Corpach, where the bodies of Highland nobility were kept en route to Iona for burial, on to Loch Eil where seventeen sea walls were built to protect the railway from fierce storms.

The *Jacobite* rattles along, exhaling steamy clouds of magic into the air. Glenfinnan Viaduct comes into view and, for sheer romance, it's hard

...thirsty?

The colourful tea garden terrace of Sheena's Backacker's Lodge in Mallaig brims with pots and tubs. It's a happy place to watch the world go by.

to beat the sight of the loco in full steam puffing around the magnificent sweep of twenty-one arches, 100 feet high. Children recount the time when Harry and Ron missed the train and zoomed around the viaduct in a flying car.

The train halts at Glenfinnan station where there's a tearoom and bunkhouse in converted carriages. There's time to look around a small museum before we continue past Bonnie Prince Charlie's hiding place and dark Loch Dubh.

The notorious Beasdale Bank is a steep and steady climb. The valiant Jacobite rasps and wheezes for all it's worth up the 1 in 48 gradient but, puffed out, the famous engine begins to slide backwards.

Florence, the guard, announces that we need to try the climb again. Widely regarded as a bonus, passengers greet this news with whoops of delight. Thomas the Tank Engine aficionados recall similar problems for James, the red engine, on Gordon's hill.

A second attempt and we're back on track, past the sheltered bays of Arisaig, the most westerly station in Britain. Crossing a peaty moor, the train heads to Morar, renowned for silver sands and the deepest inland loch in Britain, where monster Morag, Nessie's cousin, lives.

At the end of the line, Gaelic signs bid you welcome, *Failte Mallaig*. The delicious reek of the sea engulfs carriages as passengers leave the train to swamp the fishing village. The vibrant harbour is opposite the station – before refrigerated lorries, the fish went from boats to the station to market.

Mallaig's main catch is shellfish, especially prawns. Fish merchants around the harbour welcome visitors, and a tasty souvenir of traditional kippers and peat-smoked salmon can be sent by post to your home.

For great views of Mallaig's lively harbour, Loch Nevis and Knoydart, try the 1.75 mile circular walk signposted from East Bay car park.

Visit Mallaig's wee heritage centre on the site of the former railway-men's dormitory, next to the railway line. Don't miss Mary Ethel Muir Donaldson's evocative portraits of Highland families and their way of life. Born in England in 1876, this remarkable social historian studied chemistry and optics in order to process her own glass negatives and prints. On her travels around isolated Scottish villages, she towed weighty camera gear in a large wooden box she called 'Green Maria'.

Take the train back to Fort William or stay longer, hire a bike from Off Beat Bikes and cycle to the extraordinary Silver Sands along the coast between Arisaig and Morar. Bikes can be hired in Fort William and booked on to the train in advance, although numbers are limited.

...hungry?

The sea air in Mallaig will whet your appetite; fortunately there's plenty of choice.

Nuri's van is amid the queue of vehicles waiting for ferries to Skye and the Small Isles. Take a seat at a cable reel table and Nuri, from Barcelona, will cook your food to order. Children love the wee pots of baked beans with added onion.

Mallaig's Fishermen's Mission Café is the place to meet local and foreign fishermen, and the second hand book sale is irresistible.

The Cabin takeaway in Davies Brae serves from a hatch in the door – freshly landed fish and chipped potatoes peeled on the premises. Make a donation to their RNLI collection and you can help yourself to a fork!

The Fish Market Restaurant on Station Road serves super-fresh seafood and is always busy. Try the chowder with a plate of langoustines.

Send smoked kippers home by post from Jaffy's Seafood at Mallaig. Kippers are herrings, split from tail to head, then gutted, salted and smoked.

If you're cycling to the Silver Sands, stop at Café Rhu in Arisaig for a bowl of broth and haggis roll.

7

Go West!

Whale watching   White beaches   Emerald forests

Ardnamurchan, the Land of the Great Seas, is the furthest point west on the British mainland. Reaching the far-flung peninsula on the north-west coast of Scotland is an adventure in itself but well worth the effort. The spectacular destination, around two hours' drive from Fort William, the largest town in the West Highlands of Scotland, is the haunt of sea eagles, whales, golden eagles and red deer.

For many visitors, the excitement begins with a short ferry crossing from Corran to Ardgour on Loch Linnhe. The alternative is a forty-mile route around Loch Linnhe and Loch Eil. The Corran Narrows crossing is one of the oldest trade routes in the Highlands. Before the arrival of the first car ferry in 1935, drovers would swim cattle from one side to the other. Today it's a roll-on roll-off journey of five minutes.

The road from Ardgour winds past whitewashed crofts and road signs in Scots Gaelic. In Strontian the post office is also a petrol station, grocer, newsagent and tearoom. Before setting out, it's worth checking the programme of events at the Sunart Centre – entertainment often includes traditional and contemporary music, films and shinty, a fast and furious game played by two teams with a leather ball and curved stick.

From Strontian to Ardnamurchan Point, it's single-track road and drivers are requested to use passing places to allow locals to overtake. The reward is often a friendly beep by way of appreciation.

Hugging the sheltered bays of Loch Sunart, where otters cavort, the road threads its way through an ancient emerald forest of feathery ferns, mossy banks and wild roses. Stop at Ard Airigh (pronounced *aard are-ee*) in the Sunart oakwoods to visit a beautiful wildlife hide of turf roof and local timber, crafted by local people. In the hush, read Gaelic poems on the walls and peer quietly across the sparkling loch. Here are wildcats, pine martens, red squirrels and golden eagles. In the wildlife log, a visitor counted nine common seals, the rare ones, on the day before my visit.

At Glenborrodale, golden eagles and merlin are among the star species of the RSPB nature reserve. Look out for a wee roadside nursery, one of my favourites, where woodland plants are assembled on a table-top theatre, each with a handwritten label.

Deer grids punctuate the road and high wire fences prevent fatal landings on passing traffic. Black-faced sheep and lambs wander the highway freely, to munch at the verge or snuggle into potholes. It is with much reluctance that they give way. Visit the Ardnamurchan Natural History Centre at Glenmore for wildlife exhibitions and live footage from hidden cameras.

At Kilchoan, the Ferry Stores and Post Office is a treasure trove of

groceries, essentials and useful things. Look out for the jolly sheep painted on the unleaded petrol pump and the deer on the diesel. Minke whales, dolphins, ferries and a lighthouse appear on the mural in the playground of the primary school. There's an honesty box at the harbour for visitor moorings and the friendly community centre is a good stop for tea, internet access, a local heritage collection, sporting facilities and the most westerly tourist information office on the mainland, open all year.

Ardnamurchan Point is a prime site for whale and dolphin watching in summer. Scanning the sea from rocks below the lighthouse, designed

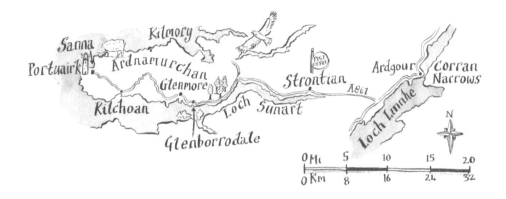

and built in 1849 by Alan Stevenson, is an easy way to lose track of time but it can be hugely rewarding. Stevenson's tower stands 36 metres high and is built from dressed Ross of Mull granite, which sparkles when the sun strikes flecks of mica in the rock. Between April and October you can climb the 152 steps and two ladders to the top of the tower for panoramic sea views.

Discover what life was like for the keepers and their families at the superb visitor centre. The job description calls for an ideal 'man of parts', with respect for the sea, a temperament for isolation, good working knowledge of engines, skills to operate radar, foghorn and radio. He should also be a useful cook and companion, a handyman of the highest quality, be self-sufficient with a small parcel of land and a handful of cattle and have his children educated under a teaching-by-post system.

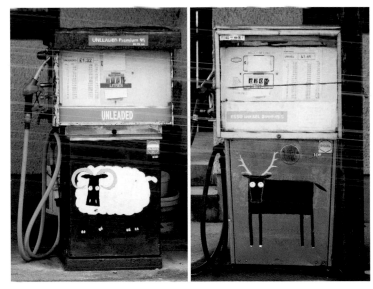

He needs to be be prepared to move on within five years. As for the pay, 'A lighthouse keeper will not make a fortune but he will be at peace with himself and the world.'

The engine room is deliciously oily, a Heath Robinson world of cogs, gauges and tubes that once operated the booming foghorn's diesel-driven air compressor. Cupboards overflow with charts and gubbins. You can imagine the ideal 'man of parts' turning up at any moment with a mug of tea and stories of the sea.

Ardnamurchan beaches are magical. The hideaway Singing Sands are reached by a forest track from Arivegaig. Portuairk and Sanna are para-

There's no shortage of good food on the peninsula including the Inn at Ardgour, a great place to watch the comings and goings of the Corran ferry. The Kilchoan House Hotel is the last bar before the ferry to Tobermory on the Isle of Mull. For a small fee you can camp in the grounds, not far from the midge machine. There's free camping in the fields of the family-run Sonachan Hotel, and breakfast is served in the bar. Local seafood is served in the bistro and you can get cosy with the wood-burning stove in winter or laze on the deck in summer. After climbing the lighthouse tower, reward yourself at the stable block café where there's good coffee and a lovely cobbled floor.

dise beaches of white sand and icy clear water that makes you gasp as it grips you around the middle. Trace the prints of Sanna's tottering sheep and lambs to sheltered dips in dunes studded by wild flowers and thyme. The scenery is spectacular, and the walk from Portuairk to Sanna Point is like a beautiful dream. Views of the Small Isles of Eigg, Rum and Muck are heavenly. Kilmory is another favourite, reached by a bridge over a gurgling stream and through a parade of yellow flag iris in late spring. The beaches feature in collections of Ardnamurchan walks from local stores.

Seaward

A seaside canal Artists Ancient woods

The remote Crinan Canal in Argyll and Bute is known as Britain's most beautiful shortcut. Opened in 1801, the waterway links the Sound of Jura and the west coast of Scotland with Loch Fyne and the Clyde Estuary. The alternative route, around Knapdale and the Mull of Kintyre, would add 100 miles to the journey.

The peaty black canal travels 9 miles through fifteen locks from Ardrishaig on Loch Gilp to the sea at Crinan – once a bustling port, now an idyllic haven.

From 1847, passenger boats on the canal followed 'the Royal Route' taken by Queen Victoria, from the Clyde, via Crinan, to Fort William and Inverness. The passenger steamer SS *Linnet* had priority over all other vessels. Bound 'for the North and Oban', it connected with onward boats at Crinan. The Clyde puffers also used the canal. For Scotland's west coast and islands, they were a lifeline: delivering coal and collecting whisky.

Today, setting out along the towpath from Crinan on the sea to Ardrishaig on Loch Gilp is a blissful weekend treat, and walking in the opposite direction is equally beautiful. The coastal scenery is magnificent and you can watch pleasure boats working their way up and down the locks, just as the puffers used to.

Allow a day for the return trip of 18 miles, or three hours for one way.

Alternatively, hire a bike from Crinan Cycles in Lochgilphead.

At Crinan harbour, a visit to the family-run Crinan Hotel near the sea lock is a must. Frances Macdonald, one of Scotland's most highly acclaimed contemporary artists, is at the helm with her husband, Nick Ryan. Together, they have made the hotel a heavenly oasis; staying there is a real treat.

From the restaurant and rooms, panoramic views of the mountains of Mull, the islands of Scarba and Jura and Loch Crinan are breathtaking. After a day walking the canal, a freshly landed seafood supper is a mouth-watering prospect. Push the boat out for a balcony room and you can sit out with a lighthouse and the whitewashed buildings of Crinan harbour at your feet.

Around the hotel, Frances's magnificent seascape paintings capture the luminous beauty and restless moods of Argyll and the Western Isles. Her trademark application of colour with a palette knife gives texture to the rugged landscape.

The work of her son, Ross Ryan, printmaker and painter, is also on

...tired?

Staying at the Crinan Hotel is a very special experience. If you are on a budget, the friendly Empire Travel Lodge, a converted cinema in Lochgilphead makes a great alternative.

...thirsty?

Halfway along the canal, the Cairnbaan Hotel, beside Lock 5, makes a welcome stop for refreshment.

Lochgilphead's oldest and best-loved pub is the Comm, opposite the children's playground and paddling pool on Front Green. For pensioners there's a special price deal of half a pint and a dram. Illuminated signs above the wee bar request model behaviour: 'Pay Honourably Be Good Company'.

show. Look out to sea from the hotel and you might see him zipping across the waves in a dinghy, on his way to a remote and enchanting boatshed studio where it would be hard not to feel creative. His work is large and it's a tight squeeze under the boatshed studio's sloping slate roof. Ross enjoys the construction process involved in creating the final print. Fish, boats and fishermen are recurrent themes in his work.

Passionate and knowledgeable about the sea, Ross is the local coast-guard and organiser of the annual Crinan Classic Boat Festival in July, an informal gathering of wooden boats that combines relaxed summer racing with whisky-tasting.

Ross inherited a magnificent racing yacht, *The Truant*, from his godfather, Bob Davidson. Commissioned in 1909 by Sir Ralph Gore, Commodore of the Royal Yacht Squadron, she enjoyed a glorious career before ending up in an Irish potato field. Rescued in 1952 and now fully restored, she is available to charter for adventures from the hotel.

From Crinan, the tranquil and beautiful shipping 'shortcut' winds through magnificent coastal scenery alongside emerald green Crinan

Wood, ringing with birdsong. High on the hill, ancient oaks are sculpted by the wind. Moss, lichen and thirteen different types of fern thrive on moisture-laden air from the sea. For views over Crinan harbour and distant islands, it's worth taking the signposted diversion from the canal path to explore this special place.

Look out for the studio of painter and printmaker Fraser MacIver at the Wagon Press. His exuberant canalside garden and colourful wagon appear like pages in a picture book, and on fine days Fraser sells prints on the towpath. Cross the bridge and see more of his work at the wagon. To announce your arrival, simply honk the horn!

...hungry?

Lochgilphead hosts Ardrishaig Farmers' Market in Chalmers Street on the second Saturday of each month. 10 a.m until 1 p.m.

Pick up local smoked salmon and cheeses from Cockles Fishmonger and Delicatessen on Argyll Street, Lochgilphead.

Eat and drink in the Mainbrace Bar of the Crinan Hotel while watching comings and goings through the sea lock. Or treat yourself to a memorable meal in the hotel's renowned restaurant.

Let's Get Away From It All

Go-slow lifestyle Gulf Stream gardens Spectacular seabirds

If your idea of heaven is unspoilt villages, unpolluted air, lush pastures and quiet country lanes, then pack your bags for the Rhins of Galloway, a stunning peninsula in south-west Scotland.

Often described as 'Scotland's forgotten corner', there is a real sense of being in another world. The climate is mild and there are spectacular sea views at every turn. The Rhins feel like a heavenly island, just 20 miles long.

The pace of life is sleepily slow. Mobile signals are invariably intermittent, a good sign. There are no banks, so plan ahead and take enough cash for simple pleasures like lighthouse visits, ice cream and cake. There are no petrol stations either. Arrive with a full tank and hold back enough to get you to filling stations in Stranraer.

Unmarked lanes wind in all directions and the scent of wild flowers hangs heavy in the air. Rather like Dorothy in the poppy field en route to Oz, visitors are soon overcome. Losing yourself is lovely, but if you want to get back to Kansas, take an OS map.

Tumbling to the sea, the pretty town of Portpatrick is a hub of gentle activity. Children play in the sandy harbour, black guillemots nest in the walls and abundant fish almost leap on to the lines of anglers.

Allow around four hours for a magnificent circular walk of just over 6 miles to Killantringan lighthouse near Black Head. The route heads up steep steps out of Portpatrick and across dramatic cliffs overlooking secluded coves before turning inland across the moor and back to town.

'Pay as you play' golf courses extend a warm welcome to visitors. Coastal scenery around Portpatrick's clifftop course is spectacular and there's great fun for families at the town's immaculate putting green.

The Mull of Galloway lighthouse and RSPB Reserve is at the most southerly point in Scotland. Views to the Cumbrian fells, the Isle of Man and Ireland are breathtaking. The dramatic headland is one of Britain's most important wildlife sanctuaries; home to more than 3,500 nesting seabirds, including puffins. The RSPB Visitor Centre is open from Easter to October and 'Big Brother' cameras broadcast live TV coverage of seabirds on the cliffs.

After climbing 115 steps to the top of the lighthouse tower, there's welcome refreshment at the Gallie Craig coffee house. The award-winning turf-roofed building blends seamlessly into the contours of the landscape and views from the open terrace over the sea are magnificent.

PARADISE GARDENS

Outstanding gardens flourish in the warm ocean air of the Gulf Stream. While they're all special, these are favourites.

There are carpets of snowdrops in Dunskey Gardens and Maze in February and March. Take a magical walk through Dunskey Glen down to a secluded beach and visit the walled garden, plant nursery and popular tearoom, where locals meet for lunch.

In 1974, Tessa Knott of Glenwhan Garden took a leap of faith and bought a ruin and land at Dunragit over the telephone. Since then a glorious garden has been created out of rough pasture; an extraordinary achievement. There's a tearoom and small nursery with no-nonsense handwritten plant labels: 'Rose, climbing. Colour – pot luck', 'Rudbeckia, huge, 6ft.' On a balmy spring day, amid palm trees and reflective pools, Logan Botanic Garden feels like some exotic distant oasis. Vivid colours, heavy scents and plants from warmer climates flourish. Tearoom and nursery too.

...hungry?

Shop at the pretty market garden of Jim McIntyre and his wife Cathy at Port Logan Old School House. Freshly picked salad and tomatoes, combined with award-winning smoked salmon from the Colfin smokehouse make a great picnic. Jim's garden used to be the playground of his primary school. He tells the story of how he rode to school every day on his wee pony, Kirsty, who would be tethered in the schoolyard while he attended lessons. What lovely memories!

Head to Campbell's restaurant on the harbour in Portpatrick. Owner and fisherman Robert Campbell serves up freshly caught seafood.

Buy fresh fish off the boat from the sea anglers at Port Logan, though they'll often refuse your money and share a good catch for free.

The fully functioning Corsewall Lighthouse Hotel welcomes non-residents for lunch and dinner.

Enjoy refined afternoon tea on the lawns of Knockinaam Lodge, a hideaway hotel where Sir Winston Churchill held a top-secret meeting with General Eisenhower in the Second World War.

Treat yourself to Cream o' Galloway ice cream; there's 23 per cent fat in the premium real raspberry, which is completely scrumptious so it must be good for you!

10

The artistic centre of Galloway is Kirkcudbright, where the painters form a scattered constellation, whose nucleus is in the High Street, and whose outer stars twinkle in remote hillside cottages.

-Dorothy L. Sayers

Fish and Paint

Artists' colony   Secret garden   Town cat

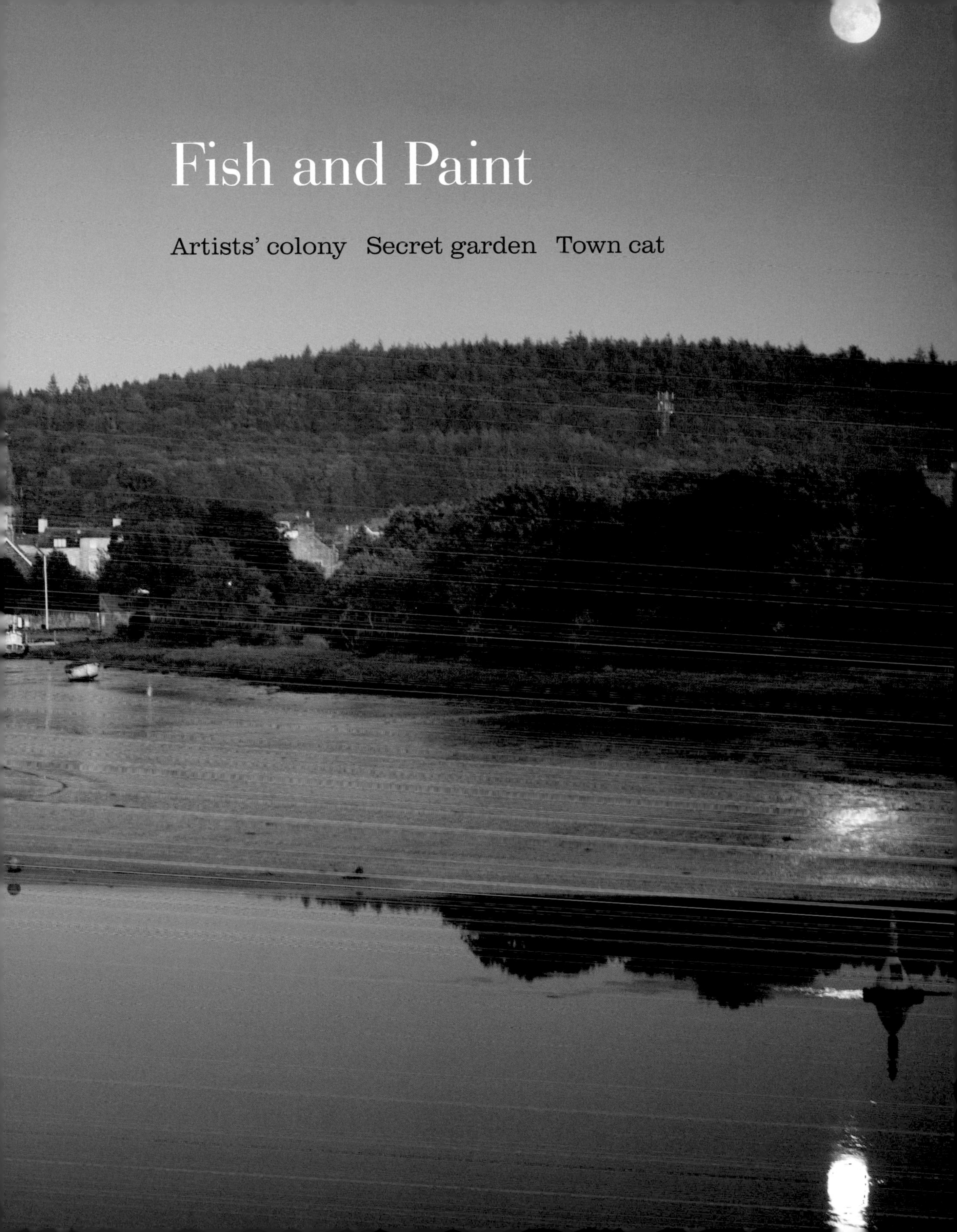

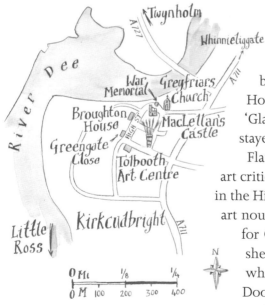

Little has changed since Dorothy L. Sayers' 1931 description of Kirkcudbright (pronounced *Kir-coo-bree*), in *Five Red Herrings*. Colourful heritage, snug cobbled streets and eighteenth-century boulevards make the artists' town on the banks of the River Dee a great weekend visit.

Start your visit at the historic Tolbooth art centre where an excellent free audiovisual presentation traces the development of the artists' colony led by E. A. Hornel, leader of the Glasgow School.

Attracted by the character of local people, combined with the townscape, landscape, coast and light, Hornel moved to Kirkcudbright in 1895. More of the 'Glasgow Boys' joined him for the summer and many stayed longer.

Flamboyant 'Glasgow Girl', Jessie M. King and her art critic husband E. A. Taylor took up residence at Greengate in the High Street. Fresh from Paris, Jessie was famous for her art nouveau designs for Liberty fabrics and her illustrations for Oscar Wilde's children's stories. At Greengate Close, she established an important centre for women artists who stayed in cottages named after the paintwork 'Red Door', 'Blue Door', 'Yellow Door'. When the neighbours turned to Jessie for advice, the town was awash with colour.

Don't miss the opportunity to visit Hornel's splendid pink limewashed home at Broughton House, administered by the National Trust for Scotland. Far from being the ramshackle garret of a starving artist,

smart 'Broo-Hoose' is proof of Hornel's huge commercial success.

His studio appears untouched – easels, canvases, paint pots and brushes are all about. Under a north-facing skylight, he worked on a south-facing wall. Using local girls as models, much of his work celebrates the people and traditions of Galloway.

In the magnificent wood-panelled gallery, considered to be one of the finest rooms in Scotland of its period, the refined bachelor read antiquarian books surrounded by exquisite furniture, art and ceramics.

Hornel's garden is an enchanted place, densely packed with plants and curious objects from his travels. In this lush hideaway you sense the artist was creating a secret world.

Visit the picturesque ruins of MacLellan's Castle, built in 1582 and Greyfriars Episcopal Church, which features in the cult 1973 horror movie, *The Wicker Man*. Look out for the memorial to Ceasar, the wandering town cat, a rotund ginger tom with a big personality. Mrs McKinnel was one of many

...hungry?

Enjoy award-winning fish and chips from Polarbites café. Picnic benches by the harbour are great for watching fishing boats.

Sunday mornings are sleepy in Kirkcudbright, making it a good time to explore the lovely lanes and countryside beyond the town. The road to Little Ross lighthouse is a lovely cycle ride with wonderful views back to the town across the bay.

shopkeepers who 'had a share in him'. Ceasar first showed up at her hardware store when he was about six months old and took to sitting in the sunny shop window, or outside on stacked bags of compost. 'He looked cuddly but he had a fierce side. Everybody knew him. Every day he'd go back and forth through town and all the cars would stop for him!' she told me.

Kirkcudbright's busy commercial harbour is a stone's throw from Charlie Easterfield's beautiful tree-trunk carving of a mother and daughter, *In Memory of Loved Ones Lost at Sea*. I find it especially moving in association with the town's other adult and child sculpture – an impressive bronze warrior shields a young boy on the War Memorial.

Sunday mornings are sleepy in Kirkcudbright, making it a good time to explore the lovely lanes and countryside beyond the town. The road to Little Ross lighthouse is a lovely cycle ride with wonderful views back to the town across the bay.

At Dhoon Bay, picnic tables overlook a sandy beach where low water exposes the timbers of the schooner, *Monreith*, wrecked in 1900.

For speed fiends there's the quirky David Coulthard Museum and Pitstop Diner further afield at Twynholm. And for gardeners like Hornel, who wish to be reminded of their travels, there are three excellent nurseries for souvenirs. Just out of town, Elizabeth MacGregor specialises in violas and cottage garden plants. Cally Gardens at Gatehouse of Fleet offers rare perennials and grasses, and at Buckland Plants in Whinnieliggate you'll find woodland and shade-loving treasures.

The Vikings introduced haaf net fishing on the Solway over a thousand years ago and still groups of sturdy fishermen stand deep in the incoming tide to catch wild Atlantic salmon in rectangular nets.

The Crossing Place

World heritage site   Area of outstanding natural beauty

The Solway Firth, on the frontier of south-west Scotland and north-west England, is one of the most natural and least industrialised estuaries in Europe. While the serene landscape is awash with bloody history, today it's a great place for a quiet weekend.

The weekend begins just 5 miles from Carlisle at rural St Michael's church in Burgh (pronounced Bruff) by Sands. The church stands within a Roman fort on Hadrian's Wall, which extends from Bowness-on-Solway, on the west coast of Britain, to Wallsend on the east.

Emperor Hadrian built the wall in AD 122 to mark the northern limit of his empire and, after the Romans left Britain, local people recycled the building blocks to construct homes and churches.

Solway takes its name from the Norse, *Sul wath*, meaning muddy ford, reflecting the strategic importance of the crossing place used by Celts, Britons, Romans, Angles, Vikings and Normans.

When Scottish reivers, or raiders, of the Middle Ages, stormed across the estuary, the parishioners of Burgh by Sands raced up St Michael's fortified pele tower to shower the invaders with missiles fired from arrow loops.

In 1307, warrior King Edward I planned to cross the Solway and sub-

due a Scottish uprising led by Robert the Bruce. But England's most ambitious monarch was in poor health and died of dysentery at his camp on Burgh Marsh. His body was laid in state at St Michael's church before being taken to Westminster Abbey, where his tomb reads 'Here lies Edward I, the Hammer of the Scots. Keep troth.'

Follow signs from the church to the King's monument and a circular walk of forty minutes around the melancholic salt marsh and incongruous sandstone column surrounded by heavy railings and curious bullocks. There's something pathetic about it all. How the mighty are fallen.

From Burgh to Drumburgh (pronounced Drumbruff, a straight Roman road slices across the marsh, perfect for chariot-racing. There's a small rise at Boustead Hill, though a 'pimple' might be a fairer description in this flat-as-a-pancake landscape.

> The tide advances with such rapidity upon these fatal sands, that well-mounted horsemen lay aside hopes of safety, if they see its white surge advancing while they are yet at a distance from the bank.
>
> Sir Walter Scott, *Redgauntlet*, 1824

There are lifebelts, tide timetables and warnings of unexpected surging seas all along the roadside. To stay safe, you must pay attention.

At low water, the vast sands of the Solway appear like a desert between England and the hills of Scotland. In summer, sheep and cattle wander freely, grazing on the salt marsh as they have done for centuries.

CURIOUS

Atmospheric Burgh Marsh is at the heart of a spaceman mystery that has yet to be solved. In 1964 photographer Jim Templeton took a picture of his daughter on the marsh and was astonished to discover an astronaut, in white suit and helmet, in the print. Kodak confirmed the image was genuine and still no explanation has been found.

Lush Solway turf is springy underfoot and was used for Wimbledon tennis courts and the football pitch at the old Wembley Stadium.

All feels serene in this peaceful place, but way-markers indicating footpaths around the marshy creeks to the shores of the River Eden remind you again of tidal dangers: 'This route has natural hazards, seek local guidance.'

Hadrian's garrison of 500 foot soldiers at Drumburgh was positioned strategically to guard another of the important Solway crossing places. Again, stones from the Wall were recycled to extend Drumburgh Castle, a fortified farmhouse. Look out for Roman altars near the front door: found in a hedge by the farmer, they were thought to be birdbaths at first!

The National Nature Reserve at Drumburgh Moss is one of the few remaining peat bogs on the Solway plain. Keep your eyes peeled for lizards, adders, moths and butterflies, red grouse, curlew, red shank and grasshopper warblers.

Nearby Glasson Moss and Bowness Common are also important lowland, raised mire wildlife reserves.

Elegant street lanterns, handsome houses and cobbled fronts are clues to the bustling past of sleepy Port Carlisle. The lovely village grew up around the sea lock of the short-lived canal that linked the port to Carlisle between 1821 and 1853. The canal is long gone; so too are the hot and cold seawater baths that enticed city weekenders. Look out for another Roman altar, above the doorway of Hesket House bed and breakfast.

Take a seat for magnificent estuary views at Banks promenade in

Bowness-on-Solway, the start or finish of the Hadrian's Wall Trail. A Roman garden celebrates Maia, the most westerly fort along the Wall, garrisoned by 800 Spanish and Moroccan legions.

Don't miss the wonderful windows of St Michael's church, capturing the spirit of this border reiving, smuggling and haaf net fishing community. The Vikings introduced haaf net fishing on the Solway over a thousand years ago and still groups of sturdy fishermen stand deep in the incoming tide to catch wild Atlantic salmon in rectangular nets.

The estuary is a magnificent bird-watching venue. Many varieties of wading birds are seen easily from roadside lay-bys at high tide. There's no charge to visit RSPB Campfield Marsh Nature Reserve, a great picnic spot, a mile west of Bowness. Open all year round, the reserve is especially lively in winter when migrant pink-footed geese and wigeon fly in to graze the wet grassland.

...hungry?

Walkers on the Hadrian's Wall Path National Trail break from the route march to stop at 'Laal Bite' in the grounds of Drumburgh's Roman fort. The self service café is a great place for local information, scrumptious cakes and ice cream.

Try seasonal haaf net-caught wild Solway salmon in the local pubs.

Wander past fishing boats, lobster pots, and seaside chickens.

See Red

Sandstone Saints Seabirds and submarine mines

W est of the Lake District, there is superb coastal scenery around the distinctive red sandstone cliffs of St Bees Head. Along with some of England's largest seabird colonies, you'll find the simple pleasures of country walks, bike rides and buckets and spades on the beach.

The pretty village of St Bees has welcomed pilgrims in search of miracles for more than a thousand years. According to medieval legend, St Bega, the holy daughter of an Irish King, refused to marry a Viking chieftain, jumped in her coracle and sailed alone across the Irish Sea to St Bees.

The priory church of St Mary and St Bega is at the heart of the village. Enter through the magnificently carved Norman doorway and prepare yourself for an unusual display of photographs near the altar.

The pictures record the exhumation and autopsy of 'St Bees man', a well-preserved medieval knight whose coffin was discovered during an excavation of church grounds in 1981. He is not alone; outside the church, an inscription reads 'monks and knights unknown rest here'.

Within the grounds, the Sleeping Child Garden is dedicated to all who have suffered the loss of a young life, before or after birth. The sculptures of sweet, innocent infants are by Josefina de Vasconcellos.

Local boy made good, Edmund Grindal, Archbishop of Canterbury, founded St Bees School on his deathbed in 1538. You can just make out the school motto, carved on a lintel in the Quadrangle, opposite the priory church: *Ingredere Ut Proficias*. (Enter so that you may make progress).

Along the main street, a jumble of historic farm buildings lead to the charming sandstone railway station where the Cumbrian Coast Line deposits walkers and cyclists who are about to embark on long-distance trails.

One of the most famous is the Coast-to-Coast Walk, devised by Alfred Wainright in 1972. The journey begins at St Bees on the west coast of England and ends at Robin Hood's Bay on the east.

From St Bees, cyclists set off on the 'C2C', sea-to-sea, cycle route to Sunderland or Tynemouth. Whitehaven and Workington are alternative points of departure. St Bees is also on Hadrian's Wall Cycleway, route 72 on the national network, from Ravenglass to Tynemouth.

But you don't have to be a long-distance walker or cyclist to enjoy the undulating Cumbrian landscape; there are plenty of routes for weekenders and early summer is a great time to try them.

N

Whitehaven
Sandwith
St Bees Head
Rottington
Fleswick Bay
South Head
St Bees
A595
Egremont
Coulderton

0 Mi 1 2 3
0 Km 1 2 3 4

Lace up your boots for a two-hour, 4-mile circular route from Seamill Lane, St Bees, via Lovers' Lonnin, to the curious seaside hamlet of Coulderton, where a string of quirky beach bungalows nestle below a railway embankment at the edge of the Irish Sea. Some are ramshackle, some deluxe, many have been family owned for generations, and many have been swept out to sea.

Wander past fishing boats, lobster pots, and seaside chickens. On a clear day, there are views to the Isle of Man. At high water, it is safest to return the same way; at low water, follow the rocky shore from Coulderton back to Seamill Lane.

Alternatively, follow the coast from St Bees towards Whitehaven for a longer circular walk of 6 miles. Allow around four hours, depending on how long you like to linger on the beach or observe seabirds. From the beach at St Bees follow the steep coast path to South Head, eighty metres high and known locally as Tomlin. Sea views take in the Isle of Man and Dumfries and Galloway.

Before reaching St Bees Head, the most westerly point in northern

...thirsty?

Savour a pint of Theakston's Best Bitter or Wells' Bombardier in the evening sun outside the Manor House pub in St Bees. Try Jennings' Cumberland Ale at the Oddfellows Arms on Main Street.

England, the path dips to the secluded suntrap of Fleswick Bay. Keep your eyes peeled for semiprecious stones in the shingle: striped agate, ruby cornelian and red jasper.

The path then climbs back to the clifftop, with peaceful pastures on one side and a squawking wall of sound on the other. In spring and summer, rowdy seabirds perform acrobatics around their nests on rocky shelves. The impressive cast includes fulmars, herring gulls, kittiwakes, guillemots, including black guillemots, and razorbills, with occasional star turns from puffins too. Observe the action from RSPB viewpoints along the path.

The path continues to St Bees lighthouse on North Head. Turn inland to follow the farm lane to Tarn Flatt Hall. From here, the route passes through the pretty hamlets of Sandwith and Rottington before returning to St Bees.

For cyclists, the 15-mile St Bees coastal circular is a medium to moderate 'do-in-a-day' ride through coastal and pastoral scenery. The route begins at Egremont, rolls into St Bees and follows quiet country lanes above the beach bungalows of Coulderton. It's well worth the diversion to see them.

From St Bees Head, the coast heads north to Whitehaven, which is enjoying a post-industrial renaissance. At the harbour, stone quays with names like Sugar Tongue hint at former trading links with far-flung countries. There's inspired public art on the waterfront, from whale tail benches to a coal-mining monument commemorating 'The End of an Era'. Look out for the sailor spiking an original Whitehaven cannon, in preparation for John Paul Jones's failed 1778 raid on the town during the American War of Independence.

For panoramic views over the magnificent harbour and fascinating history, visit the Beacon Museum on West Strand.

The Haig Colliery Mining Museum is an unpolished gem. Extraordinary stories and excavations under the sea make this a must visit. Twenty minutes' walk from the harbour, it is open seven days a week, with free admission.

...hungry?

Hartleys beach shop and tearoom on the prom at St Bees is a favourite with locals, who pop in for ice cream in a chocolate cone all year round.

Large picture windows overlook the sands, where coast-to-coast walkers traditionally dip their boots in the Irish Sea before walking them into the North Sea two weeks later.

For picnics, there are benches on the seafront, close to the lovely playground.

St Bees beach welcomes dogs all year round; there's even a sandy dog loo, next to the public loos, in the car park by the promenade.

In spring and summer, rowdy seabirds perform acrobatics around their nests on rocky shelves. The impressive cast includes fulmars, herring gulls, kittiwakes, guillemots, including black guillemots, and razorbills, with occasional star turns from puffins too. Observe the action from RSPB viewpoints along the path.

13

It's a fierce wind that whips around the coast at Formby Point, creating

disappeared in a mighty sandstorm

Another Place

Iron men   Prehistoric footprints   Dunes and pinewoods

mmense and restless sand dunes. Last seen in 1739, Ravensmeols village

hat whipped up massive dunes.

Much about this weekend on the Sefton coast, within easy reach of Liverpool, is extraordinary, including 100 spectacular iron men on Crosby beach; the largest sand dune system in England; the awe-inspiring sight of prehistoric footprints on the beach; and the weird sound of natterjack toads in the dunes.

Sculptor Antony Gormley's massive installation of one hundred figures, cast from moulds of his own body, stretches 2 miles along the Sefton coast. How you discover the iron men of *Another Place*, depends very much on the weather and state of the tide.

At high water, the Irish Sea sloshes over their heads. On stormy days, the figures stand firmly resolute as surging waves spatter them. But on warm, sunny days, when the mood is relaxed, you half expect them to wave at passing ships. On high days and holidays, the locals like to dress them up.

Watching them, watching ferries leave England, stirs poignant memories of emigration. To witness 100 iron strangers staring out to sea is, as locals would say, a gob-smacking experience.

Up until the 1960s, most people crossed the Atlantic on liners sailing from Liverpool to New York. In season, passengers embarking on the great adventure traditionally feasted on fresh Formby asparagus. Demand from the liners made the delicacy big business and, at its peak, over 200 acres of flat-floored asparagus fields sheltered behind Sefton's mighty sand dunes. Now just a handful of growers remain. At Marsh Farm, David Rimmer harvests asparagus spears traditionally, by hand. Offcuts are fed to his discerning gourmet cattle.

It's a fierce wind that whips around the coast at Formby Point, creating immense and restless sand dunes. Last seen in 1739, Ravensmeols village disappeared in a mighty sandstorm that whipped up massive dunes. This is often a place for a cosy hat, even in high summer.

In the late 1880s, inspired by timber crops growing in the dunes of Arcachon in south-west France, English landowners followed suit, planting a forest of Corsican and Scots pines around Formby Point. Attracted by abundant seeds, and pine cones, native red squirrels soon moved in. When the National Trust acquired the land, a reserve was established to protect the landscape from development, but while the pine forest remains, the red squirrels are in decline. The parapox virus, carried by

---

...hungry?

Buy seasonal fresh asparagus direct from Larkhill and Marsh farms in Formby. Head inland to Little Crosby for good food at the Courtyard Café, a pretty converted barn in a medieval hamlet. Dine out on local produce at the stylish Warehouse Brasserie in Southport.

From 'The Birkdale Nightingale'
Bufo calamito – the Natterjack toad

On Spring nights you can hear them
two miles away, calling their mates
to the breeding place, a wet slack in the dunes.
Lovers hiding nearby are surprised
by desperate music. One man searched all night
for a crashed spaceship.

Jean Sprackland

grey squirrels, which are immune to it, is deadly for the reds.

Horseboxes are a common sight at Lifeboat Road car park; the vast expanse of firm sand is an ideal workout for riders and mounts. It's a training regime that worked brilliantly for Red Rum, three times winner of the Grand National.

Clear, deep footprints in the mud of Formby beach appear to be freshly imprinted, yet these are the 10,000-year-old tracks of hunter-gatherers in pursuit of deer, wild boar and extinct breeds of cattle. Under the hot sun, animals and humans unwittingly left their mark. The footprints baked hard and tides carried silt to conceal them until coastal erosion revealed this extraordinary time warp. Some prints were made within

...thirsty?

Traditional pubs abound; three of the best are the Volunteer Canteen, five minutes' walk from Waterloo Station; the tiny Crows Nest and the Edinburgh are both within walking distance of Blundell-sands and Crosby Station.

a short time of each other; others are hundreds of years apart. All of them will be washed away by tides that, at once, reveal and destroy the prints.

The pinhole glimpse of a lost world is profoundly moving. To touch the hollows where huntsmen, mud-larking children and pregnant women ran and played is to make a tingling connection with our prehistoric past.

TICKET TO RIDE

It's as easy to get around this weekend by train as by car. Mersey-travel Northern Line trains stop every fifteen minutes at stations all along the coast.

Between Waterloo Station and Hightown Station, you can wander along the shore in the company of Antony Gormley's magnificent iron men. Allow about three hours for a gentle walk, following the natterjack toads on the way-markers of the coastal path, which stretches all the way from Seaforth to Southport. The rare toads, known locally as Birkdale Nightingales, breed and hibernate in Sefton's dunes.

Don't miss the splendour of shipping magnates' mansions at Beach Lawn, situated at the mouth of the River Mersey so that owners could, quite literally, watch their ships coming in. Thomas Henry Ismay, founder of the White Star Line, which built the *Titanic*, resided at number thirteen.

Low tide reveals a 4,000-year-old submerged forest near Blundellsands sailing club on the Alt Estuary.

From Hall Road Station, walk to the beach and mid-point of Antony Gormley's installation, which stretches over 2 miles. A 2-mile stroll inland from the station follows Dibbs Lane, an ancient path to the medieval hamlet of Little Crosby.

Formby Station is the stop for immense sand dunes and prehistoric footprints at Formby Point. There are magnificent views from the Point to north Wales and Snowdonia and Cumbria on clear days. Visit Cabin Hill Nature Reserve for wild flowers and rare willows. Buy fresh asparagus in season from Marsh and Larkhill farms.

Freshfield Station is at the start of the lovely fisherman's path through tranquil woodland to the shore. In spring, gorse colours the dune heath yellow; in autumn, heather turns it purple.

14

Where the Dee Meets the Sea

Marsh mayhem   Viking settlers   Island trio

Three tidal islands, extraordinary bird-watching, challenging golf and spectacular sunsets make the Wirral peninsula on England's north-west coast a special place to visit. Flanked by the River Dee to the west, and the River Mersey to the east, the beautiful peninsula has speedy access to the cities of Chester, Liverpool and Manchester. Wales is on the doorstep and ferries sail to Ireland from the local docks.

Twelve and a half miles long and five and a half wide, the marshy Dee estuary is one of the most important wetland sites in north-west Europe. The winter arrival of over 80,000 birds from Iceland, Greenland and the Arctic puts it in the top ten for over-wintering wildfowl and waders.

Exceptionally high tides between September and March bring mayhem to the marsh. It's wildlife showtime. Take a front row seat among twitchers along the shore and watch the gripping drama unfold.

As the sea slides over the land, thousands of birds rise from reedy roosts in alarm. Small creatures abandon bolt-holes to flee inland. Alert to the prospect of dinner, the raptors show up: peregrine falcons, kestrels, sparrow hawks and harriers swoop in for the kill, jostling with black-headed gulls and short-eared owls. As the waters rise, the small fry run for their lives: mice, shrews and voles zigzag over the marsh, criss-crossing frantic stoats, weasels and foxes.

For wildlife exhibitions and information about the estuary, visit Wirral Country Park at Thurstaston. This is a great place for picnics at any time of year, with clear views to Wales, the conversation of wittering birds in the estuary, paragliders taking flight over sandcastles and fishing boats, and spectacular sunsets. There's a real sense of being on the edge of the land.

Around 1,000 years ago, the peninsula was Viking territory; 50 per cent of men from old Wirral families have their strongest genetic matches in Scandinavia and many villages take their names from Norwegian Viking settlers: Thurstaston, or Thorsteinn's Tun, was the site of a Viking farmstead.

The River Dee meets the Irish Sea around Hoylake, a top spot for kite-flying, parakarting and sand-yachting. From the RNLI station, the *Lady of Hilbre* lifeboat has to be skilfully launched by tractor due to the tide range over the immense flat beach.

The seaside resort of West Kirby is just half an hour away, along the beach and over the boardwalk through the swaying reeds of Red Rocks

Marsh, home of rare natterjack toads. Walk beside the famous championship links of the Royal Liverpool Golf Club, host of the Open in 2006. The ninth tee offers panoramic views of islands in the Dee estuary and Welsh hills.

At low water, it is possible to cross the sands at West Kirby and visit the tidal islands: Little Eye, Middle Eye and Hilbre. The easy walk takes around an hour each way but be aware of the serious risk of quicksand and being cut off by the tide. Before setting out, check the safest route and tide times posted on the noticeboard at Dee Lane slipway.

The islands are of international importance and groups of six or more require permits in advance from Wirral Country Park Visitor Centre. Take binoculars to observe grey seals hauled out on West Hoyle Bank; around 400 of them loll around in August. However, the islands offer little shelter and no facilities so be prepared: pack a picnic, raincoat, sun cream and a hat for sun or wind. Dogs must stay on leads and visitors on the paths.

At West Kirby, sandstone walls enclose windsurfers and boats on the marine lake, described as 'the Amphitheatre of Sailing' when built in 1899. In spring, the lake hosts the Wilson Trophy, the world's largest dinghy team racing event. Take a pew along the parade and be entertained by thrills and spills on flat water in high winds.

FOUR WIRRAL WALKS

From Banks Road car park, Heswall, follow the coast path to pretty Parkgate village, 3 miles away. Looking over peaceful creeks and silted marshes to the mountains of north Wales, it's hard to believe this was a bustling eighteenth-century port. Stroll along the quayside for award-winning ice cream, traditional pubs, fish and chips and restaurants.

The Wirral Way follows the former railway line, running nearly 12 miles from Hooton to West Kirby. It's great for family cycling, walking and horse riding with estuary views. The unassuming Harp Inn on the quayside at Little Neston is a gem. Regulars include dogs, with their own page on the pub website, and bird watchers by the fire in winter.

The Wirral coastal walk skirts the peninsula from Seacombe ferry terminal on the Mersey in the east to the Wirral Country Park Visitor Centre at Thurstaston on the Dee in the west, nearly 15 miles in all.

Stroll around Ness Botanic Gardens, created in 1898 by plantsman and cotton merchant Arthur Bulley. See the famous collections of rhododendrons, camellias and azaleas; there's also a café and plant sales.

...hungry?

A recent lifestyle survey put Heswall among the UK's top three most desirable waterside places to live, along with Lymington in Hampshire and Sandbanks in Dorset. Explore the muddy shore and quiet creeks around Sheldrakes bar and bistro. Roses Tea Rooms boast the Tea Guild's Award of Excellence, rather like the Oscars of café society. Savour good books and coffee at Linghams independent bookshop and lunch, brunch or afternoon tea at Emma's Coffee Shop in pretty Lower Heswall.

At Thurstaston, GJ's Café is open all year round for homemade soup, hot waffles and Welsh rarebit, handy for visitors to the nearby Caravan Club site. Church Farm sells fresh organic produce; seasonal asparagus and strawberries are a speciality. Lose yourself in the lavender maze during July and August. There's a café and caravan site too.

West Kirby offers a wide choice of restaurants and bars. Palms Fine Foods make picnic baskets to order, perfect for an island outing. Treat yourself to a fresh-fruit ice cream sundae at Sands Café Bar. After a bracing walk around the marine lake, locals head to Marigolds for quality fish and chips.

15

A Touch of Class

Seaside splendour   Mountain scenery   Sheltered gardens

On a beautiful evening, the splendour of Llandudno is magical: elegant hotels, dressed in seaside pastels, grace the north shore promenade, a necklace of white lights adds sparkle and exotic palm trees suggest that your weekend away is somewhere much further than the north Wales coast.

Llandudno is the dream-come-true of the influential Mostyn family. Using the General Enclosure Act of 1845, known in Wales as Deddf y Llaadrad Mawr, the Great Theft Act, they turned common land by the sea into a grand resort for the middle class. Gracious buildings and wide boulevards, fit for Victorian horse-drawn carriages and cabs, were laid out on a grid pattern, to create a sense of airy refinement.

Handsome canopies and intricate ironwork are still part of the scene along Mostyn Street, yet the town is not set in aspic. The Oriel Mostyn Gallery, established in 1901 by Lady Augusta Mostyn, was the first in the world to show exclusively the work of women artists; still forging ahead, it has an exciting reputation for bold contemporary art.

Llandudno is on an isthmus, or neck of land, which connects the Great Orme with the hinterland. Two impressive beaches sweep around either side of the town.

At West Shore, David Lloyd George unveiled a statue of Lewis Carroll's white rabbit in 1933 to celebrate Alice Liddell's regular visits to the fam-

ily's Llandudno holiday home. *Alice's Adventures in Wonderland* and *Alice Through the Looking Glass* were dedicated to the little girl. You can't miss the smartly dressed bunny, just a hop from the site of her family's house, near the swans and model boating lake; an ugly but necessary cage protects him. The sandy beach faces the Conwy estuary, with tropical amber sunsets over Puffin Island and the Isle of Anglesey.

The North Shore appears like a golden stage, between two dramatic headlands, Great Orme's Head and Little Orme's Head. In summer the scene is vibrant: red and white deckchairs, traditional Punch and Judy shows, lifeboat displays, donkey rides and community hymn-singing on the sweeping prom, wide enough for twenty day-trippers to stroll happily arm in arm. There's no nasty neon to spoil the effect.

Opened in 1878, Llandudno's pier is one of the finest in Britain. The cast-iron work is outstanding; strong columns

FIRST CAR
LAST CAR
12
9
3
6
A.M.
P.M.
TRAMS
LEAVE
ON - THE HOUR
20 - PAST THE HOUR
20 - TO THE HOUR

...hungry? thirsty? tired?

Hungry or thirsty, you're spoiled for choice
   Lovely Llandudno has to be one of my favourite seaside resorts; after toboggan rides at the ski centre, donkey rides on the beach or people-watching from a bench, you'll be ready for refreshment and with plenty to choose from, it's difficult to select just a few.
   The popular Fish Tram Chips café and takeaway is opposite the lower tram station; cross the tracks to the friendly Kings Head pub. Find fruit-packed smoothies at Number 19 café, lavish opulence at the Empire and Osborne House Hotels and stylish bed and breakfast at the Cliffbury.
   'Haulfre' is Welsh for 'sunny spot' and the Sunshine Café opened here in 1933. It is hidden on the hill, but look in their direction and, whenever the Welsh flag is flying, you will know the café is open for business.

support the structure, delicate balustrades and fine lattice-work railings embellish it. Saunter along, free of charge, past exotic domed kiosks to the landing stage where the first holidaymakers, wealthy Victorians from Liverpool, disembarked from passenger ships. There was once a swimming pool at the pavilion; look out for the plaque dedicated to Walter Beaumont 1855–1924. One of the pier's high divers, he is remembered for 'selfless acts of saving lives in Llandudno Bay'.

Forget the cares of the world and visit the extraordinary camera obscura in the pleasure grounds of Happy Valley, on the slopes of the Great Orme. Immense views of the coast are breathtaking.

Hacked out of the Great Orme's vertical limestone cliffs, Marine Drive is Llandudno's superb corniche. Pedestrians can walk the scenic 2.5-mile circuit free of charge; drivers pay a £2.50 toll. Circumventing the headland on a bright, clear day brings the Wicklow Mountains, Isle of An-

glesey, Puffin Island and Conwy Castle into view. There will be climbers too, especially in winter, when wind off the sea dries the rock quickly.

It's said that the Vikings named the Great Orme headland 'Horma Heva', meaning 'sea monster', and that's just how it looks as it rises out of the deep. Walkers taking the challenging summit path trail, Igam Ogam, zigzagging up from West Shore, or footpaths from Marine Drive, catch their breath at the peak, with panoramic views to Snowdonia, Anglesey, the Isle of Man, Blackpool and the Lake District.

It's hard to resist alternative routes to the top. If you have a head for heights, ride the UK's longest cable car ride, departing from Happy Valley. Travelling at twenty-five metres above the ground, gondolas glide over the outdoor ski and snowboard centre, past villages, farms and the largest known prehistoric copper mine in the world, where miners worked with bone and stone. Views over Llandudno Bay and the Irish Sea are thrilling.

If you'd rather not dangle, take the tram. The Great Orme's cable hauled street tramway system is one of just three in the world; experience the others in San Francisco and Lisbon. Beautifully restored tramcars rattle out of Tyn-y-Coed village on the edge of the town. Towards Halfway Tram Station, cable cars glide overhead, and cheery passengers exchange greetings.

Look out for the Great Orme's livestock: black Welsh cattle, sheep and a herd of goats, introduced from Pakistan and India in the late nineteenth century. Locals use them to forecast the weather; when rain is on the way, the herd shifts to the sheltered lower slopes.

From the south-facing terraces of Haulfre Gardens, which once belonged to Victorian grocer and tea merchant Thomas Lipton, you get a real sense of Llandudno's town plan. Below, to the left, there are blue slate roofs dating from 1849; to the right are the red tiled roofs of the 1900s. On sunny benches, visitors and locals meet and chat, surrounded by lavender and agapanthus basking in the sun; the living is easy and reminiscent of warmer climes.

16

Set off at low tide and head across the wide sandy bay

Tŷ Coch stands out amid the cluster of fishermen's

Secrets of Wild West Wales

Hideaway beaches Lush country lanes Poetic landscapes

...owards the natural harbour of Porthdinllaen where the redbrick inn,

...ottages on the shore.

Welsh language and culture remain strong on the Llŷn peninsula, which points out to sea like a witch's bony finger. This is a landscape of whitewashed farms in patchwork fields, deep country lanes and high hedges brimming with bramble, fern and wild flowers. Footpaths and cycleways entice you to explore sandy beaches, picturesque harbours and a wide range of marine habitats.

The simple pleasures of rustic campsites on coastal farms attract families who return year upon year. For sunset suppers on the beach, seek out hidden bays along the coast between Porthysgaden and Porthtowyn. There's good mackerel fishing off the rocks and dolphin watching too.

There's an exhilarating 3-mile circular walk, from the National Trust car park on Golf Road in Morfa Nefyn. Set off at low tide and head across the wide sandy bay towards the natural harbour of Porthdinllaen where the redbrick inn, Tŷ Coch, stands out amid the cluster of fishermen's cottages on the shore. Scramble over rocks to explore Lifeboat Bay and the RNLI station, then turn inland up a steep hill to the spectacular championship golf course with thrilling views from every tee, the mountains of Snowdonia to the east and the Wicklow Mountains to the west. Follow the path across the course and back to the start.

On Daloni Metcalfe's farm in Tudweiliog an

The Other

There are nights that are so still
That I can hear the small owl calling
far off and a fox barking
miles away. It is then that I lie
in the lean hours awake listening
to the swell born somewhere in the Atlantic
rising and falling, rising and falling
wave on wave on the long shore
by the village, that is without light
and companionless. And the thought comes
of that other being who is awake, too,
letting our prayers break on him,
not like this for a few hours,
but for days, years, for eternity.

R. S. Thomas

...hungry?

For a seafood feast, follow the trail of hand-painted signs in lanes around Tudweiliog to the country hideaway of 'Mary Crabs' and 'Gareth Lobster' at Selective Seafoods. Local fishermen supply them with live crab and lobster and it's Mary's job to dispatch them. 'I'm going to die with a hammer in my hand!' she says.

The superb quality of the catch is due to dangerous riptides around Ynys Enlli, Bardsey Island, 2 miles off the tip of the Llŷn peninsula. Currents stir up rich pickings for greedy crustaceans. 'We never have to put additives and bulking agents in our crab meat,' says Gareth proudly.

Visit farmer's daughter and chef Marian Williams at Caffi Porthdinllaen, a handsome wooden café close to the eponymous beach near Nefyn. Great coffee and home cooking.

There's often a queue at weekends outside the fish and chip shop in Aberdaron; always a good sign! Friendly cafés in the village too.

extraordinary potato shack 'Cwt Tatws' became an unofficial chapel where Hywel Harris, leader of the Methodist Revival, preached in the eighteenth century.

From the tiny stone building, Daloni sells Welsh onion tarts, home made cakes, fresh farm eggs and the work of contemporary Welsh artists to holidaymakers wandering through the meadow to the beach. Cwt Tatws has to be one of Britain's most beautiful and unusual seaside stores.

The story goes that that 20,000 saints are buried on sacred Bardsey Island and, in the Middle Ages, three pilgrimages to windswept Bardsey were said to equal one to Rome. Still popular today, the island attracts those seeking spiritual peace and outstanding wildlife. Day trips sail from Porth Meudwy and Pwllheli and it is wise to book ahead.

For spectacular views of the peninsula, take binoculars, a flask and a picnic to the Old Coastguard Lookout on the summit of Mynydd Mawr, the Big Mountain, 6 miles from Aberdaron. Drive up if you must, though it seems a shame when footpaths are clearly marked and the scenery's magnificent.

Rare choughs in red stockings perform aerial displays on the salty wind that whips off the sea, views along the coast are breathtaking and,

...thirsty?

The Lion Hotel in Tudweiliog is an award-winning CAMRA (Campaign for Real Ale) favourite and it's hard to beat the views from the Tŷ Coch inn on the beach at Porthdinllaen.

Enjoy drinks on the beachside terrace at Gwesty Tŷ Newydd Hotel in Aberdaron. The neighbouring Ship Inn offers good food and accommodation too.

in high summer, the heathland becomes a vivid patchwork of purple heather and yellow gorse.

From Mynydd Mawr, the mile-long sandy bay and unspoiled village of Aberdaron is clearly visible. St Hywyn's church teeters on the shore; sermons are accompanied by the sound of the sea. Leave pebbles with special messages at the cairn by the side of the altar. On the last Sunday of October they are all returned to the sea.

Hugely inspired by the landscape and people of the Llŷn, the outspoken and celebrated poet R. S. Thomas was vicar here between 1967 and 1978. His poems are sold in the well-stocked Eleri village stores.

HIDEAWAYS

So many secret bays and beaches, some easily accessible, others to be hunted down! Take a map and tide tables to discover these favourites.

Porth Oer aka Whistling Sands, where grains of dry sand above the high tide line squeak underfoot. A popular family beach with seasonal café and lots of fun for junior for body-boarders.

Porth Iago Reached by a muddy, bumpy private track, pay 50p for the privilege and scramble down steep grassy slopes to a perfect hideaway cove.

Porth Ysgo A hidden gem in the cliffs between Porth Neigwl and Aberdaron. From a tumbledown farmyard, follow the stream down the valley to the headland, the disused manganese mine and wonderful views to Ynys Gwylan Fach and Fawr, big gull and little gull islands. Steep steps to the beach keep crowds away.

Porth Colman From the small slipway, local fisherman Sion Williams runs wildlife and fishing trips.

Traeth Penllech. A track leads to a vast stretch of sand in this quiet bay near Porth Colman. Best at low tide.

17

Colour Therapy

Grand designs   Dylan Thomas   West Wales dolphins

Stir your creative spirit with a weekend in the vibrant Welsh seaside towns of Aberaeron and New Quay in Ceredigion or Cardigan. Bold splashes of colour, leaping dolphins and dramatic connections with Dylan Thomas make this weekend an invigorating experience.

The paint-box town of Aberaeron is pure colour therapy, even on the dullest day. Rows of rainbow houses are elegantly arranged in cheerful streets around the historic harbour; one in four is listed as being of special architectural or historical interest, largely due to the efforts of Reverend Alban Jones-Gwynne, who used a Private Act of Parliament to transform the harbour of a traditional Welsh fishing village into a nineteenth-century port of international maritime significance, at his own expense.

Shipyards and sawmills sprang up around the boom-town. Blacksmiths moved in, to hammer out fittings for sailing vessels in Vulcan Place. Sea captains bought elegant new houses and named them after far-flung destinations like 'Gambia' and 'Melbourne'. Labourers slaked their thirst in thirty-five pubs, including the Dolphin Inn where shipyard owner, John Harries, paid wages from the side window in the hope that they would be spent at the bar!

Aberaeron's expansion continued in the 1830s when the Reverend's son, Colonel Alban Gwynne, commissioned genteel Alban Square, a town hall and a church. But in 1911, the arrival of the railway killed off the port.

Today, Aberaeron hosts a breathless whirl of events including a Country and Western Festival in June, Cardigan Bay Seafood Festival in July, and in August, the Aberaeron regatta, the Festival of Welsh Cobs and Ponies, the annual tug of war across the harbour – in which the losing team get a soaking – the famous Rugby Sevens, a flamboyant carnival and a mackerel festival which involves a monster fish parading around the harbour, a ritual burning and a big knees-up.

For more sedate moments, there is a gentle stroll of just under 2 miles or a cycle ride along the route of the old railway tracks, from town to the enchanting National Trust gardens and the handsome villa designed by John Nash at Llanerchaeron.

Seven and a half miles south of Aberaeron is the hillside seaside town of New Quay, where Dylan Thomas enjoyed one of the most productive periods of his life, writing poems, radio and film scripts. It's also where his friend William Killick took a shot at him after a drunken pub brawl.

The Black Lion Hotel was Thomas's favourite watering hole, perhaps be-

...hungry?

Take a mug of tea to the beach from the Fisherman's Shed at Aberaeron, so much friendlier than a throwaway cup. Opening hours are extended for 'high waters, holidays and sunny days'. The best ice cream for miles around is at the Hive on the Quay, and the seafood is good too. Dine in style at the Harbour Master Hotel, overlooking yachts and swans.

Buy freshly caught crab, lobster and seasonal fish from local fishermen at the Fresh Fish Shop near New Quay pier.

cause the kindly landlady cared for his baby daughter Aeronwy, named after the river running through Aberaeron, while he worked hard in the bar. It wasn't unusual for him to leave the baby overnight and fetch her in the morning.

New Quay residents are said to have inspired many of the characters in his play for voices, *Under Milk Wood*. In *Quite Early One Morning*, first broadcast on BBC radio in 1945, Thomas describes a walk though the sleeping town and along the cliff path. You can trace his steps on the Dylan Thomas trail, available from New Quay and Aberaeron tourist offices.

The quirky Queens Hotel on Church Street doesn't have a Dylan Thomas trail plaque, though it does deserve one, being the only bar in town to have refused him credit. Ironically it's just the kind of place where you'd expect to find him. The atmospheric backroom is stuffed with eclectic books from landlady Rose Spencer's vast collection, some for sale, some to be borrowed and some just to be enjoyed in situ at tables dressed in red checked cloths. Scrumpy cider and real Welsh ales are served from kegs on the bar and there's an old-fashioned bar billiards game in the corner; Rose will teach you the rules.

Visit the Cardigan Bay Boat Place on the stone pier that shelters New Quay's sandy beach; a live webcam link relays seabird activity on Bird Rock. Near the slipway, the old schedule of tolls and duties levied on ships and vessels reveals that everything had its price, from young trees for planting to feathers, coffins, cigars and bath chairs. Avoiding these expenses made smuggling a real alternative to farming in eighteenth-century New Quay.

Close to the lifeboat station is the Cardigan Bay Watersports Centre where you can have a go at kayaking, sailing, windsurfing and powerboat training. And don't miss the Marine Wildlife Centre's colourful free exhibition about West Wales' 200 bottlenose dolphins in Cardigan Bay. There's also the opportunity to take a trip on a research boat. Volunteers from the Centre carry out land-based surveys to observe dolphins around the harbour, posting their findings on a chalkboard at the pier. When I was there, it read 'August 23rd Mother and calf chasing fish close to harbour wall'. Just moments later, I got to see them for myself. Surprising the families fishing for crabs at the end of the pier, the playful pair popped up, as if to say hello, before a game of chase around the boats – a close encounter that left everyone elated.

Splashdown

Remote rural beaches Industrial villages Inspiring landscape

pend a Welsh weekend pottering around the quiet industrial heritage of the beautiful north Pembrokeshire coast. The simple pleasures of mooching on secluded beaches and discovering one of Britain's best-preserved Bronze Age settlements make this a great escape.

Laid-back Porthgain is gathered around a village green, close to the lovely harbour. In the nineteenth century the community grew around brickworks and two quarries, known as Jerusalem and Caersalem, which kept local people in employment until closure in the 1930s.

The crisp sea air is pure and the industrial harbour is quiet now but Porthgain is an atmospheric place; it's easy to imagine how the hillside must have resounded to the din of ships loading up with hard dolerite road stone bound for Ireland, the hissing steam crusher grinding slabs of rock into assorted sizes, the narrow gauge railway rattling back and forth over the headland and clouds of dust everywhere.

Workers would have slaked their thirst in the vibrant Sloop Inn, which opened for business in 1743 and remains firmly at the heart of the Welsh-speaking community. There's a warm welcome and local seafood is so good that regulars wisely book well ahead. Call in for breakfast, tide

timetables, the latest scrap metal and red diesel prices, takeaway sand-wiches, great beer and a fascinating gallery of photographs showing old Porthgain at the height of its industrial powers.

Porthgain is a place where you can be happily busy doing not much at all; join an impromptu game of football or cricket on the village green or sit on the harbour wall watching rowers from the Porthgain gig club train for open-sea races. Theirs is the only club in Wales to row a Cornish pilot gig, a six- or four-oared boat traditionally used to guide sailing vessels into harbour. Visit the galleries in Y Stryd – the street, a cluster of pretty stone cottages – or follow the 2-mile stretch of coastal path up and over the head land to a secluded beach and the exotic Blue Lagoon at Abereiddy.

The clifftop walk from Porthgain to Abereiddy takes about an hour; allow longer to explore secluded Traeth Llyfn beach. Over 100 steep steps lead to the sheltered shore, which is best at low tide (part of the beach is cut off at high tide). Swimming here is not advisable because of dangerous currents and rocks.

...hungry?

Surrounded by lobster pots on the quayside, the Shed Wine Bar and Bistro in Porthgain has earned glowing reviews for freshly landed local seafood.

The café at Melin Tregwynt is small and charming. Try a bowl of traditional Welsh cawl (lamb broth). The mill shop and café are open seven days a week.

The iron age fort of Trwyncastell crowns the headland just before reaching the intensely coloured Blue Lagoon at Abereiddy. You'll probably hear the shouts and sploshes of leaping swimmers well before you see them. The scary prospect of launching from a cliff into a deep, flooded slate quarry attracts people from far and wide. Injuries are frequent when people hit the water badly – leap at your own risk!

There's plenty of sporting action along this coast: coasteers scrambling over rock and into water; surfers in the waves; fishermen on the shore; kayakers in sea caves under the cliffs, although these are out of bounds at seal pupping time; and divers in the lagoon and Porthgain harbour.

From the thrills of Abereiddy it is a ten-minute journey back to Porthgain on the zippy Strumble Shuttle bus, which regularly links the villages around the coast.

The coastal route from Porthgain to Strumble Head is a challenging walk of around 10 miles. The inland route of deep country lanes, thick with high hedges and wild flowers, makes a lovely drive or cycle ride.

The Pembrokeshire landscape is good hunting ground for artists. John Piper (1903–92) had two cottages near Strumble Head: one to live in; the other for painting.

The exposed mini mountain of Garn Fawr features often in his work. Garn Fawr is one of Britain's best-preserved hill forts. Follow signed paths from the car park to discover the stone huts, animal pens and field systems of a settlement that may date from 1500 BC. Views from here to St David's Head, Strumble Head and the Presili Hills are breathtaking.

A suspension bridge links the mainland to the islet of Ynys Meicl and Strumble Head lighthouse. It's a magnificent spot that seems miles from anywhere until the stalwart shuttle bus puts in an appearance to deliver bird and sea watchers and their binoculars to the headland. This is a top spot for sightings. Look out for gannets circling above the sea, often an indication of dolphins and porpoise nearby.

Hop on the shuttle at Strumble Head for a twenty-minute ride inland to Melin Tregwynt where colours of the Welsh landscape are woven into beautiful cloth. You may tour the mill on weekdays and peep over the shoulder of workers making designer throws and blankets for luxury hotels around the world. Admission is free but prepare to spend in the chic shop.

From the mill there's a path to the shore: Abermawr beach and Aberbach cove await. Strong sea winds make them perfect for kite-flying. Pebbly Abermawr is sandy at low tide, smaller Aberbach is good for rock pools.

...tired?

The Old School Eco Hostel in Trefin is a favourite with cyclists and walkers. The village also has a pub and gallery-cum-café.

Tuck yourself into a tipi at the small but beautiful Trellyn Woodland Campsite near the small port of Abercastle; fresh lobsters and vegetables for supper. It is hugely popular, so book well ahead.

Wake up to spectacular sea views at Pwll Deri Youth Hostel, from Strumble Head. Dramatic coastal scenery from the dining-room windows is jaw-dropping stuff.

Headspace

Seabirds Islands Seals

Magnificent west Pembrokeshire is all about the forces of nature. Sea-salt breezes carry a coastal symphony: the raucous chatter of seabirds, the thunder of rolling waves and the haunting moan of Atlantic grey seals in sheltered coves. The windswept scenery of the Marloes and Dale peninsulas in the Pembrokeshire Coast National Park is spectacular. When you want to connect with the elements, this is the place to be.

Pembrokeshire coastal bus routes allow you to break free and ditch the car on arrival. The country lanes are perfect for cycling and footpaths criss-cross the fields while the Pembrokeshire Coast National Trail hugs the shore.

At Marloes Sands, a vast golden beach is studded with rocks and backed by a dramatic range of towering cliffs. The sands are revealed only at low water so take care to time it right. In winter, when raging seas lash the shore, the clifftop is an excellent vantage point to observe the drama below. The ten-minute walk from here to the shore deters casual visitors, so you can often be alone with your thoughts in this special place.

The National Trust manages the area and in the car park there's useful information about the four geological groups that make up the extraordinary cliffs around the beach. Outstanding examples of Skomer Volcanic, Coralliferous, Gray Sandstone and Old Red Sandstone are irresistible to geologists.

Seabirds are everywhere; pack binoculars and bird guides to identify them. In spring and summer, Grassholm Island turns white when the largest gannetry in southern Britain takes up residence. Skomer and Skokholm Islands host internationally important colonies of puffin, razorbill, guillemot and Manx shearwater. Choughs nest in sea caves, skylark and meadow pipit in open land, and prickly gorse bushes are alive with stonechat, linnet and whitethroats.

The pools of Marloes Mere are a haven for water birds, including Black Ducks. In the 1800s, the remote mere kept Harley Street doctors supplied with huge quantities of medicinal leeches.

Marloes village, on the north side of the peninsula, goes about its business quietly. There's a fine arts and crafts-style clock tower, built as a memorial to the fourth Baron Kensington, renowned for his punctuality. The church of St Peter the Fisherman reflects the traditional occupation of villagers, as does the Lobster Pot & Inn.

There never were any deer in the deer park beyond Marloes village but there are Welsh mountain ponies. Introduced by the National Trust, they roam freely and help to maintain the diverse structure of the heathland.

From Wooltack Point you can observe seabirds fishing in the waves and Atlantic grey seals basking on the Garland Stone. Enjoy magnificent views towards Skomer, Grassholm and Skokholm too. From Martin's Haven, weather-dependent boat trips depart for the islands in summer.

Diverse habitats above and below the water promote abundant animal and plant life and attract divers to explore the clear water. Visit Skomer Marine Nature Reserve visitor centre and Lockley Lodge in Martin's Haven to learn about the importance of precious sea slugs and squirts, octopus and kelp. R. M. Lockley, naturalist, writer, conservationist and famous Skokholm resident took refuge at the Lodge on days when the weather was too severe to cross to the island.

Between August and December, the headland resounds to strangely human groans, echoing from coves below the cliff path. Peer very carefully over the edge and you'll see beaches littered with furry seal pups and vocal mothers loudly defending their space. Looking like silvery sardines in the water, the pups are a joy to observe. I watched one at play with a floating pallet in a sheltered cove. Much to its mother's distress, the pup flopped aboard the raft and made for the open sea. In hot pursuit, she dived underneath to nudge pup and pallet back to the safety of a sea cave. Moments later, they were off again.

It's important to stay quiet, still and out of sight when observing seals. They are easily disturbed and mothers won't come ashore to feed pups if they sense intrusion. They may even abandon their young altogether. Keep a low profile and your patience is usually rewarded.

If you like to keep moving, the sheltered, unspoiled village of Dale, once a den of smugglers, is paradise for sailing and water sports enthusiasts. Hire wetsuits, boards, sailboards and kayaks, or charter a boat for fishing or diving trips.

For a perfect picnic, seek out the sheltered white sands of secluded Watwick Bay, one of the many lovely beaches around Dale.

...thirsty?

After all the activity, chill out at the friendly Griffin Inn in Dale with a glass of Felinfoel Double Dragon ale and a plate of smoked mackerel.

...tired?

At Marloes youth hostel, a converted farmhouse close to the clifftop where the sound of the waves will lull you to sleep.
In Marloes village, the Clock House is a bright and breezy cafe and bed and breakfast. Relax on the pretty terrace in the company of a huge carved puffin called Scraggamuffin.

Circle of Friends

Tea with Aunty Vi   Magnificent limestone cliffs   Military manoeuvres

PRINCE WILLIAM
WAS IN THIS SHOP
WITH A GROUP OF
ETON STUDENTS
IN JULY 1999

Elizabeth II 2002

Jubilee portrait
Mail

Mencap Gardens
Stackpole Estate

For all your Fresh Vegetable, Soft Fruits &
Herbs, shrubs and flowering plants

Open All Year
Mon – Fri 8.30-4.30
Sat   9.00-5.00

— Gypsy Caravan —
Bed and breakfast

Genuine Gypsy Caravan in idyllic settings

Bed and Breakfast for two persons

the arc
of Asia

SALE HERE

Real
Lancashire
**Eccles
Cakes**

Real Lancashire
Eccles Cakes
CONTAINING PURE BUTTER
AND
CHOICEST VOSTIZZA CURRANTS

Stackpole
Barafundle Bay
Bosherston
Stackpole Head
Broad Haven South
St Govan's Head

0 Mi   1
0 Km 1   2

ublime beaches and an exhilarating circular walk around Stackpole Head in the south-west corner of Pembrokeshire, the UK's only coastal National Park, make this weekend perfect for time away with friends or family.

The six-mile walk starts at Bosherston, but before setting out, visit the Olde Worlde Café where Mrs Weston, or Aunty Vi to regulars, has been serving tea for over seventy years. In 2009 she received an MBE in recognition of her services to hospitality and tourism. Opened by her parents in 1922, the café exudes time-warp charm. Tables, chairs and fruit trees are dotted about the garden and, in case of inclement weather, there's a cheery wooden pavilion that would grace any village cricket pitch.

Mrs Weston is a fervent royalist and, as a reminder of the momentous occasion when Prince William dropped in unexpectedly, she displays a picture of him, alongside his brother, above the ice-cream counter. Whilst she was being photographed for this chapter, a breeze caused a newspaper cutting of the younger prince to flap about on the wall. 'Let's do the picture when Harry settles down,' she said, without a hint of irony.

The walk begins at Bosherston Lily Ponds, three flooded limestone valleys on the National Trust's Stackpole Estate, formerly the Welsh country residence of the Earl of Cawdor from Nairn in Scotland. In June, a floating waxy carpet of exquisite water lilies bloom across the lake, dragonflies hover and otters scout for eels. There's good coarse fishing too, predominantly pike, with tench, perch and roach. Permits are on sale at Mrs Weston's café, and fishing is at pegged points.

Cross bridges over the ponds to the dunes of Broad Haven South. The beach is a favourite with body-boarding families in summer and experienced surfers riding barrelling waves in winter. Follow the path's short steep climb to the top of the limestone cliffs and you are rewarded with spectacular coastal views. The granite lump of distant Lundy Island is visible on a clear day.

From here it is an easy, level walk across the clifftops, but keep a close eye on young children who may be tempted to charge ahead, blissfully unconcerned with a sheer drop to the sea.

Stackpole Head is the haunt of seals and seabirds and climbers too, but only when seasonal restrictions to protect birds nesting on the ledges of the sea cliff are not in force. The schedule is posted at Mrs Weston's café. Turning inland, the path descends through woodland to Barafundle beach. Walls built to prevent livestock straying from the Cawdor deer park enclose this dreamy secluded place, which remains extra special because it can't be reached by road.

Take the steep steps from the beach to Stackpole Quay, one of the smallest harbours in Britain, built to load eighteenth-century sailing ships with limestone from the Earl of Cawdor's quarries. Now the snug quay shelters boats of local fishermen and launching is possible with permission of the National Trust. From here the walk turns inland, back to Bosherston, although you could hop on the popular Coastal Cruiser shuttle bus, a great service, specially adapted for walkers, wheelchairs, mountain bikes, dogs and surfboards.

To the west of Stackpole, Castlemartin's carboniferous limestone cliffs offer world-class climbing. The spectacular Green Bridge of Wales is an immense natural arch carved by the waves, and the detached pillars of

...hungry?

Visit the Olde World Café in Bosherston where the redoubtable Mrs Weston has been serving quality leaf tea for over seventy years: 'We've never used tea bags, I don't like them.' At the end of the coastal walk to Stackpole Quay there's thirst-quenching homemade lemonade, crab salad and local cheese at the Boathed café.

Pick up fresh vegetables, fruit and flowers from the Mencap walled garden and shop at Stackpole Home Farm.

Dine out at the Stackpole Inn where good food is cooked to order. There's a relaxed atmosphere and bedrooms for those who'd like to stay longer.

Stack Rocks, crowded with nesting seabirds through spring and summer, attract bird-watchers. Protected species along this coast include chough, peregrine and razorbill. Grassland edges and dunes are of national geological and biological interest, but Castlemartin is also a military range used by tanks and helicopters to practise beach landings and village attacks all year round.

To meet the demands of access, recreation and nesting birds, the Ministry of Defence, conservationists and climbers perform a finely tuned balancing act. Access to the range is restricted when live firing is taking place; before attempting a visit, it's best to consult www.pembrokeshireranges.com. The firing range schedule is also posted at the Olde Worlde Café. Flexible restrictions agreed with the British Mountaineering Council identify 'no climbing areas'. Red clifftop markers indicate 'no go' zones until the chicks have fledged or birds have failed to nest.

The extraordinary hermitage of St Govan, a sixth-century monk, is just south of the firing range. However, the road from Bosherston to the chapel is closed when the military are on the move. The monk's tiny chapel and cell is wedged between great slabs of rock, reached by a steep staircase. Count the steps there and back – local people say the total is never the same. Pursued by pirates from Lundy, seeking to kidnap him for a handsome ransom, St Govan was hiding in a crevice when the rock face opened up to protect him. Impressed by the welcome, he decided to stay.

Saddle Up

Pagan landscape   Headline beach   Clifftop golf

The landscape of the Gŵyr or Gower peninsula, west of the city of Swansea, became the first of the UK's forty-seven Areas of Outstanding Natural Beauty (AONB) in 1956. There's a distinct air of Welsh romance about the limestone cliffs and hidden bays, ruined castles and wild horses on the salt marsh. Whatever the season, whatever the mood, time spent here is richly rewarding.

With a bucketful of award-winning beaches, there's too much choice for just a couple of days, so take a weekend to whet your appetite and get acquainted with the coast from the heights of Cefn Bryn, a sandstone ridge known as the backbone of Gower. Commanding views are inspirational: a patchwork blanket of lush green fields, golden shores and shimmering sea is spread at your feet. To be on Cefn Bryn at the end of day when the sun slips from the sky to the sea is a spine-tingling experience. The atmospheric summit is also associated with pagan ritual.

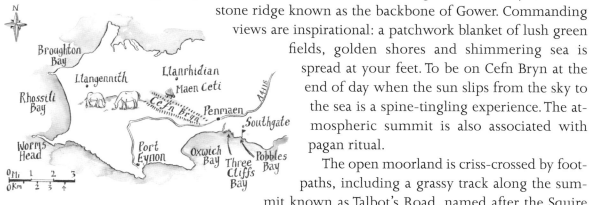

The open moorland is criss-crossed by footpaths, including a grassy track along the summit known as Talbot's Road, named after the Squire of Penrice Castle, who used the route after a day's hunting in Parc le Breos. Travelling on horseback is still one of the best ways to explore the Gower. Beginners and experienced riders can saddle up at local stables for a day of trekking with fantastic views and a relaxed pub lunch.

One of Cefn Bryn's most famous features is Maen Ceti, or King Arthur's Stone, a huge boulder deposited by an ice age glacier. Legend has it that King Arthur found grit in his shoe and hurled it from Llanelli to Cefn Bryn, whereupon it swelled with pride having been touched by the hand of greatness. There are alternative theories: many believe the boulder sheltered a double-chambered neolithic tomb for communal burials, while others reckon it was aligned with the heavens to serve as a prehistoric clock.

Herds of cattle and ponies wander freely across unfenced land at Cefn Bryn, one of ten locations on the peninsula where local people, mostly farmers, have for centuries exercised a legal right to graze a registered number of livestock. Commons land covers almost half of the total land area of Gower and the biggest threat to grazing is traffic accidents, which kill and injure livestock. Drivers are urged to slow down, especially at night.

Beneath Cefn Bryn, grazing livestock congregate to drink at Broad

...thirsty?

Join pony trekkers and horses for lunch at the friendly King Arthur pub in Reynoldston. In fine weather, take a seat outside to admire the ridge of Cefyn Bryn; on colder days there are log fires to tempt you in.

Go for Three Cliffs Gold in the Joiners Arms, Bishopston. Beer festival, folk dancing and a brewery in the garage make this a lively local.

...hungry?

Gower is the home of traditional Welsh laverbread, or cooked chopped seaweed, which goes well with cockles from the muddy flats of the Burry estuary.

Try Gower cockle and laverbread bake, freshly prepared by landlord Mike Beynon and his aunty Margaret at Llanrhidian's eighteenth-century Dolphin Inn. A great place to watch birds of prey and roaming horses on the marsh.

Gather a feast of local flavours, including salt-marsh lamb, from Llangennith produce market in the village hall on the last Saturday of each month, April to September.

Let them eat cake at the Three Cliffs Coffee Shop in Southgate, famous for a huge range of delicious home baking.

Pool. From May to August the shallow water is alive with aquatic plants and dragonflies. Between September and April it is the haunt of bird-watchers on the lookout for passage migrants like spotted redshanks.

One of Gower's landmark beaches is Three Cliffs Bay, winner of national popularity polls for good looks. Have your camera ready for the viewpoint on the A4118, near Penmaen village. A trio of peaks shelter the magnificent beach, which is reached by steeply sloping paths. While spectacular Three Cliffs hogs the headlines, its lovely neighbour Pobbles Bay is quietly enchanting.

To reach Pobbles on foot, walk from Three Cliffs at low water or from the National Trust car park at Southgate village. Pass Pennard Golf Club on the cliffs where Gus Faulkner, club professional and father of 1951 Open champion Max Faulkner, was responsible for eliminating rabbits on the links; he had permission to shoot them before 10 a.m. The glorious seventh hole famously features the romantic ruins of medieval Pennard Castle. From here there are breathtaking views of Three Cliffs Bay, horse riders on the shore and the meandering Pennard Pill on its way to sea. It's the perfect spot for a Welsh picnic.

Shiver Me Timbers!

Saints Ghosts Movies

eave the fast lane behind and escape off the M4 motorway in South Wales to explore Glamorgan's rich coastal landscape, marked by ancient history, extraordinary geology and strange goings-on.

In the bid to keep Christianity alive in Britain after the departure of the Romans, St Illtud was dispatched to Llantwit Major, or Llanilltud Fawr in Welsh. The warrior knight, who reformed his unruly ways to become a monk, established a fifth-century church and mission centre where royal children and saints from all over the world were educated and Welsh kings were buried.

Nothing remains of the important seat of learning, although foundations may lie under the present St Illtud's church which, thanks to a series of extensions over hundreds of years, provides an object lesson in the history of ecclesiastical architecture.

Described by John Wesley as 'the most beautiful as well as the most spacious church in Wales', St Illtud's nestles in a sheltered hollow close by the babbling Ogney Brook. Inside, there's a treasure trove of carved Celtic stones, medieval wall paintings and a fifteenth-century stone screen behind the altar.

Just beyond the narrow, twisting streets of ancient Llantwit Major, the Col-huw valley leads to the beach at Col-huw Point, popular with

fossil hunters, surfers and sea kayakers exploring dramatic caves along the coast.

There's an extraordinary natural arch known as the Bow of Destiny beneath the roof of Tresilian cave, on the shore between Llantwit Major and St Donat's. Couples were married in here up until the eighteenth century, and legend tells of a pirate buried up to his neck in pebbles and abandoned to the incoming tide. The eerie chamber, known as Reynard's Cave, is said to be the lair of semi-human foxes in local folklore.

Allow a couple of hours to walk 3 miles along the cliff path from Col-huw Point, past St Donat's Castle, to the lighthouses at Nash Point, with views along the way to Somerset and Devon across the busy Bristol Channel. But take care, the cliffs are eroding and rockfalls are frequent.

The Channel serves ports at Bristol, Barry, Cardiff, Newport and Avonmouth. Look out for ships painted white to keep imported fruit cool and oceanographic research vessels, painted red and green.

In 1925, American newspaper magnate William Randolph Hearst brought glamour to Glamorgan when he acquired St Donat's medieval castle after seeing it in the pages of *Country Life* magazine. Movie stars and statesmen, including John F. Kennedy, Charlie Chaplin and David Lloyd George attended the tycoon's lavish seaside parties, a lifestyle that inspired Orson Welles' film *Citizen Kane*.

Today the castle is an international sixth-form college and innovative arts centre. Dynamic modern architecture merges with the medieval stone; this unique venue is a great way to add cinema, theatre, art and music to your weekend.

Nash Point is an atmospheric place. On the beach, rockfall from near-vertical soft cliffs appears like smashed digestive biscuits over wide wave-cut platforms.

Behind the beach, smugglers would hide chains of horses in a sheltered wooded valley to carry their tax-free booty inland.

A treacherous sandbank lurks beneath the waves, marked by a

...hungry?

Stop for tea at Ogmore Farm where former London fashion buyer Judith Yates serves scrumptious homemade cakes. The farm also offers two-hour trekking rides on beautiful local beaches.

Many a dark deed was planned at at Llantwit Major's Old Swan Inn. Smugglers climbed the concealed staircase for shady meetings in the attic.
No need for cloak and dagger at the Net community café near St Illtud's church; pop in for proper ice-cream milkshakes, internet access and a friendly welcome.
Join dog-walkers and the winter surfers warming up in the Beach Café at Colhuw; it's open all year round.

navigation buoy equipped with a bell. When the wind blows on a foggy day, the sombre clanking of the bell – to the rise and fall of the waves – is enough to chill you to the core.

On the clifftop, two lighthouses stand apart from each other, designed to be lined up for safety by ships going up the Bristol Channel. Still operational, the higher light welcomes visitors between April to September. Although no longer in service as an aid to navigation, the foghorn blares on occasion for civil weddings taking place in the tower.

From Monknash beach, turn inland to follow the lane to the Plough and Harrow, oozing character and serving ale since 1383. The pub stands in the middle of the Monknash Grange, a monastic farm once tended by 300 monks. It was the scene of much skulduggery. Stories tell of shipwrecked bodies stashed in a chamber at the end of the bar awaiting their coffins for burial. These were victims of the 'Wreckers of Wick', who confused ships approaching the docks in Barry and Cardiff by tying lanterns on wandering sheep.

Unsurprisingly, the pub has ghosts. The landlord explains that they 'manifest themselves through activities such as tugging at the staff, moving furniture and holding conversations in an empty bar'. Be brave – go for the warm welcome, roaring fire, good food, beer and cider. The bus stopping at the top of the lane will take you safely back to Llantwit Major.

The spectacular cliffs and vast sands of Southerndown beach have often been seen in the BBC *Doctor Who* series. A walled garden is all that remains of Dunraven Castle, which overlooked the beach. It was used as a convalescent home during the First World War, and patients and staff reported sightings of another of Glamorgan's ghosts here: the shadowy figure of a young woman in blue who walked in a cloud of fragrant mimosa visiting the bedsides of dying soldiers.

For information about events in the area, visit the Heritage Coast Information Centre at Dunraven Park. Continue along the coast to wander around romantic riverside ruins at Ogmore Castle, where grassy slopes are perfect for picnics and lazing in the sun. Admission is free.

Hop across fifty-two stepping-stones in the ford of the Ewenny and Ogmore rivers to the thatched village of Merthyr Mawr where David Lean came to film blockbuster *Lawrence of Arabia* on mighty sand dunes along the beach.

The Wreckers' Coast

Dramatic coastal scenery   Weird geology   Cream tea heaven

23

'From Hartland Point to Padstow light, is a watery grave by day or night.'

From Morwenstow in Cornwall, to the lighthouse at Hartland Point in Devon, the Atlantic coast is awash with deadly rocks, shipwrecks, and spectacularly weird geology – perfect inspiration for Robert Stephen Hawker, Cornish hero, opium smoker, poet and eccentric vicar of Morwenstow from 1834 to 1875. It's a dramatic place to visit for a weekend.

Shipwrecks off the coast claimed hundreds of lives during Hawker's time, and while many locals were tempted to leave dead sailors on the shore, Hawker ensured they all had a Christian burial in the churchyard.

The captain of the doomed *Caledonia*, which sank in 1843, is buried under the ship's famous white figurehead, a Scottish girl in kilt, tam-o'-shanter and sporran. There were just two survivors: a member of crew and a tortoise.

In the church, a window in the south aisle portrays the vicar, who wrote the Cornish anthem 'Song of the Western Men'.

During forty years at Morwenstow, Hawker spent much of his time smoking opium to relieve depression. His bolthole, Hawker's Hut, was a driftwood shack on the cliffs between Higher Sharpnose Point and Hennacliff, the highest in Cornwall. His constant companions were a pet pig Gyp, and Berg, his dog who carried the church keys in his mouth.

Follow the footpath from the church across the meadow to Hawker's Hut, now in the care of the National Trust. The simple shelter enjoys spectacular views of Lundy Island and Trevose Head. It's a short walk from here to the exposed ridge of Higher Sharpnose Point; breathtaking, but give it a miss if you have vertigo!

From Hawker's windswept cliffs, head inland by car or foot to Docton Mill at Lymebridge where banks of wild flowers grow to the gush and gurgle of a millstream and waterfalls. The pretty garden is open between March and November.

Narrow country lanes plunge down sheltered valleys to the unmade road at Welcombe Mouth. Low water reveals a sandy beach and wave-cut platform of folded rocks. Stride out along the undulating South West Coast Path to Speke's Mill Mouth where a rare coastal waterfall surges fifty metres over the sheer cliff – a favourite with climbers. Surfers head here for the reef break and you might spy seals, dolphins and porpoise too.

From Speke's Mill Mouth it's a twenty-minute walk to Hartland Quay and geology nirvana. Sandstone and mudstone rocks reveal earth-shattering events of around 300 million years ago. The rocks have been responsible for dramas in more recent times, many of them recorded in the Shipwreck Museum at Hartland Quay.

From A Croon on Hennacliff

Thus said the rushing raven,
unto his hungry mate:
'Ho! gossip! for Bude Haven;
There be corpses six or eight.
Cawk, cawk! the crew and skipper
Are wallowing in the sea;
So there's a savoury supper
For my old dame and me.'

R. S. Hawker

...hungry?

This is cream tea country. There's 'Smugglers' Choice' tea at Rectory Farm, opposite Morwenstow church, homemade jam and scones at Docton Mill and Gardens, with warming soup and local ice cream from Hartland Point's kiosk. Liable to shake, rattle and roll in high winds, the friendly little café is tethered to the ground by strong rope.

The Bristol Channel meets the Atlantic Ocean at Hartland Point. The lighthouse alerts shipping to dangerous waters and there's a stern warning below the cliffs. The MS *Johanna* foundered there in 1982; her crew survived but the broken vessel left to the mercy of the sea makes a dramatic sight. There's great shore fishing around the point, one of the best bass-fishing marks in north Devon.

If you venture inland, the craft shops, potteries and galleries of pretty Hartland village are 3 miles away. Augustinian monks built Hartland Abbey, near Hartland Quay, in the twelfth century. Gertrude Jekyll, a regular guest of the Stucley family who remain in residence, influenced the lovely gardens. The abbey is open between April and October.

24

Beach Break

Surf Sand School

Back to school for surf lessons on Cornwall's Atlantic coast, where the teachers wear wetsuits, the classroom is a golden beach and the playground is the pounding ocean.

Surfing is booming although the scene has changed dramatically since the heady days of the 1960s and the Beach Boys' 'bushy, bushy blond hairdos'. Now, balding novices and silver surfers are just as likely to catch a wave alongside the sun-kissed bleached-blond dudes.

Coastal car parks are a sign of the times; locals park salty motors beside gleaming executive cars, people-carriers and midlife-crisis soft-tops, all of them loaded with wetsuits and 'sticks'.

Take time to select your surf school carefully. Opt for small classes and qualified instructors, who are familiar with local beaches and tides. It pays to be flexible too; working around the weather means that locations and lesson times may have to change for your safety.

Sarah and Cheyne of the Constantine Bay Surf School have a lifetime of local experience and a great surfing pedigree: Cheyne's dad runs the renowned Constantine Bay Surf Store and he is named after Bondi hero, Cheyne Horan. No pressure there, then. With seven fantastic bays on their doorstep, Sarah and Cheyne tailor lessons and locations to suit their students' ability.

Taster sessions are hugely popular with beginners. Students head for

the beach in the surf school uniform of wetsuits, boards and bibs. Beach safety and ocean awareness are the first and most important lessons, along with how to carry a board safely into the sea and how to protect yourself when you fall off, which you will.

Before taking to the water, the class practise surf moves on the beach, learning to paddle, catch the wave and get up on their feet. When the instructors feel they are ready, the group wade out to sea. There are whoops of delight, fits of giggles, wobbly wipe-outs, and great gulps of sea water as debutants take to the waves. The instructors shout encouragement and monitor progress closely. The class is called ashore to refine techniques before heading back for more. The thrill is exhausting and exhilarating at the same time.

THE MAGNIFICENT SEVEN

There's a string of seven great bays around the rocky coast of north Cornwall.

Trevone Bay

A wide flat sandy beach. Discover Tinker Bunny's seawater bathing pool in the rocks and, in the fields above the beach, a dangerously deep and spectacular blow hole known as the 'Round Hole'.

...hungry?

After a session in the sea, stop by Food For Thought in the car park at Harlyn Bay, where Charles and Lynne serve up breakfast and treats like Thunder and Lightning: dripping syrup and oozing Cornish cream on a bread roll.

Padstow Farm Shop sells fresh food from local producers, traditional Cornish pasties and buns made with Persian saffron, scrumpy and wines from the Camel Valley Vineyard Farm – great for Cornish picnics.

For fabulous seaside style, there's nothing like spoiling yourself with a visit to Rick and Jill Stein's outstanding Seafood Restaurant and Hotel in Padstow.

Harlyn Bay

A popular sheltered family beach with sloping sands and gentle surf, surrounded by low cliffs. A large Celtic Iron Age cemetery of 130 stone cist burials was discovered here in 1900; see the finds at the Royal Cornwall Museum in Truro.

Mother Ivey's Bay

Gently sloping Polventon beach, on the doorstep of a large caravan park, offers good fishing for bass and ray. There's a toll road to Trevose Head Lighthouse on the headland and the nearby RNLI Padstow lifeboat station is open to visitors.

Booby's Bay

Not for surfing novices but great rock pools and sand dunes. Swimming is dangerous due to strong currents.

Constantine Bay

Adjoining Booby's Bay, more great rock pools, sand dunes and dangerous swimming. Again, it's not for novices; the reef at the southern end of the beach is a challenge for expert surfers only.

Treyarnon Bay

Location, location, location – Treyarnon youth hostel is in an idyllic spot above the sandy beach and rocky bathing pool. Beware strong rip currents at some states of the tide. Said to be the birthplace of British surfing in the early 1960s; Stuart Charles, winner of the Cornish longboard championships, was the professional lifeguard here.

Porthcothan Bay

While the surf is often small and messy, as they say in surfspeak, this is an unspoiled and easily accessible family beach. The friendly Porthcothan Stores sell or hire everything for a perfect day at the seaside.

After watching Nick and Jane Darke's fascinating film *The Wrecking Season*, exploring the mystery of long-haul drift washed up on the Porthcothan shore from as far away as Labrador and the Amazon basin, I view flotsam and jetsam on the strand line quite differently. Catch it on DVD (www.thewreckingseason.com).

The South West Coastal Path

Try the easy 5.5 mile stretch from Padstow to Harlyn. Spectacular coastal scenery and lush farmland make this a walk to remember. There's a regular bus service between Harlyn and Padstow for the journey back.

On the Towan

Literary inspiration   Miles of beach   A world heritage site

Nothing that we had as children made as much difference, was quite so important to us, as our summer in Cornwall.

-Virginia Woolf

The faded glory of a pioneering port whose industry shaped the nineteenth-century world and mile upon mile of dreamy beaches make Hayle and St Ives Bay an intriguing combination.

The port of Hayle has long served the Cornish mining industry but it gained a worldwide reputation for innovative engineering and manufacture of steam engines during the massive industrial expansion of the nineteenth century.

Two foundries dominated the town. Bitter rivals, they sought to outdo each other at every opportunity; from the calculated act of building quays so far into the Hayle river that they would restrict the opposition's access to the harbour to impromptu street fighting.

Their feuds became known as 'the thirty years' war' and even now the town is divided. The east end is Copperhouse, site of the Cornish Copper Company's smelting and iron works and the west end is Foundry, where John Harvey's company made one of the largest steam engines in the world.

The Cornish Copper Company made the chain links for the Clifton suspension bridge, and some of the biggest Cornish beam engines and pump engines made by Harvey's were used to distribute London's water supply and drain the Severn tunnel.

The global significance of Hayle's industrial heritage is recognised by the town's inclusion in the Cornwall and West Devon World Heritage Site. Take a walk to discover Brunel's viaduct, the harbour, quays and canal so

vital for trade, Foundry Square's handsome boom-time buildings and Loggans steam-powered mill, the largest listed building in Cornwall. Wander past the open-air swimming pool to a glorious blaze of colour and fairy lanterns in the subtropical gardens of the King George V Memorial Walk, beside Copperhouse Creek and the RSPB nature reserve.

The modest town takes its name from the Cornish word for estuary, heyl. The mild climate makes the huge, shallow estuary the warmest in Britain. Although still polluted by heavy minerals from the mining industry, there's much activity in autumn and winter when migratory birds stop to feed en route to their destinations. At Ryan's field, the RSPB have created a saline lagoon, four islands and a salt marsh to attract even more feathered friends.

Beyond the town are the towans (Cornish for sand dunes), a spectacular arc of sand from the mouth of the Hayle estuary to the lighthouse at Godrevy Island – a shoreline so vast that each stretch of the towans takes a name: Harvey's, Black Cliffs, Riviere, Mexico, Phillack, Upton, Gwithian, St Gothian Sands and Godrevy. The huge seaside is per-

fect for land-based wind-powered sports, including speed sailing, land yachting and kite-flying and the best surfing is at Gwithian, where archaeologists discovered a fifth-century oratory submerged by the sands. There are stories of a buried city beneath holiday chalets on the towans.

The 'red river' flows across Godrevy and Gwithian beaches, so named because it carried iron ore run-off from the mining industry, which stained the sea red. There was industrial activity on the beach too; tin was extracted from the sand. Look out for the cutting blasted through rocks at Sheep's Pool; wide enough for horses and carts loaded with sand.

From the National Trust car park there's an easy half-hour walk around the cliffs of Godrevy headland, close to the island and lighthouse that inspired Virginia Woolf. Look out for grey seals, dolphins and basking sharks.

Although her 1927 novel *To the Lighthouse* is set in the Hebrides, it was Godrevy that inspired Woolf's story of a summer outing. Her childhood holidays were spent at Talland House, a Victorian villa above Porthminster beach, with heavenly views across St Ives bay to Godrevy Island.

...hungry?

Plenty of tasty choices this weekend, all distinctly different. Hayle heaves with pasties, including 'the finest hand-crimped Cornish pasties in the whole of Cornwall' from Philps bakeries. Queues outside the door, always a good sign, and frozen pasties to cook at home. Johnny's Café in Hayle has a great vegetarian menu.

Even on wintery days it's fun to gaze out of the big windows of the Sunset Surf Beach café on Gwithian Towans, overlooking huge seas in St Ives Bay. From here I've watched snow falling softly over the dunes, a rare sight indeed. The popular café is a gem, offering surf hire, internet access and surf webcam.

Don't miss the quirky, dinky Jam Pot café on Gwithian Towans, a whitewashed Grade II listed Cornish roundhouse with a pot-bellied stove to beat the chill in winter. For a great breakfast, there's the National Trust beach café at Godrevy, and for laid-back style, just chill at the friendly Sandsifter Bar and Restaurant on Godrevy beach.

26

Ocean Drive

England's only Cape   Mysterious landscape   Mining heritage

From St Ives to St Just the B3306 road squeezes between high stone walls that have enclosed ancient fields farmed since the Bronze Age. With the Atlantic to one side, hills and moors to the other, it's a wonderful drive.

Between the tourist magnets of St Ives and Land's End, there's wonderful West Penwith, a wild, windswept place, strewn with the chaos of giant boulders, ancient stones, burial places and country paths shrouded in mystery. There's no doubting its appeal. The western extremity of Cornwall is an intriguing place to spend a few days.

The rough and ragged coast makes rewarding but arduous walking. In the past, the fastest route around the headlands was by sea. Today, one of the best ways to discover West Penwith is by car. From St Ives to St Just the B3306 road squeezes between high stone walls that have enclosed ancient fields farmed since the Bronze Age. With the Atlantic to one side, hills and moors to the other, it's a wonderful drive.

D. H. Lawrence succumbed to the power of West Penwith when he moved there in 1915. In his semi-autobiographical novel *Kangaroo*, he recalls night-time falling over 'dark, shaggy moors, that were like the fur of some beast, and upon the pale-grey granite masses, so ancient and Druidical, suggesting blood sacrifice'. With his German wife Frieda, Lawrence walked the lonely moors, cliff paths and hills. Locals feared they were wartime spies and monitored their movements; the police eventually expelled the couple.

St Senara's church is at the heart of isolated Zennor village. A West Country schooner hangs from the ceiling, in memory of unnamed sailors drowned at sea and W. A. Proctor, lost in the Pacific on a single-handed voyage from Newlyn. There's a famous mermaid carved into a wooden pew. They say the mermaid disguised herself to hear chorister Matthew Trewhella sing in church before luring him into the sea at nearby Pendour Cove. Some people hear him singing there at sunset.

Allow time to explore Zennor's quirky Wayside Folk Museum and call into Lawrence's local, the atmospheric Tinners Arms. Climb the hill, a mile from the village, to ancient Zennor Quoit. The stone chamber tomb on the moor dates from 2,500–1,500 BC.

Back on the road, it's hard to miss the award-winning Gurnard's Head gastro pub with rooms; the name is emblazoned across the roof. Work off lunch with the 2.5-mile walk from the hotel along the South West Coast Path to Bosigran Iron Age hill fort and sea cliffs, a favourite with climbers.

After your walk, turn off the main road to visit the lighthouse at Pendeen Watch; here is some of the most dangerous coastline in Britain where, after many shipwrecks, the craggy headland was flattened to make way for the lighthouse in 1900. The coastal path takes you from

CURIOUS

Zennor churchway was the traditional route used to transport the dead for burial at church. But the origins of the ancient track, which cuts through prehistoric fields up to 3,000 years old, are shrouded in mystery. Many believe it is connected to the supernatural, witchcraft and places of mystical energy. Three cross heads that marked the way are now in Zennor churchyard.

the lighthouse car park to pebbly Boat Cove and sandy Portheras Cove.

Redundant engine houses, pitheads, shafts and chimneys are reminders of Cornwall's mining industry. The Pendeen village community has strong links with its mining past: at Trewellard, a group of volunteers known as 'the greasy gang' restored the Levant mine steampowered beam engine, now in the care of the National Trust and open to the public. The workings extend a mile from the shore and 600 metres below sea level.

Working up until 1990, Geevor tin mine and World Heritage Site is the largest preserved mining site in the UK. Allow plenty of time for the underground tour and stunning sea views from the café.

Along the road to Cape Cornwall, the extraordinary Botallack mine teeters on cliffs high above the Atlantic swell. In deep submarine caverns, miners worked to the terrifying rumble of waves hurling boulders around the seabed over their heads.

St Just-in-Penwith oozes character. At the heart of the grey granite community is the *plen an gwary*, a grassy theatre where medieval miracle plays were staged in Cornish. Miners' cottages huddle along streets leading to the sea and the ancient church features a wall painting of St George and the dragon.

Cape Cornwall, gifted to the National Trust in 1987 by the Heinz food company, is signposted from the market square. The rugged headland is flanked by Porth Ledden's strange rock formations to the east and pebbly Priest's Cove, with its fishing boats and tidal pool, to the west. A highlight of the annual Cape sports day in summer is a swim around the Brisons rocks, which lie about a mile offshore.

Surfers relish the surging swell rolling across the Atlantic to Whitesand Bay, crashing on Sennen and Gwenver beaches almost at the end of England. Colourful buildings around the more sheltered working harbour at Sennen Cove are a reminder of the pilchard fishing station.

Two dogs, Tyson and Bilbo, play vital roles in this seaside community. Bilbo is Britain's first fully trained canine lifeguard and Tyson is head of security at Sennen lifeboat station.

...hungry?

There's a cheery café, gallery and parish community centre in the former schoolhouse of Morvah village.

Refresh body and mind at the Cook Book Café in St Just. It's an oasis of calm amongst the bookshelves. Your verse is welcomed in the visitors' book, an intriguing collection of impromptu poems.

End the journey on a high note, with good food, panoramic views, surfers and sunset on the terrace of the Beach Restaurant at Sennen.

27

Fish and Ships

Artists' colony   Victorian internet   High drama

14

This fascinating weekend combines the quaint former fishing villages of the Cornish riviera with the harsh reality of fishing for a living along Cornwall's south coast.

Newlyn is England's premier fishing port, renowned for the export of salt pilchards since 1555. Newlyn Tidal Observatory on the south pier determines the mean sea level of the whole of the UK and at least 50 species of premium line-, trawlnet-and pot-caught fish are landed every day. But the fishing industry is in decline and Newlyn's famous pilchard works closed in 2005.

Commercial fishing is still one of the most dangerous industries in the UK: to fish for a living is to risk your life. Tom Leaper's lifesize bronze sculpture of a young fisherman is a reminder of the true price of fish and a memorial to all the fishermen lost at sea from the harbours of Cornwall and the Isles of Scilly.

Marie from Liverpool runs the small, busy Newlyn Harbour café, a steamy little gem on the Strand. Packed like pilchards, fishermen come here for strong tea, Guinness stew and to catch up with *Fishing News*, EU quotas and legislation that affects their lives. Join the conversation and you'll get a unique insight into the reality of life as a modern commercial fisherman.

Many are incensed at having to throw high-value dead fish back into the sea: chucking fish out of the nets goes against the grain. An average trawler uses between 200 and 300 litres of expensive fuel over a two-day fishing trip and, as any fisherman will tell you, there's no guarantee of a good catch.

Walk into the Fishermen's Arms, the Swordfish Inn, the Dolphin or the Star Inn, complete with a handsome green parrot in the upstairs window, and you'll hear more talk of a sea change in the fishing industry.

The Newlyn Water Trail, is a great way to explore the back streets on foot. A guide is available from the local newsagent. Starting at the Fishermen's Mission, the trail weaves through the village to a string of water wells, shoots and pumps where women

gathered water in pitchers for domestic use – a scene captured by many artists of the Newlyn School, who painted real people in real surroundings in the 1880s.

Follow the Heritage Walk through cobbled 'courts' and hillside streets like La Rue Des Beaux Arts, made famous by artists. The Newlyn Art Gallery continues the tradition of exhibiting the work of contemporary artists while a collection by the original Newlyn School is at Penlee House Gallery in Penzance.

From Newlyn it's a short bus ride to quaint Mousehole, a tourist attraction that rhymes with 'cows'll'. Car parking spaces are few; even out of season the lanes are dotted with homemade signs declaring 'Parking for locals'.

In high season the village can feel distinctly overrun by visitors, but time it right and its charm will be evident.

Mousehole is renowned for a storybook cat, romantic Christmas

lights around the harbour and the tradition of eating star-gazey pie on 23 December. The fish heads poking through the pastry are a tribute to Tom Bawcock, who braved a storm to return with seven different types of fish after weeks without a single catch.

When the weather's kind the harbour is sheltered, but come November it's 'baulks down, boats up' as the locals protect themselves from fierce storms. The harbour entrance is closed with huge timber baulks from Canada. Look out for spares lying around the harbour wall.

CURIOUS

Newlyn people are known as Buccas, after the Bucca-boo storm devil. To keep him sweet, fisher-men put out scraps of food and slops of beer.

From Mousehole there's circular walk to Lamorna Cove, which lies at the end of a lush wooded valley 2.5 miles away. Head up Raginnis Hill, past the wild bird sanctuary founded by two sisters in 1928, and follow the signposts.

'Home of the Victorian Internet' boasts Porthcurno, one of the world's most important cable stations. Here a network of underwater cables from America entered England to deliver top-secret wartime messages, which were decoded by ace teams working in bomb-proof, and gas-proof tunnels. Allow plenty of time to visit the fascinating Telegraph Museum and tunnels.

The open-air Minack Theatre is astounding. Theatre and costume designer Rowena Cade, an extraordinary woman, created the magnificent amphitheatre, perched on the cliff, digging much of it out of the rock-face herself over a period of fifty years. Plays are performed under the stars with a backdrop of crashing Atlantic waves. Even if you can't attend a production, it's well worth visiting to explore the amazing setting. For sheer romance, the Minack is a must-visit.

...hungry?

Newlyn
Due to health and safety restrictions, Newlyn fish market is not open to the public but freshly landed fish is served up at the bright blue Newlyn Seafood Café. Savour Newlyn crab soup with harbour views at the Red Lion pub.

Don't miss vanilla ice cream made with Cornish milk and served with clotted cream from May to October at Jelbert's.

Mousehole
Art aficionados wishing to pay homage to Mousehole artist Jack Pender (1918–98) can stay in the Pender room, formerly his studio. The Ship Inn on the harbour is the place for stargazey pie and Cornish fish stew.

Formerly a pilchard-processing factory, the Cornish Range in Mousehole is now a relaxed restaurant with rooms and a pretty garden.

Minack
The Minack Theatre café enjoys superb views over the shell-white sands of Porthcurno beach, with occasional dolphins and basking sharks in the turquoise waters below.

Lamorna
For tree-high views through the valley to the shore, with great food in luxurious surroundings, reserve a table at the Cove in Lamorna.

28

A favourite with Victorian day-trippers from grand hotels, beautiful Kynance has lost none of its looks or popularity. Investigate serpentine rocks, polished smooth by the sea, to reveal distinctive snakeskin patterns.

Getting to the Point

Coves Cliffs Communications

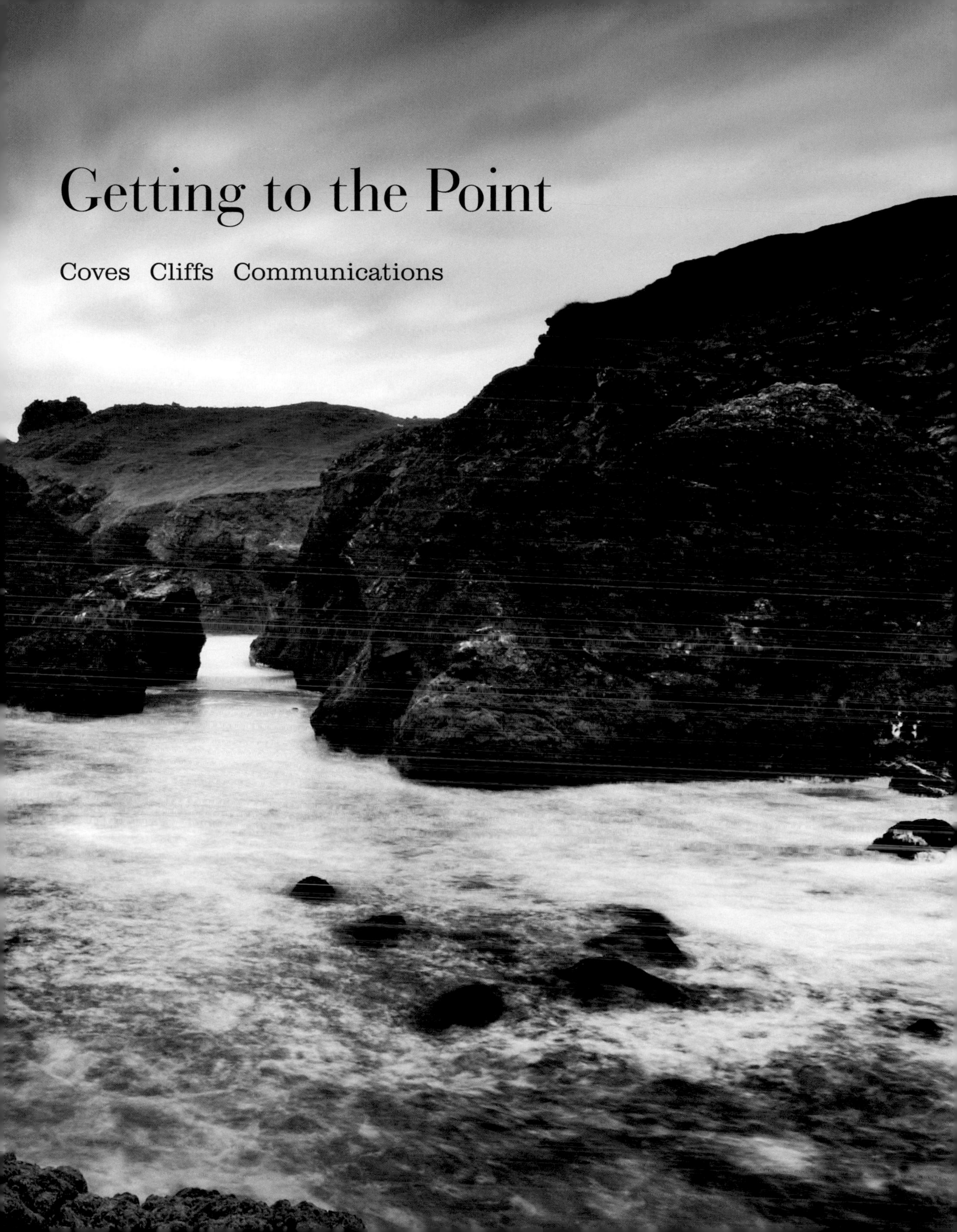

For clifftop walks with ever-changing views, for fishing coves and sandy beaches, a long weekend around Lizard Point – the most southerly tip of mainland Britain – is a perfect change of scene. Much of this wild and spectacular coast is owned, and made accessible, by the National Trust. From Gunwalloe in the west to Lankidden in the east, from lifeboat stations to wireless stations, there's fascinating variety all the way.

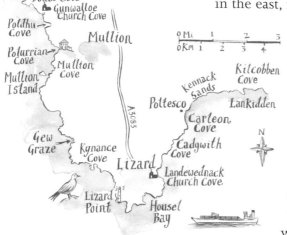

Gunwalloe Church Cove is an atmospheric place. Standing on the shore, within precarious reach of the sea, lovely St Winwaloe's fifteenth-century church rises above a froth of salt-tolerant pink tamarisk in spring. Known as the church of the storms, it has shipwrecked sailors buried in the graveyard.

Strike lucky and you might find gold and silver coins among the pebbles at Dollar Cove; in 1527 the King of Portugal's treasure ship was shipwrecked near here. Sections of the St Winwaloe's rood screen are made from the wreckage.

Soft sand and dunes, a café and lifeguards make popular Poldhu Cove a family favourite. A clifftop memorial marks the pioneering achievement of Guglielmo Marconi, who transmitted the letter 'S' in Morse code from

Poldhu to Canada, without wires, in 1901. For the full story, visit the exhibition at the nearby Marconi Centre, which was built to commemorate the centenary of the event. It is also the home of Poldhu Amateur Radio Club GB2GM.

Regarded as the start of the Lizard proper, the secluded sandy beach, at Polurrian Cove, popular with families, is reached by steep paths from majestic Polurrian Hotel or a ten-minute walk from the car park in Mullion village.

Mullion Island provides sanctuary for nesting seabirds and Mullion Cove's strong harbour walls protect a clutch of fishing boats against fierce winter storms that wreak havoc. Climate change forecasts suggest that the harbour walls face more violent, more regular storms in future, making costly repairs futile. It seems inevitable that one day Nature will be allowed have her way and reclaim the cove. At low water, there's a sandy beach in the harbour.

A favourite with Victorian day-trippers from grand hotels, beautiful Kynance Cove has lost none of its looks or popularity. Investigate serpentine rocks, polished smooth by the sea to reveal distinctive snakeskin patterns. Take tea at the eco-friendly café and pack a torch to explore caves with domestic names like the Parlour, the Kitchen and Drawing Room.

Many visitors park at Kynance for the magnificent 5.5-mile circular

...thirsty?

Sunset views and good food make the Halzephron Inn at Gunwalloe a favourite with locals and visitors, though it's often packed to the rafters in summer. Family tables outside.

For lobster, crab and Cornish brews, visit the Cadgwith Cove Inn. Upstanding locals hang out in the bar; pints in one hand, the other through rope straplins in the ceiling. Get there for sea shanties on Fridays.

Marconi's wireless technology played a vital part in the arrest of infamous Dr Crippen. Receiving the news that the murderer and his accomplice were among passengers on the SS *Montrose* en route to Montreal, Scotland Yard sent a fast boat to arrest the fugitives. And when the *Titanic* struck an iceberg, SOS messages from onboard Marconi operators played a key role in the rescue of 700 survivors.

walk north to Gew Graze, known as Soapy Cove, where soapstone rock was quarried to make porcelain. The route returns via Predannack Manor Farm. Alternatively, walk twenty minutes south around the coast to the Lizard, just under 2 miles away.

After all the natural beauty, you may wish to turn a blind eye to 'Britain's Most Southerly Gift Shop' at Lizard Point, although some feel impelled to pop in for a serpentine ashtray or a 'No hand signals, I'm eating a pasty' sticker before visiting the Lizard lighthouse.

A clifftop memorial marks the biggest rescue in the history of the RNLI. In 1907, without loss of life, brave lifeboat crews and local people saved 456 men, women and children after the White Star liner SS *Suevic* foundered on a reef off the Point in dense fog.

Cornish choughs were once so common and significant in Cornwall that the birds feature on the county's coat of arms, alongside a miner and fisherman. As coastal grazing declined, so did the choughs. With the recent reintroduction of animals on the cliffs and slopes – to create short grass in which the birds forage for insects – chough numbers are up again at Lizard Point. Look out for their aerial acrobatics in glossy black plumage with red stockings and beaks.

Visit the world's oldest surviving wireless station on the clifftop, at Housel Bay where Marconi received wireless communication from the Isle of Wight, in January 1901. The record-breaking achievement encouraged him to shunt along the coast to Poldhu, from where he transmitted to Canada.

The beach is hard to reach and can be cut off at high tide. Take the cliff path from Lizard Point and climb down to the sandy cove. For refreshments, visit Housel Bay Hotel on the clifftop.

For Kilcobben Cove and Landewednack Church Cove, follow signs from Lizard village to Church Cove. Park at the car park, just beyond the church. Follow the track on foot to a signpost pointing across fields to the lifeboat station at Kilcobben Cove or continue down the track to hideaway Church Cove.

This coast overlooks one of the world's busiest shipping lanes; every day over 400 ships move up and down the Channel past Lizard Point.

At Kilcobben, the Lizard RNLI lifeboat is wedged between sheer cliffs forty-five metres high. They offer just enough shelter to launch in almost all conditions. A steep cliff railway plunges the crew down to the station, which is open to the public but beware 200 steps. Hurry to see the old station building; construction of a new one begins soon.

The winding walk from the car park above Cadgwith Cove to the shore passes the lovely Breton-blue metal church of St Mary's. Looking like an oversized heavenly shed, this 100-year-old place of worship brims with seaside character.

Step inside for blue pews, fishing nets and lobster pots on the altar. From here it's a short stroll downhill to thatched houses end on to the sea and fishing boats on the shore.

Spend three lovely hours walking the easy, 4.5-mile circular Serpentine Route, starting at Cadgwith car park via Ruan Minor to the tranquil wooded valley of Poltesco. Atmospheric deserted buildings at Carleon Cove reveal how the local economy moved on from pilchard fishing to working serpentine stone.

Bathing is safe at Kennack Sands, a popular family beach where the National Seal Sanctuary occasionally releases rehabilitated animals.

Overlooked by an Iron Age cliff castle, the sheltered cove at Lankidden is the haunt of sea anglers, swimmers and basking sharks, though you can often have the place to yourself.

...tired?

Thanks to a partnership between the National Trust and the Youth Hostel Association, the Victorians' favourite, the former Polbream Hotel at Lizard Point, is now a five-star hostel with superb sea views.

29

Gardeners' Delight

Heaven on earth   Feng shui design   D-Day embarkation

A lush weekend lies in store with a visit to Glendurgan and Trebah, two of Cornwall's greatest gardens, on the Helford River in Cornwall.

Secluded valleys, tidal creeks, stone quays and mudflats inspired Daphne du Maurier's scandalous novel *Frenchman's Creek*. Ancient oak woods offer tantalising glimpses of secret havens where a sophisticated French pirate might just anchor his sailing ship and creep ashore to seduce an English lady yearning for adventure.

In valleys that tumble to the shores of the river, the twin gardens of Glendurgan and Trebah are equally exotic. The climate is subtropical, the soil acidic and the springtime blooms of magnolia, rhododendrons and camellias are breathtaking.

The sculpture of a sleek fox sidling along the wall of the National Trust's garden at Glendurgan recalls the extraordinary Fox family who began planting a deep valley garden here in the 1820s. Quakers and passionate gardeners, Alfred and Sarah Fox regarded Glendurgan as 'heaven on earth'. Today the garden covers twenty-five acres.

Rare plants from faraway places abound, thanks to the family's shipping connections. Huge hydrangeas imported from Japan mingle with

...thirsty?

There's been a ferry across the Helford Passage for over 300 years and the terrace of the Ferry Boat Inn is still a great place to watch comings and goings on the river. In the summer holiday season, ferries sail from here to Glendurgan and Trebah.

rhododendrons from the Himalayas and tulip trees from North America.

Glendurgan is a fantastic place for children. With six daughters and six sons to entertain, the Foxes planted the wonderful laurel maze in 1833. Still going strong, it's a great place to lose yourself, but be sure to save some energy for the Giant's Stride, a towering maypole, around which generations of Fox children and visitors have whizzed at top speed to become airborne.

Another of the joys of Glendurgan is the hidden fishing village at the bottom of the garden. Around twenty families once lived in this heavenly hamlet, fishing Falmouth Bay for pilchards, pollack, mackerel, bass, lobster and crab. Donkeys carried the fish to market in Falmouth and a long line of them was a sure sign of a good catch!

The shingle beach is perfect for paddling and investigating rock pools. The coast path wanders around the shore with lovely walks to the blacksmith village of Mawnan Smith, Rosemulllion Head and the Helford Passage.

Another of the Fox family planted the extraordinary garden at Trebah,

Glendurgan's close neighbour. Inspired by his brother's patch of heaven at Glendurgan, Charles Fox began the creation of his own twenty-six-acre paradise in 1831.

The garden path zigzags to the shore of the Helford River through tree ferns, bamboo jungles and rare specimen plants. While the atmosphere is magical and inviting, there's nothing haphazard about the planting because Charles Fox, a keen student of Chinese culture, was very careful about what went where.

Planning views of the garden from the house, he used a megaphone to instruct gardeners on the exact location of precious new plants in accordance with the principles of feng shui. The head gardener built scaffolding towers to indicate the height of the plant at maturity and the youngest gardener would shin up it with a white flag so that Fox could spot them easily from his window. Left a bit, right a bit.

Beyond mounds of sky-blue hydrangeas around Mallard Pond at the foot of the garden, there's safe swimming at sandy Polgwidden Cove. In stark contrast to the pleasures of the garden, a memorial on Yankee Beach pays homage to the courage of 7,500 young American soldiers who embarked from here for the June 1944 D-day assault on Omaha Beach, Normandy.

GARDENS NEARBY

If you just can't get enough of glorious Cornish gardens, there are more nearby. Stay for bed and breakfast at Carwinion, where there's a magnificent bamboo collection. Have fun with the woodland cam-era obscura at Trewithen and explore another Fox family jungle at Penjerrick.

...hungry?

The Red Lion Inn at Mawnan Smith is a great traditional pub. Within whitewashed cob walls and under a thatched roof, there are three friendly bars. Local food is on the menu with fish, chips and mushy peas on Fridays.

Eat well and simply in the glasshouse café of a former market garden at High Cross Constantine. Recently revived, the Potager Garden is constantly evolving. Craftspeople working in studios onsite include a traditional wooden boat builder.

Heads and Tails

Simple pleasures Fishing villages Operation tiger

South Hams in deepest Devon is a chocolate-box world of thatched pastel cottages in steep wooded valleys or combes. The rolling landscape invites you to slow down to explore country lanes, secret sandy beaches and exposed promontories with curious names like Gammon Head and Start Point, taken from the old English *steort*, meaning tail.

Pretty cottages cluster around a neatly mowed green at East Prawle, Devon's most southerly village, where there's a quirky pub, well-stocked shop and café. Steep and narrow lanes plunge to the small National Trust car park at Prawle Point: you can walk from here to the National Coastwatch Institution lookout on the hill where a team of eagle-eyed volunteers survey dangerous waters offshore. Views to Bolt Head in the east and Start Point in the west are breathtaking and there's unusual geology too; green hornblende schist at East Prawle, a series of ice age shore- and wave-cut platforms and cliffs and the glinting mica schist of Start Point.

The lookout station is staffed 365 days a year with a wildlife exhibition in the visitor centre. Take binoculars to observe basking sharks, migrant birds in spring and autumn and rare cirl buntings with yellow and black striped faces. Spy the rusting remains of the cargo ship *Demetrios*, wrecked in 1992, and secluded Maceley cove, tucked in the shelter of Gammon Head.

Lannacombe Beach is another sandy haven but, like so many hideaways, there's a different feel in high summer when tailbacks of overheated cars and drivers snarl up single-track lanes to the shore.

On a clear day, there are great views of sweeping Start Bay from the headland car park, a good place for quiet contemplation at peaceful times. If you're feeling lively, scramble five minutes down the footpath to Great Mattiscombe Sands where sea-washed rocks on the beach are perfect for bouldering, or climbing without ropes. Stroll to exposed Start Point lighthouse which is open to visitors between Easter and October. Look out for the fast-moving Skerries tidal race in turbulent water around the tower.

Heading west from Start Point, a walk of around 7 miles along the South West Coast Path takes in clifftop views, fishing villages and the shingle ridge of Slapton Sands which runs from Torcross to Strete Gate. The regular bus service linking Slapton with Dartmouth and Plymouth is popular with walkers.

...hungry?

Stop for delicious Devon cream tea at gracious South Allington House, a Grade II Georgian manor that offers bed and breakfast too. Don't leave your visit too late; Barbara Baker's lovely scones often sell out.

Savour sea air, lobster and Start Bay scallops at the Cricket Inn, Beesands. After kite-surfing or beach-fishing in Start Bay, visit the cheery Seabreeze café in Torcross for breakfast, lunch or cream tea. They do bed and breakfast too. Devour pancakes with maple syrup at the shorefront Rocket House café.

...thirsty?

There's no such thing as minimalism at the Pig's Nose Inn at East Prawle. The pub serves local ales from the barrel and bursts at the seams with live bands on music nights, eclectic bric à brac, a library of books and outdoor jackets for smokers to borrow.

The simple pleasure of great fish and chips washed down with a glass of local apple and root cider on the seafront patio of the Start Bay Inn at Torcross is the kind of treat that makes expats misty-eyed.

In Slapton village, there's good food and accommodation at the historic Tower Inn. Log fires and candle-lit suppers are cosy on chilly days and the pretty beer garden, complete with fourteenth-century Chantry tower, makes a charming refuge in summer.

From a viewing platform over the sea, visitors peer at the remnants of Hallsands hamlet crumbling on the shore. Originally protected by a pebble ridge in the bay, the fishing community was put at risk by dredging for shingle in the early 1900s. Battered by high tides and gales, the houses, pub, grocers and post office succumbed to the waves in 1917. A sign advises that there's no access to the beach because the old right of way has 'been taken away by the sea.'

Fishing continues at Beesands where anglers line up on the beach, and boats, lobster and crab pots are piled up by the sea wall. Visit the Fish Shack for freshly caught crab or diver-caught scallops in a granary bap. There's a seaside village green and playground, picnic tables along the shore and cosy cottages with wooden shutters to protect them from stormy seas.

Torcross village straddles the shingle ridge of Slapton Sands, a fine dividing line between the seawater of Start Bay and fresh water of Slapton Ley National Nature Reserve. Home to otters, eels and the camera-shy Cetti's warbler; the Lower Ley is the largest natural lake in south-west England. Look out for the lovely boardwalk through the marsh.

Playing their part in the war effort, local people were evacuated from their homes and land in 1943 when Slapton became an invasion battle training area. As they rehearsed the assault on Utah beach in Normandy, landing craft carrying troops, tanks and live ammunition were attacked in the dark by fast-moving German torpedo boats. In the ensuing chaos 946 US servicemen lost their lives. The appalling death toll of Operation Tiger was higher than that of the actual landings on Utah beach in June 1944. By the side of the road, an American Sherman tank, recovered from the sea in 1984, bears witness to one of the greatest tragedies of the Second World War.

...tired?

Close to the coast at Prawle Point, Mollie Tucker's Field welcomes a handful of caravans.

For a spiritual escape, join the Anglican Community of the Glorious Ascension at Lamacraft Farm where the brothers unite a working life with monastic life. They offer accommodation in self-catering cottages and, occasionally, the community house.

Cliffhanger

Jurassic shores   Old rope   Fabulous food

31

Soak up the atmosphere of an historic maritime warehouse at Sladers Yard café in West Bay.
On the banks of the River Brit, West Bay's Riverside Restaurant serves delicious seasonal, locally sourced ingredients simply. Treat yourself to Lyme Bay Dover Sole or local lobster.
Bridport's lively Electric Palace Cinema combines café, cinema, comedy and children's events. Chill out at the pretty garden café behind Bridport's Arts Centre and feast on the impressive 'Crustacean Creation' seafood platter at the Hive Beach Café in Burton Bradstock. If you can't manage that, plump for freshly landed spider crab with a glass of dry white Dorset wine.

From West Bay to the Isle of Portland in Dorset, Chesil Beach extends 18 miles along a stretch of the Jurassic Coast, England's only UNESCO World Heritage Site, which extends 93 miles between Dorset and east Devon.

Chesil Beach takes its name from the old English *ceosil* meaning shingle. Pebbles are the size of peas around West Bay, graduating to spuds around Portland to the east. Smugglers landing in thick fog had only to pick up a stone from the vast beach to figure out where they were. For good luck and protection, fishermen traditionally tied a pebble with a hole in it to the stern of their boat before setting off.

West Bay's Jurassic pier offers great views of towering sandstone walls at East Cliff and Burton Bradstock. They are especially magnificent at sunset. From the end of the pier, the undulating edge of mainland England is on show, all the way from Portland Bill in Dorset to Brixham in Devon. The headland of Golden Cap rises to the west. At 191 metres above sea level, it is the highest point on the south coast.

The dynamic cliffs are restless; rockfalls and landslides are frequent and can happen at any time. It has not quite got to the point where hard hats are issued to day-trippers on the shore, but leaflets issued by the National Trust, which owns much of the coast, warn that a falling rock can reach speeds of up to 100 metres per second and weigh several tonnes. Even a seagull taking flight can trigger a high-velocity rockfall. Best stay away from the foot of the cliffs then.

The upside of all this plummeting rubble is the feast of fossils that lies along the coast. The cliffs are a treasure trove of weird stuff, one of the richest sources of Jurassic reptiles, fish and insects in the world. Fossil fiends of all ages will find rich pickings further along the coast, around Charmouth.

West Bay has a long history of shipbuilding. In the eighteenth century, prolific yards here built a huge variety of vessels from fishing boats to warships for the navy. Visit the maritime warehouse at Sladers Yard to see traditional wooden boats being built alongside a gallery of exquisite furniture and work from local artists.

Holidaymakers enjoy the crabbing and amusements around West Bay's harbour, one of the busiest on the south coast. For something more sedate, hire an elegant rowing boat to while away an hour on the meandering River Brit with the peaceful rustle of reeds and the gentle drip of the oars.

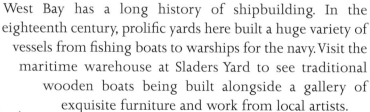
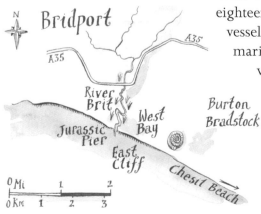

The bustling market town of Bridport is a short bus ride or pleasant twenty-minute, walk from West Bay. Visit the museum and local history centre to discover how the settlement, noted in the Domesday Book, became the most important centre of rope- and net-making in Britain by the thirteenth century.

Geoff Hurst's 1966 World Cup goals landed in one of Bridport's nets, which were traditionally made from flax and hemp grown in sheltered valleys around the town. Now Bridport makes nets from synthetic fibres; they still catch footballs, and the space shuttle when it lands back on Earth.

Bridport is great for retail therapy, with independent shops like Girl's Own Store, a haven of organised domestic bliss, and Malabar Trading for silks, ceramics and treasures from distant lands. There's a street market in the centre of town every Saturday and Wednesday and the Women's Institute hosts the West Dorset Country Market in North Street on Saturday mornings, with further delights of a farmers' market at the Arts Centre on the second Saturday of every month.

While there's a popular sandy beach at East Cliff, fossil fiends are more richly rewarded at Burton Bradstock, especially after a rockfall, although overhanging and dangerous cliffs make the hunt here unsuitable for children. For them, there are sea breezes and grassy slopes, perfect for kite-flying, opposite the Hive Beach Café, one of the best in Britain. There's a large terrace for summer sun and patio heaters for winter's chill. The atmosphere is lively and the service friendly, from breakfast to dinner. Good food comes with impeccable local connections; tags on the line-caught sea bass indicate the fisherman and boat that supplied them.

GETTING AROUND

Enjoy the views from the top deck of the award-winning CoastLINX53 bus, which travels between Exeter and Poole, stopping at Bridport, West Bay and Burton Bradstock. Day trip tickets offer unlimited travel.

Book your seat for a thrilling taxi ride by RIB (rigid inflatable boat) just fifteen minutes between West Bay and Lyme Regis.

32

Set in Stone

White rock   Wave watching   Lighthouses

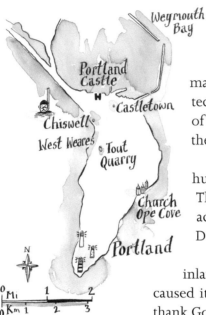

For extraordinary sculptures, a stony-faced castle, sunsets, seafood and spectacular views of one of the world's best storm beaches, make a trip to intriguing Portland in Dorset.

Situated at the very end of Chesil Beach, scarred Portland has famously supplied the world with smooth, white, durable limestone from up to eighty quarries on the island. After the Great Fire of London in 1666, Sir Christopher Wren used 60,000 tons of Portland stone, raised by hand, to rebuild St Paul's Cathedral. All the First World War graves on the Western Front and the United Nations building in New York are also made of Portland stone.

The storm beach curves to meet the island at Chesil Cove, making a connection with the mainland. Here, the steep bank protects the low-lying village of Chiswell and the pebbles are biggest of all along the 18-mile stretch. Notices ask visitors not to remove them.

When fierce weather slams the shore, stones from the ridge are hurled to the seabed and flung back again by wave action. The sound and fury is fantastic. John Meade Falkner captures the action in *Moonfleet*, a tale of friendship and smuggling, set on the Dorset coast:

'It is that back-suck of the pebbles that you may hear for miles inland, even at Dorchester, on still nights long after the winds that caused it have sunk, and which makes people turn in their beds, and thank God they are not fighting with the sea on Moonfleet beach.'

Clear water and abundant sealife around the cove make it a popular diving site in calm weather. Local notices remind exhibitionists not to cause offence to residents by changing in and out of diving gear on the public highway.

John Maine's terraced land sculpture at West Weares is a massive monument to Portland's geology and masons. Commissioned to celebrate the completion of sea defences protecting the village, it's a great place to picnic with the setting sun.

At Tout Quarry, extraordinary art is evolving where Victorian quarrymen left off. It is wonderfully surreal, so prepare to be taken by surprise as fantastic sculptures creep up on you. It's all very Indiana Jones. Antony Gormley was the first artist to work the vacated hollow in 1983; his plummeting life-size figure, *Still Falling*, is on the rock face.

Of the three lighthouses at the bill at the southern end of Portland, only one is operational. The higher old lighthouse is privately owned and the lower lighthouse is a members-only bird observatory. The

sprawling car park at the foot of stripy Portland Bill indicates the high-summer popularity of the visitor centre. Be warned.

On the east coast of the island, there's a sprinkling of beach huts around sheltered Church Ope Cove, overlooked by the ruins of Rufus, or Bow and Arrow Castle and St Andrew's church. It is a short walk to the quirky Portland Museum, snugly packed in two small thatched cottages and well worth a visit.

Weymouth Bay and Portland Harbour are the sailing venue for the 2012 Olympics. There's a hub of maritime activity along the shore near the former naval dockyard in Castletown, including boat builders, a chandlery, dive shops, pubs and a passenger ferry to Weymouth.

Two floating concrete Mulberry Harbours, used during the Normandy landings, lie offshore and fishing boats vie for space on the small stretch of beach that remains. The Merchant's Incline walk traces the route of the horse-drawn railway, which transported quarried stone to the jetty. From Portland Heights, at the top of the hill, there are far-reaching views over Chesil Beach and the Fleet Lagoon.

Henry VIII's no-nonsense castle stands at the water's edge like a squat British bulldog, snarling in the face of would-be invaders from France and Spain. The Governor's Garden, designed in 2002 by Chris Bradley-Hole, is a smooth, cool amphitheatre of Portland stone and native plants. Crab sandwiches in the tearoom are delicious.

GETTING AROUND

On the road from Wyke Regis to Portland, Chesil Beach Centre is the place to pick up useful information about the storm beach, the Fleet lagoon and Portland.

Portland's circular coast path, 8 miles, is a great way to explore the island.

...hungry?

From the roof terrace of Quiddles seafood café on the esplanade at Chesil Cove, there's a grandstand view of the magnificent storm beach. Pounding waves rattle the stones below. Quiddles is the Portland name for squid, a local delicacy. Just a stone's throw from Quiddles is the Cove House Inn. Make the most of wintry days: wrap up warm for the beach and defrost by the fireside. For a relaxed romantic meal, book a table at the BlueFish Café, also in Chiswell.

The Lobster Pot café, at the foot of Portland Bill lighthouse, is a favourite with locals, who go all year round for sea views, cream scones and a proper cup of tea, made with leaves.

Be inspired by the arty and exotic courtyard garden at David Nicholls' White Stones gallery and café in Easton. Good food in a great venue makes it one of my favourites.

With a simple picnic of freshly caught dressed crab from fish merchants in Castletown, watch the waves from West Weares.

33

Island of Adventure

The Famous Five   A Victorian playground   An unsolved mystery

The Isle of Purbeck is forever associated with Enid Blyton. Throughout the 1950s, the prolific children's author used the idyllic backdrop of Dorset coast and countryside in many of her books. Corfe Castle inspired Kirrin Castle; Stoborough Heath, the 'Mystery Moor'; and Brownsea Island is both 'Whispering' and 'Keep Away Island'. Fans will be delighted to discover that much is unchanged and a visit to Purbeck is super fun, whatever your age.

Enid took holidays at the smart seafront hotels of Swanage and, just like the Famous Five, she loved to be outdoors, swimming around both piers before supper. While only sad traces of one pier remain, the other has been restored to its former glory by a determined group of volunteers. Brass plaques on sponsored new planks make a great read, best enjoyed on an early morning stroll. From A&J: 'Our life's a pier, our love the ocean'; from the Reeves family: 'Chips in the Dark'; and from Peter to Jezabelle: 'Will you marry me?' I can't help wondering, what became of them?

The first Swanage pier was built in 1860 to export paving stone from local quarries. Having discharged their cargo, ships often returned with curious ballast because stone contractor John Mowlem and his business partner, George Burt, were into recycling on a grand scale. Together the pair scavenged unwanted chunks of London.

THE SWANAGE RAILWAY

TODAY'S TRAINS

STEAM	DIESEL Trains
0950 *	14.30
10.30	15.10 *
11.10 *	15.50
11.50	16.30 *
12.30 *	17.10
13.10	17.42 *
13.50 *

1810
1910
2010 — LAST TRAIN TO NORDEN
2200 } Herston (Request)
2300 } Harmans X
Corfe Castle

* PULLMAN OBSERVATION CAR
SUPPLEMENT PAYABLE ON TRAIN

CURIOUS
Look out for the spectacular mural on the disused Pier Head building. Created by community artists Nina Camplin and Antonia Phillips, the images reveal a glimpse of the interior from wartime 1940s to present dereliction. Meet the artists in their blue-painted wooden gallery and studio, the Art Hut, on the seafront.

Prep-school masters taught pupils to swim at Dancing Ledge pool, blasted out of the cliffs near Worth Matravers, close to the South West Coast Path, it's a dangerous scramble to the water.

The city's grand cast-offs became ballast used to give Swanage a makeover. Cast-iron lamps from Hanover Square were planted on the Parade and the stone façade of London's Mercers' Hall became the face of Swanage Town Hall. At Purbeck House, George Burt's home on the High Street, there's an archway from Hyde Park, mosaic tiles from the Palace of Westminster and a balustrade from Billingsgate market. No wonder Thomas Hardy described the Victorian entrepreneur as 'the King of Swanage'.

Burt's pièce de résistance is the fabulous playground at Durlston Head, within walking distance of Victorian day-trippers landing at the pier. The centrepiece is an immense forty-tonne Portland stone globe, standing 41 metres above sea level. Poised like a mighty bowling ball, about to hurtle down the cascade of stone steps and over the cliff, it is surrounded by tablets of stone bearing improving inscriptions, intriguing facts and fragments of poetry.

The path along limestone cliffs from the Globe to Anvil Point lighthouse provides a great vantage point; take binoculars to spot seabirds and dolphins.

Purbeck's further attractions include the huge arc of sand around Studland Bay and the opportunity to get your kit off at the UK's most popular naturist beach. The well-signposted section of naturist beach at Studland is haf a mile long and accessed from the National Trust car park at Knoll beach.

Combine a great view of Swanage Bay and local seafood al fresco at Gee Whites on the Old Stone Quay, Swanage. Their cooked-to-order gooey chocolate crêpes are a big hit with children and adults alike. Timmy would have wolfed them down.

Take tea and admire George Burt's keen eye for recycled grandeur at Purbeck House, now a hotel, on Swanage High Street.

Having been improved by erudite quotations in stone at Durlston Country Park, let yourself go at the café. The Lookout serves great local produce; cream teas, homemade pork pies, Portland crab salad and Dorset apple cake are all on the menu.

Call into the Bird's Nest Buffet on Swanage station platform for an environmentally sound mug of tea, take it on the train and return the mug at the end of the journey. No waste – brilliant. Look out for the bird's nest in the glass case, a reminder of the days when the buffet carriage was a wreck.

If nude sun-bathing was the Famous Five's kind of thing, Enid didn't let on. Fans can follow the tracks of their adventures on the charming Swanage Steam Railway line to Corfe Castle. Alight at the station and you step back in time. Overlooked by the dramatic ruins of the fortress, it is a scene set for adventure. Visit the railway museum on the platform, the National Trust castle on the hill and the Ginger Pop shop for everything Enid.

Mystery surrounds a lonely chapel at St Aldhelm's Head, the most southerly point of the Isle of Purbeck. Reach it by foot from the car park at Worth Matravers, via the coastal path – the circular route is about 5 miles long. You can also get to the chapel by road, following a rough track to the sea.

St Aldhelm's is so isolated you feel you might shatter the peace. A reassuring sign reads 'You are very welcome here, whether to pray or to sit and rest'. The origins of the strangely square chapel are unknown but an age-old story tells of a father who witnessed the death of his newly wed daughter and her husband as they sailed from here into a storm. Broken-hearted, he is said to have built the beautiful clifftop memorial.

Head back to Worth Matravers for cider from the cask at the Square and Compass tavern. The pub's been in the Newman family for over 100 years and their collection of fossils and antiquities is in a curious museum at the end of a long, low drinking corridor – just the kind of place you might find Uncle Quentin.

St Aldhelm's is so isolated you feel you might shatter the peace. A reassuring sign reads 'You are very welcome here, whether to pray or to sit and rest.'

34

In Retreat

Seven Sisters   Skinny-dipping   Cinque port

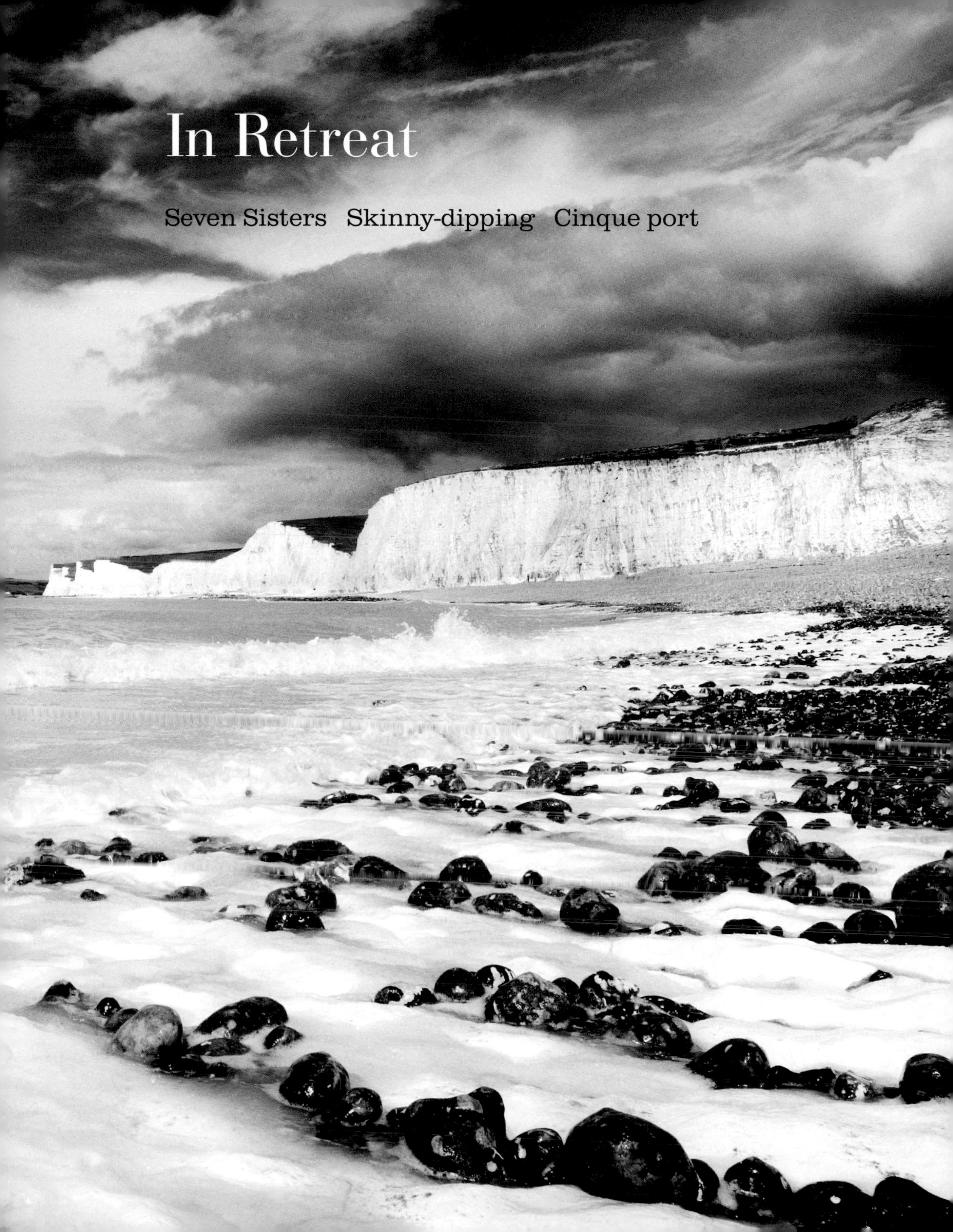

The relentless gnawing of the sea has created one of Britain's most iconic landmarks: clean white chalk cliffs that are the full stop of mainland England. They are part of our national identity and taking time out to explore them is richly rewarding.

Teetering on the English Channel, Birling Gap, on top of the Seven Sisters cliffs, makes a good place to start. The small settlement is shrinking, due to coastal erosion: between 1873 and 1997, 89 metres of land fell into the sea. Much of the old coastguard station is gone and what remains is decidedly precarious.

Between the Birling Gap Hotel and the coastguard station buildings there is a wooden stairway from the clifftop to the shore. To the west lies a patchy sandy beach where brave naturists skinny-dip in the chilly English Channel.

A great double-decker bus service shuttles regularly along the coast.

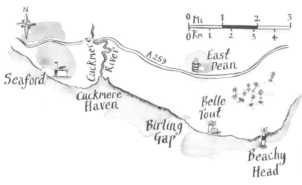

You can hop on at Birling Gap for a ride to Beachy Head. However, it would be a shame to miss the 2.5-mile walk between the two along the South Downs Way over magnificent chalk downland of national and international importance.

The steep slopes of the South Downs were traditionally used for grazing; crops were grown on the lower, flatter land. In the 1960s, the Downs changed drastically as herbicides and pesticides wiped out much of the natural habitat. Without grazing sheep and cattle, the wild flowers and grasses were overcome by scrub and brambles. Now the sheep and cattle are back and one of Britain's richest wildlife habitats is alive with rare butterflies and flowers between late spring and August.

In 1832 a lighthouse was erected at Belle Tout Hill but sea fog dulled the effect and so Beachy Head lighthouse was erected in 1902. Belle Tout lighthouse was almost another victim of coastal erosion, so in 1999, the owners relocated: all 850 tons were moved seventeen metres backwards.

On the approach to Beachy Head, a memorial commemorates the epic Dieppe Raid of 1942 which was partly controlled from the clifftop radar station. The site also honours PC Harry Ward, the old soldier who patrolled the Downs on his horses Princess Patricia and Jumbo until his retirement in 1966. Harry risked his life many times on the cliffs in an attempt to save others.

CAFE DELICATESSEN

FRITH & LITTLE

Bread Cheese Wine

illy

OPEN

The sight of Beachy Head lighthouse, dwarfed by 168 metres of the highest chalk cliff in England, is strangely unreal. It's one of those iconic images, seen so often that first-time visitors feel they have somehow been here before. Call into the Countryside Centre for a trip back to the Bronze Age, an account of the headland's Second World War defences and a meeting with spooky Walter, the Downland shepherd. Admission is free.

Foodies should take the short bus ride from Beachy Head to East Dean. There's great coffee and good food from Sussex and around the world at Andy and Kathy's lovely deli, Frith & Little, opposite the friendly Tiger Inn, where the stuffed head of Bob the big cat beams from behind the bar. Try a pint of Legless Rambler from the pub's own micro-brewery or tea and cake at the Hikers Rest café next door.

...hungry?

Plan ahead and order a superb picnic lunch or BBQ pack to take away from Frith & Little's great deli at East Dean.

...thirsty?

Call into the quirky Birling Gap Hotel and Thatched Bar (with tiled roof); Victorian colonial style meets the 1930s on the brink of a cliff.

A few miles away, the Cuckmere River swirls to sea at Cuckmere Haven, an area that faces great change. Rising sea levels and the high cost of maintaining flood defences and man-made diversions have fuelled a strong argument to allow the river to find its way to the sea in a more natural way. But how to manage the future of this ancient estuary has divided the local community.

Follow the river to sea from the Seven Sisters Country Park Visitor Centre at Exceat – a walk of 1.5 miles – or, better still, enjoy wonderful views of the ancient estuary and Seven Sisters from Seaford Head Local Nature Reserve. Walk to this inspirational place from Seaford Esplanade (about 2 miles) or park at South Hill Barn, off Chyngton Way.

Seaford was once a prosperous Cinque Port on the River Ouse, exporting Sussex wool to the Continent. In the sixteenth century, the natural harbour became blocked by shingle and, adding insult to injury, a mighty storm caused the river to divert to Newhaven. Seaford, bereft of river and harbour, was abandoned.

Revived as a seaside resort in the Regency style, the town has an

Martello Tower no. 74, the last in a long line of forts from Aldeburgh to Eastbourne. The deceptively spacious tower houses the intriguing Seaford Museum. Discover remnants of medieval Seaford at the atmospheric Crypt Gallery, where modern art is exhibited in a beautiful vaulted cellar.

DOG SQUAD

Take your dog to the Seven Sisters Country Park and you might meet the Dog Squad: local people working with the tenant farmer and local police to tackle the serious problem of dogs and sheep-worrying. Dogs and cliffs aren't a good combination either; there are too many tragedies every year. Warnings at Birling Gap urge visitors to keep their hounds on a lead.

...tired?

The Boathouse bed and breakfast at Birling Gap has been on the move. Perched on the edge, Mrs Nash decided in 2009 that it was time to have the whole building picked up and set 30 metres further back from the cliff, still in a fantastic location.

The Beach Boys

Extraordinary fishermen   Hastings' oldest quarter   Seaside traditions

35

I n the early morning on Hastings shore you can witness a spectacle that's part of our island heritage and likely to leave you in awe of the men who risk their lives at sea to put food on our tables.

Just beneath the UK's steepest funicular railway at East Hill is a shingle beach known as the Stade. This place has been at the heart of the defining occupation of Hastings folk for generation upon generation – fishing.

Hastings' inshore fleet has been launching boats from the stade for over a thousand years. Working in the rich waters of Rye Bay, the fishermen make daily or overnight trips. Most boats are family-owned and the men are not paid wages but given a share of the catch.

On the Stade, elongated net shops and tackle houses climb upwards like skyscrapers because space is at a premium. They are unique to Hastings and reminiscent of children's naive drawings. This is a working beach with many hazards including a miniature railway that runs along the seafront. Step carefully over the tracks and you enter a shantytown of winch sheds, cables, bulldozers and the tractors of Britain's largest beach-launched fishing fleet.

Colourful boats, beached like lolling seals, are stranded on the shingle bank above the high-water mark, each loaded with net marker flags and dan buoys. Many are surprisingly small, yet so much depends on them. On the Hastings District Register there are 339 boats under ten metres in length and for every fisherman it's reckoned that there are ten people ashore employed within the industry.

To launch and land their boats, the fishermen have invested in second-hand modified tractors, bulldozers and power winches. Launching stern first into the surf is one thing – landing is something else. There's just one arm of the harbour wall at Hastings: it provides some shelter but boats landing directly on the beach are always at risk. Heavy seas are especially dangerous for smaller punts. If they hit the shingle bank with the sea 'up their back' they can be turned broadside and smashed to smithereens. 'You judge the waves, it's about timing, knowing how far your boat's going to carry you,' explained skipper Roland Kelly of *Girl Kayla RX 256*.

Boats returning to shore look like aircraft coming into land and aiming for the runway. In surging surf, to avoid being swept aside by breaking waves behind them is a matter of life or death.

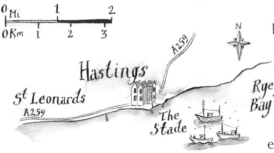

On the final approach there is one last glance backwards before the skipper thrusts the vessel up on to the shingle bank. There's a mighty crunch on contact, a bow strop is thrown over to the 'boy ashore' who connects it to a power winch line. This hauls the boat over a track of timber 'trows', sloshed with vegetable oil to keep everything moving smoothly. It's an impressive display of teamwork.

At the market, along the beach freshly landed fish is packed in ice and sold to wholesalers. If the big blue doors on the east or west side are open, you are invited to look inside. Upstairs is the café where you can stop for tea with the fishermen.

Don't miss a visit to one of the best museums on the British coast in the former Fishermen's Church of St Nicholas. It's stuffed to the gunnels with fascinating exhibits including *Enterprise RX 278*, one of the last of the traditional boats used by the Hastings fleet. Visitors are welcome to climb aboard. A short film shows the real-life rescue of a fishing boat in stormy seas and brings home the dangers of the job.

Hastings Old Town continues up the hill beyond Winkle Island, the community's traditional gathering place. The extraordinary Working Leaf and Flower Museum supplies flower and plant props for film, theatre

...tired?

Along with traditional bed and breakfast accommodation, Hastings offers boutique chic: handsome Cavalier House is just a minute from the sea and Black Rock House is a stylish favourite.

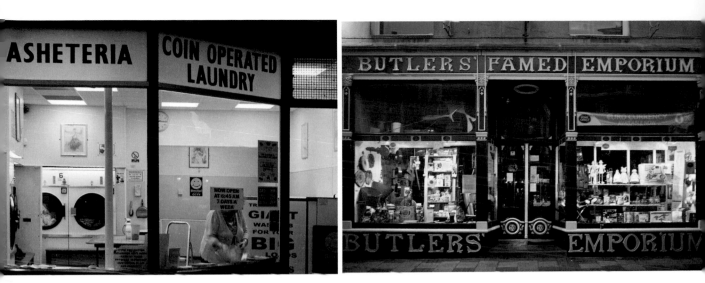

and television productions worldwide. Independent shops in winding streets are perfect for weekend mooching; there are vintage clothes stores, antiques, junk, specialist food shops and a café courtyard for Sunday brunch.

For a great night out, visit the wonderful Electric Palace independent digital cinema, which hosts the Hastings Film Festival, Shot by the Sea. Ticket sales and enthusiastic volunteers keep the not-for-profit organisation afloat.

For spectacular views over the Old Town, castle and pier, ride the West Hill Lift through a tunnel in the cliff.

Beyond the Old Town, Hastings has plenty more to offer. The traditional seafront features splashy turquoise fountains, the White Rock theatre, a boating lake, amusement arcades promising 'Slots of Fun' and the pier with a weekend market. The church of St Mary in the Castle is both a community arts centre and a place for worship on Sundays.

Hastings Museum and Art Gallery makes a great free visit. Discover an Indian Palace alongside exhibitions of famous Hastings residents including John Logie Baird, inventor of the television, and Robert Tressell, author of *The Ragged Trousered Philanthropists*. In the gallery, look out for Keith Baynes' lovely *Harbour Scene With Yachts, Hastings*.

The up and coming area around Norman Road in St Leonards-on-Sea is the latest local hotspot. Escape the madding crowd in the cool elegance of St Leonards Gardens.

...hungry?

Form an orderly queue at Put and Tush's stall on the shore for hot fish rolls filled with the freshly landed catch of the day. If you don't want bread, you get double fish! There's plenty to eat in the Old Town. Queue again at Judges popular bakery or pick up a sandwich from Penbuckles Deli. The First In Last Out (Filo) pub in the Old Town combines a brewery with good pub grub and brunch, and the Land of Green Ginger Café claims to make the best coffee in Hastings.

For views and waitress service, there's West Hill Café on the cliff.

Join locals for tea and cake at QOL neighbourhood café in Norman Road.

For a romantic supper, try St Clements Restaurant, serving freshly landed fish.

Go Native

Oysters Seduction Shopping!

RASPBERRY
EAST INDIA PALE ALE
OYSTER STOUT
WHEAT BEER
PILSNER

BREWERY

For a weekend of passion by the sea, take a tip from eighteenth-century lover Casanova, who devoured fifty shucked oysters a day and recorded 122 conquests in his diary. A weekend in Whitstable might be one you'll never forget.

Whitstable's native oysters are in their prime from September to the end of April and while you could lock yourself away with the molluscs for the whole weekend it would be a shame as there's plenty to do in the sassy seaside town.

Public transport links are good, and for a relaxed break, you don't need a car. At any time of year, it is easy to unwind by simply strolling along the seafront, stopping to explore bijou shops and ending a perfect day on the beach with your loved one and the setting sun.

The small port retains its character because the workshops of shipbuilders, blacksmiths and sail-makers around the beach prevented it from becoming a full-on garish resort. Narrow lanes with names like Squeeze Gut Alley took fishermen to the shore and whisked smugglers from the scene of the crime.

A favourite walk is the easy stroll from shingly West Beach to grassy green Tankerton Slopes. Start at the Old Neptune pub, a twisted, battered survivor of many storms. Wander past Marine Terrace where flotsam and

jetsam combine with weatherproof plants to create stylish seaside sanctuaries. Wedged in a garden not far from where she was built in 1890 is the beached hulk of the Whitstable oyster yawl *Favourite*.

On the bench at Cushing's View is where actor Peter Cushing escaped Hammer horror movies to gaze at the sunset with his wife, Helen. They loved the town and the town loved them. After Helen's death, Peter lunched regularly at a table set aside for him in the Tudor Tea Rooms. The movie star died in 1994 but his memory is cherished at Whitstable museum where film stills and his lucky rabbit foot are on display.

The Royal Native Oyster Stores is where the catch was traditionally sorted, graded and packed before being sent on the train out of town. Now it's a hugely popular seafront restaurant with eels, razor clams, scallops and oysters on the menu.

Whitstable's harbour opened in 1832 to serve the 'Crab and Winkle' railway line, the first in the world to carry passengers regularly. Trains no longer stop at the harbour, but fish and shellfish are still landed, processed and sold as they have been for years. Look out

for the catch of the day and recipe ideas in the fish market.

While slippery oysters are sexy, boiled whelks are not. Three generations of the West family cook two tonnes of these predatory snails every week. The unsung molluscs cost less than oysters and can be eaten all year round. Buy them unshelled by the pint from the seafood stall on the harbour or shelled by the gallon from the kitchen at West Quay. Add a splash of Mrs West's homemade vinegar with natural shallot, chilli, garlic or lemon flavours and enjoy the hand-picked morsels of meat like a true connoisseur.

Sail away for a day on the beautifully re-stored Thames barge, *Greta*, based at South Quay. Built in 1892, the barge is home to skip-per Steve Norris and first mate Alfie the dog. The lovely *Greta* is available to hire for private parties and wedding breakfasts.

The wonderful Whitstable Brewery Bar on East Quay is relaxed and friendly with huge windows overlooking the sea. Especially good is chilled 'fluffy' oyster stout, as described by the barmaid and 'tart' raspberry wheat beer. If your luck is in, the perfectly placed table at the end of the pier will await. This is the place to watch the evening sun light up the sky as it slides be-hind the Isle of Sheppey.

Feel like king of the hill on the steep slopes of Tankerton, where ship-shape beach huts are on parade below. For the full Whitstable experience, rent a hut for the weekend and wow your loved one with a Casanova

...hungry?

There's plenty of good food in Whitstable. Romantics should book table ten at the Pearson's Arms restaurant on the sea wall with great views across the Thames estuary and sunsets over the Isle of Sheppey. It's a hotspot for proposals of marriage over a dish of plump native oysters.

Pop into the Cheese Box for Kentish Crown cheese and wedding cakes and to Tea & Times for great sandwiches, hot chocolate and newspapers.

On the coast road between Whitstable and Faversham, the Sportsman pub at Seasalter serves freshly landed fish on a menu that changes daily.

...thirsty?

breakfast of champagne and oysters. At low water a long bank, known as 'the street', is revealed on the shore opposite the slopes. This has been a landing place since ancient times and scrunching along the shingle towards the mud of the Thames estuary is fun — but beware, the incoming tide takes victims by surprise.

Whitstable's High Street and Harbour Street ooze character. Stalwarts like Whites supply sensible nighties, and Hatchards Outfitters kept Peter Cushing in cravats. Shop for picnic treats at David Brown's deli, funky arts and craft treasure at Frank and gorgeous flowers and garden ware from Jane at Graham Greener.

There's a serious risk you might be overcome by the seductive nature of Whitstable. You wouldn't be alone. Jane from Graham Greener told me of a romantic chap who arranged for the deli to bake a cake for his lover, iced with the message 'Will', accompanied by clues to track down a stunning bouquet of Jane's flowers with the message 'You' and yet more clues leading her to Frank, where a gift read 'Marry'. The final clue took her to the beach where she found the 'Me' behind it all, a nervous, hopeful man with champagne and engagement ring at the ready. Whatever it is about Whitstable, you can certainly feel the love.

37

Yow Boys and Whoopers

Barges Oysters Island life

pend a weekend exploring secret south-east Essex. Discover historic sailing barges at Hythe Quay on the River Blackwater in Maldon and tranquil muddy creeks around Mersea Island where there's a real sense of getting away from it all.

Soft, flaky salt crystals from marshes around Maldon are renowned among chefs worldwide. Locals enjoy events including a beer festival in April, the Blackwater barge match in June, a carnival in August and a regatta and oyster festival in late summer. The fancy-dress mud race across the River Blackwater in January is a bizarre and popular spectacle.

The largest fleet of Thames sailing barges on the east coast is moored at lovely Hythe Quay. The handsome flat-bottomed barges float in as little as one metre of water, making them perfect for muddy creeks. They don't need ballast, so they are quick to unload and traditionally crewed by just two men. In 1860, 5,000 of these efficient cargo vessels worked along the east coast, and in foggy weather passing ships identified each other by the calls of the crew who would throw their voices across the water – 'whoopers' came from Maldon and 'yow boys!' came from Mersea. Even now, some Mersea and Maldon families still use the Essex dialect greeting.

Maldon merchants monitored the arrival of precious cargo from rooftop belvederes, glazed lookouts, on their homes; these are a distinctive feature of the town. This surveillance encouraged the watermen to improve journey times and led to the first sailing matches in 1863.

Beyond Hythe Quay are the islands of Osea and Northey. The Maldon Tapestry, stitched over three years by eighty local women and on display in the Maeldune Centre tells the story of the Viking encampment at Northey and raids on Maldon in AD 991. The Anglo-Saxons, led by Byrhtnoth, were defeated but the victorious Danes were so weakened they had to retreat. Look out for Byrhtnoth's statue in lovely Promenade Park on Maldon waterfront.

If you fancy messing about on the river, hire a rowing boat at Heybridge Basin on the Chelmer and Blackwater canal or watch the entertainment from the safety of the café or pub benches near the sea lock. Look out for Heybridge's curious parish church, once a sergeants' mess hall on Goldhanger airfield. When the military building became

...hungry?

Enjoy breakfast, lunch and cream teas at the Lock Tea Room at Heybridge basin. For a seafood supper at tables on the beach, visit the West Mersea Oyster Bar or take your own bread and drink to the Company Shed along the road. Beware huge queues in summer. The friendly Coast Inn claims to make the island's best fish and chips.

redundant, it was presented to the parish, topped with a bell tower and dedicated to St George in 1920.

Atmospheric Tollesbury declares itself the rural village of plough and sail. Skilled local men were much in demand on racing yachts, and roads in the village are named after America's Cup challengers. Weatherboarded sail lofts stand high on concrete blocks to avoid the risk of flooding and boardwalks on stilts zigzag through the marsh. The light vessel Trinity is moored in Woodrolfe creek; from the shore you'd hardly know that she is the residential centre of Fellowship Afloat Charitable Trust, accommodating up to thirty-six people. How that would have intrigued detective writer Margery Allingham, who loved this landscape and lived at nearby Tolleshunt D'Arcy between 1935 and 1966.

Enjoy a bracing saltwater swim at Woodup Pool, surrounded by grassy banks and picnic benches. Get up early and you might have it to yourself. The official capacity of 1,000 people doesn't bear thinking about.

Mersea, the most easterly inhabited island in Britain, is connected to the mainland by the Strood causeway, which can be impassable for

...thirsty?

Admire boats on the river by the Queens Head and the belvedere on the roof of the Jolly Sailor inn at Hythe Quay. Try the local wine at the Mersea Island Vineyard courtyard café or drink Island Oyster beer, a love potion flavoured in the cask by eight oysters.

around an hour several times a month at high water. Check the tide timetables online at www.merseaisland.com before you visit. The island's gentle landscape is perfect for a cycling tour.

Admire houseboats moored along the coast road at West Mersea, flying the flag with freshly washed laundry. Long pontoons connect the floating shacks and palaces to the shore. Paint tins, bicycles and sunflowers abound on deck and, from the roadside, the muddy romance of a home in a boat seems hugely appealing.

The king of Belgium has a weekly delivery of Mersea oysters from Mike Dawson and Ron Harvey of the West Mersea Oyster Bar. They send one million native and rock oysters to restaurants in London, Paris and Hong Kong throughout the year. Mike describes the native oyster as 'sweet and delicate' while the rock oyster has a nuttier flavour. Mike explained that wet summers are good for oysters, if not for the rest of us; marshy nutrients give plankton and, in turn, oysters, a distinctive flavour. Oyster aficionados can detect which mollusc has come from which creek. Mike recommends oysters with chopped shallots and red wine vinegar. As for letting them slip down your throat, what a waste. His advice is to chew them two or three times for the full flavour.

At Mersea Island Vineyard in East Mersea village, you can get married and then celebrate with home-grown English bubbly. Mark Rogers is an electrical engineer turned vigneron. He bought the vineyard with his wife Jacqui as a retirement project, and they have never been busier. Their son runs a micro-brewery in the grounds.

For walks along the sea wall, a sandy beach and views across the Colne and Blackwater estuaries, visit Cudmore Grove Country Park, East Mersea. From here there is a seasonal foot ferry to Brightlingsea and Point Clear.

Life and Sole

Vintage chic   Wooden huts   Rowing boats

For a fashionably retro weekend, take yourself to Suffolk where Southwold's wittily named, prettily painted beach huts epitomise the fun of classic English seaside holidays. With little regard for the weather, picnics are taken on a shingle beach in the shelter of a billowing windbreak and dips in the sea are obligatory, even if everyone comes out numb.

Many of Southwold's genteel houses overlook neatly manicured greens, while at Gun Hill a row of six Elizabethan cannon glare defiantly over the North Sea, protecting their precious slice of little England.

Southwold's gleaming white lighthouse rises from the heart of town, dwarfing red-brick cottages near Adnams Brewery to guide ships into the hidden harbour on the River Blyth. Climb to the top for panoramic views over Sole Bay and Sizewell's distant nuclear reactors.

There's plenty to do in the quaintly chic resort. Shopping is fun: Serena Hall's stylish gallery sells hand-printed seaside fabrics. CRAFTCO is a friendly co-operative gallery and shop brimming with colour and imaginative design; Cornucopia Antiques is always good for vintage clothes and a rummage; and the Dome Art and Antiques Centre is a cavern of treasure. The unique amber museum has an intriguing collection that includes an exquisite 1920s amber crown and a swarm of midges trapped for ever in petrified resin.

Lovers can get hitched or maybe just catch a movie at the snugly romantic Electric Picture Palace with only sixty-six seats, and a wedding licence.

...Hungry?

Squashy sofas and cream teas make Southwold's boating lake café a local favourite. Musicians are especially welcome at Casa Mia, a laid-back Italian piano bar and café where Ed Darragh serves line-caught fish in Guinness batter. Book ahead and she'll even provide a free courtesy car to take you home. Sitting in the salty air with oak-smoked grilled salmon and chips from Mrs T's takeaway on muddy Blackshore quay is a scrumptious experience.

If you like to eat well and walk only a short distance to bed, early reservations are advised for a stay at the Swan or Crown Hotels, owned by Adnams Sole Bay Brewery.

Southwold's twenty-first-century pier is a family-run business, open every day of the year except Christmas. The Under the Pier show is a 'mad collection of homemade slot machines unlike anything else in the known universe' – guaranteed to make you giggle. Cosy cafés with big windows are perfect for watching the sea in all its moods.

In the 1600s, Southwold's thriving fishing fleet caught herring, cod and sprats. When the harbour mouth began to silt up, the industry was badly affected and by 1800 poverty-stricken fishing families resorted to living in wooden shacks on the beach. How ironic that the town's desirable beach huts now command prices that could buy a real home elsewhere in the country.

The Alfred Corry Museum is housed in the former Cromer Lifeboat shed, which was relocated to Southwold by sea in 1988. Life has never been dull for the *Alfred Corry*. Converted from lifeboat to yacht, it was re-discovered as a derelict houseboat in Essex. Now volunteers are restoring it to its original design.

A model of the *Alfred Corry* is suspended from the ceiling of

St Edmund's medieval church, where the figure of 'Southwold Jack' strikes a bell at the start of a service. He is also the symbol of Adnams Brewery. For more maritime history visit the seafront Sailors' Reading Room, established in 1864 as a refuge and alternative to the alehouse.

Mooching around the working harbour is one of the joys of Southwold.

At Blackshore Quay there are boats in and out of the water, tarry sheds, landing stages and fresh-fish stalls. There's a vibrant seaside mural in the harbour café and wide windows overlook the outdoor action.

The cheerful Pit Stop Café, hidden away in gorse bushes between the water tower and golf club, is one of my favourite Southwold places. Happy families flock to Anne Clarke for treats like chocolate beetroot cake and Wednesday night spaghetti bolognese suppers. The Pit Stop is a Southwold institution, opened by Freddy Wells in 1949, serving Vimto and cider. When the flag is flying, the toys and games are out and Anne's got the kettle on!

To visit Southwold's neighbour, Walberswick, take a ferry not much bigger than a bathtub across the River Blyth, just as passengers have done since medieval times. You could stroll over the Bailey footbridge, but that's not half as much fun as being rowed across with dogs, bikes and assorted families.

The serious business of Walberswick is the annual British Open Crabbing Championship. Around 1,000 competitors take part in the competition, all hoping to hook a mighty crustacean worthy of the £50 prize. Monies raised by the event go to the Walberswick Sea Defence Group, which seeks to maintain the shingle ridge that protects the village, marshes and beach from the sea.

Around an idyllic green there is a handful of shops including irresistible Tinkers for 'old stuff, new stuff and tat!' The lovely beach is perfect for kite-flying and the sort of English picnics where sand goes with everything.

39

Wild Goose Chase

Twitchers Marshes Seals

Shingle ridges, flinty villages, small ports and big blue skies are just a few reasons to visit the open windswept landscape of north Norfolk. There's easy walking on the Peddars Way and the North Norfolk Coast Path and when you're weary, you can ride the coastal hopper bus to supper.

In late autumn and winter, wave upon wave of wild geese abandon distant breeding grounds and the Norfolk sky fills with travellers in search of rich coastal habitats. It's thrilling to watch swarms of birds overhead, filling the air with beating wings and raucous honking as they endlessly shuffle position in their V-shape squadrons.

Hundreds of exhausted, wind-blown migrants touch down at Holkham National Nature Reserve, a five-star haven of seablite bushes for shelter, open water, rich muddy shallows, creeks, dunes and salt marshes protected by the pine woods of Holkham Meals. Allow a couple of hours for a lovely walk on the sands from here to rainbow beach huts at the ancient port of Wells-next-the-Sea. Ride into town on the Wells Harbour Railway, one of two at the port. The steam trains of the Wells and Walsingham light railway will whisk you to the shrine of Our Lady of Walsingham, known as England's Nazareth.

Visit Big Blue Sky, a cheery emporium of art, books, textiles and great stuff from Norfolk. Dynamic Catherine Edgington has created a fun place to shop. She's passionate about keeping things local; every item shows the distance it's travelled to her inspirational store.

The village signpost at Stiffkey proclaims its alternative name, Stewkey, pronounced *Stoo-key* by residents. Local cockles are considered a delicacy because the mud in which they squelch stains their shells blue. Waders and wintering wildfowl feed at Stiffkey marshes, an apparently peaceful place but beware hidden unexploded bombs and a devil dog. It's said that fearful Black Shuck prowls these parts: an omen of death with gleaming coat and glowing eyes designed to deter the excise men from disturbing Stiffkey smugglers. Hearing the tale, Arthur Conan Doyle was

inspired to write *The Hound of the Baskervilles*. Read it over tea and cake at the jolly Stiffkey Stores.

Ferries sail from Morston to Blakeney Point at the end of a long shingle spit where common and grey seals breed. The prospect of walking

the length of the 3.5-mile spit appears easy, but intersecting dykes and channels make the boat trip a much safer bet. Learn about wildlife at the Point in the former lifeboat station, now a National Trust information centre.

In medieval Blakeney, narrow streets slope to the sea past bobbly flint cottages. There are seafood stalls on the shore and along the quay; boat crews call out the departure of more trips to see the seals.

The Norfolk Wildlife Trust visitor centre at Cley Marshes is birding nirvana: more than 300 species have been recorded. The stylish building makes the most of green technology and huge café windows overlook the marsh. The landscape has changed dramatically since medieval times when the grand church at Cley-next-the-Sea overlooked boats entering the harbour of Blakeney Haven. Now landlocked, St Margaret's is at the edge of a marsh, the harbour is long gone but the village thrives with its pottery, smokehouse, delicatessen, gallery, cafés, pubs and landmark windmill.

Crabs and lobster are on sale at Cookies shop and café in Salthouse, near the lovely elevated garden of the Dun Cow inn where there's a

...hungry and thirsty?

Brace yourself for a weekend of treats and tearooms; this selection is just for starters.

In Holkham, there's local venison and wild game on the menu of the Victoria Hotel, well situated for a visit to the state rooms of Holkham Hall. Order a picnic hamper for the beach from Marsh Larder tearooms and taste fine wines at Adnams Wine Cellar and Kitchen Store.

When in Wells-next-the-Sea, visit the Real Ale Shop at Branthill Farm for a unique collection of fifty bottled ales from fifteen different Norfolk Brewers.

Warm yourself by the open fire of the Red Lion pub in Stiffkey where there's eco-friendly accommodation under a sedum roof. Take tea with lovely vistas of the marsh and Cley beach from the café at Wiveton Hall fruit farm.

Blakeney brims with characterful pubs and the terrace of the Blakeney Hotel is a sheltered spot with lovely views over the quay. The Blakeney deli stocks all you need for a mouth-watering picnic.

Dine by candlelight at Cley Windmill and B&B on the marsh in Cley-next-the-Sea: booking is essential. From the garden of West Cottage Café in the village, there are big views of the reeds and you can pick up a simple supper of speciality bread, superb cheese and fine wine across the road at Picnic Fayre deli.

telescope to peer into the marsh. Britain's largest working military collection is at Muckleborough, and at Weybourne station on the Poppy Line volunteers run a great railway bookshop stuffed with second-hand gems. For just one more cup of tea, wander down Weybourne's Beach Lane where Gaynor Pannier's adorable little café and shop, Sea, is tucked into the whitewashed stable of Watermill House, close to the shore. Look out for a teeny donkey shoe nailed on a beam.

40

Take Flight

Seabird extravaganza   England's aviatrix   Exclusion zone

As the land drops away, the commotion of whirling birds
and the roar of the sea is thrilling.

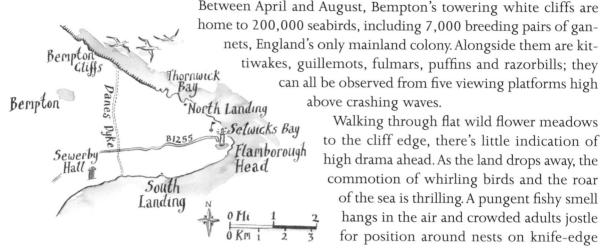

O n the East Yorkshire coast there's a pointy nose of land poking into the North Sea between Filey and Bridlington. Here the spectacular chalk cliffs of Flamborough Head peninsula play host to England's largest seabird colony. There are lighthouses, old and new, and at magnificent Sewerby Hall an intriguing exhibition celebrates high-flying Amy Johnson, the first woman to fly alone from England to Australia in 1930.

Between April and August, Bempton's towering white cliffs are home to 200,000 seabirds, including 7,000 breeding pairs of gannets, England's only mainland colony. Alongside them are kittiwakes, guillemots, fulmars, puffins and razorbills; they can all be observed from five viewing platforms high above crashing waves.

Walking through flat wild flower meadows to the cliff edge, there's little indication of high drama ahead. As the land drops away, the commotion of whirling birds and the roar of the sea is thrilling. A pungent fishy smell hangs in the air and crowded adults jostle for position around nests on knife-edge ledges – it's a wonder that any offspring make it from egg to fledgling.

For anyone new to bird-watching, friendly and helpful RSPB volunteers are on hand with telescopes to share and fascinating information about life on the cliffs.

Seabird eggs from Bempton and Speeton cliffs were collected

traditionally for food, although nests were also raided to satisfy collectors. 'Climmers' worked in teams, seizing hundreds of eggs a day. Dangling on ropes from the cliff, with little protection other than straw-stuffed caps to protect their head from rockfalls, the men were a tourist attraction until 1954 when the practice became illegal.

At Thornwick Bay there's a dramatic sea arch, clustered caverns and sandy coves popular with holidaymakers. From the sheltered bay at North Landing boat trips visit the seabird cliffs and caves. Caves can be explored on foot but don't take risks; respect the sea and know the tide times.

Flamborough Head boasts two lighthouses, although the older octagonal tower on the windswept golf course was never lit. The cliff top tower, built in 1806, is a great visit with views from the top to Bridlington and Filey. At the foot of the lighthouse Selwicks (or Silex) Bay has a huge chalk platform, rock pools and blowholes.

Look out for the toposcope monument with radiating lines that indicate distant places. It commemorates the Battle of Flamborough Head, which took in September 1779 when American colonies, supported by France, were fighting for independence from England. Locals watched from the cliffs as British warships defended a fleet of merchant vessels from attack by a squadron commanded John Paul Jones, 'Father of the US Navy'.

Beyond the pretty chalk, boulder and brick cottages of Flamborough village is South Landing where the beach is dotted with smooth egg-like white stones and fossils. The prehistoric earthworks of Danes Dyke ditch extend 2.5 miles from Catnab Cliff to Danes Dyke beach. Excavated in 1879 by Augustus Henry Lane Fox Pitt Rivers, the dyke gave up more than eight hundred prehistoric artefacts. The protected monument is a local nature reserve and a great place to enjoy woodland walks through New Year snowdrops, the spring dawn chorus or bats and moths at dusk in summer.

Hull born Amy Johnson officially opened Sewerby Hall in 1934 as a public venue for the Borough of Bridlington Council. Many of her personal belongings were donated to the Amy Johnson room, including a collection of medals, a cloth helmet, her favourite powder compact and a surprisingly flimsy flying suit.

You could spend a day visiting the Hall's zoo, gallery, cliff top cricket pitch and bandstand with views over Bridlington Bay The award winning gardens are inspirational. At the plant stall, I met a local man who had been a miner for forty years. 'Lived all my life in the dark. Now I'm finished, it's time to plant a garden.'

EXCLUSION ZONE

With the voluntary support of local fishermen, an area of one square kilometre around Flamborough Head has become a pioneering North Sea no-take zone to protect marine wildlife. This means that you can't remove anything from within the zone, either above or below the high tidemark. Fish, seaweed, shellfish and rocks must all be left where they are.

...hungry?

Make a beeline for Katy Wheelwright's cheery Ethical Catering Outdoors (ECO) caravan in the car park of the RSPB reserve at Bempton. Everything is deliciously homemade and organic, from tasty soup to rich chocolate brownies.

At Thornwick Bay, the clifftop café serves fresh Flamborough crab with salad, bread and butter. Take a break at Sewerby Hall with a visit to the Clock Tower tearooms.

Waves slosh around the foot of the village at the Dock where the Kings Beck spills out of the tunnel that carried smugglers and contraband up and away from the sea. Low water reveals a sandy beach and summer brings ice cream, deckchairs and donkeys.

The Coast is Clear

Baytown   The Boggle   Breathtaking views

There's no sign of the Prince of Thieves at Robin Hood's Bay in North Yorkshire, though the lovely fishing village takes his name.

This was the realm of eighteenth- and nineteenth-century smugglers whose highway was the sea. In Baytown, as it is known, contraband treasure passed from ship to shore through a series of village tunnels without it ever seeing daylight. Most of the community was involved, including magistrates and clergy.

Today, the steep, narrow and higgledy-piggledy lanes of Baytown are best visited out of the summer season: there's time and space to wander at will rather than play follow-my-leader with the crowds. Vehicles are not welcome in the village at any time; use the car park at the top of the hill, near the memorial that commemorates an extraordinary event.

In 1881, the brig *Visitor* ran ashore in a storm too strong to launch the Baytown lifeboat. Astonishingly, the Whitby boat came to the rescue overland, having been towed through snowdrifts by eighteen horses.

From the top of the village, there's a choice of routes to the shore. You could plunge straight down Bay Bank, but the rocky fore-shore path, past picnic tables overlooking the sea, is more interesting. This route sets the scene and you can always walk back up the other way.

Mounds of huge rocks, imported by barge from Norway, protect Baytown from pounding waves; likewise the sea wall that keeps the village in its grip. From the smooth open spaces of the modern construction, turn the corner to step back in time and enter the nar-row, cobbled lanes of the seventeenth-century fishing village.

Inviting alleyways shoot off in all directions. These are especially lovely in the quiet of evening, when the sound of chatter and distant footsteps carries above the refrain of the sea. Along the way you might meet an old married couple, heading for the shore with fishing rods and bobble hats – 'Going to catch the big one tonight!'

From 'A Smuggler's Song'

If you wake at midnight, and hear a horse's feet,
Don't go drawing back the blind, or looking in the
    street,
Them that asks no questions isn't told a lie.
Watch the wall, my darling, while the Gentlemen
    go by!

Five and twenty ponies,
Trotting through the dark –
Brandy for the Parson,
'Baccy for the Clerk,
Laces for a lady; letters for a spy,
And watch the wall, my darling, while the
    Gentlemen go by!

Rudyard Kipling

The village is pretty as a picture, and charming Sunny Place is a favourite haunt of artists. Acclaimed painter and sculptor Dame Ethel Walker, who was among the first members of the Fylingdales Group of Artists, founded in 1925, worked from a fisherman's cottage in Baytown and a studio in Chelsea.

The village is at the end of Alfred Wainwright's Coast to Coast long-distance path from St Bees on the Irish Sea, through three National Parks, to the North Sea. Blisters are forgotten and celebratory pints are downed at Wainwright's Bar in the Bay Hotel.

Waves slosh around the foot of the village at the Dock where the Kings Beck spills out of the tunnel that carried smugglers and contraband up and away from the sea. Low water reveals a sandy beach and summer brings ice cream, deckchairs and donkeys. There are rock pools and fossils too, but keep an eye on the tide.

At the Old Coastguard Station, National Trust and North York Moors National Park exhibitions include a rock pool aquarium and dinosaur tracks. Admission is free.

Walk uphill to the Bolts, where bootleggers dashed from the grasp of the excise men. Visit the smuggling exhibition at the Robin Hood's Bay Museum in Fisherhead from where there are wonderful views over distinctive red pantile roofs. Nearby is a tiny cottage with enormous whalebones at the door.

For an atmospheric night at the movies, take a pew at Swell, an independent cinema in the gallery of a converted Methodist chapel.

To explore the coast, allow two hours for a walk of 2.5 miles from Robin Hood's Bay to Boggle Hole. Check tide times: at low water it is possible to walk along the beach. Otherwise, set off from Flagstaff Steps, up Covet Hill and along the promenade. A path to the right joins the clifftop route to Boggle Hole. Return to Robin Hood's Bay along the disused railway.

Keep your eyes peeled for the Boggle, a mischievous shape-changing creature who lives in a cave on the beach. It's believed he protects local people from the forces of evil, including the excise men. Just one peep in his cave and they'd be struck down!

Warm up with a coffee in the cosy bar of Boggle Hole Youth Hostel, where wardens Peta and Andy have created a special atmosphere over the past sixteen years. They are both members of the Cliff Rescue Team, on twenty-four-hour call, and Peta's a coastguard too.

In fierce weather, seals bring their pups to the shelter of the hostel yard; it's Peta's favourite time of year. 'You can't beat being here in winter; it's so invigorating and uplifting. The light's fantastic – the whole place looks so different – and the sea roars away.'

...thirsty?

The Laurel Inn is the smallest pub in Baytown. Enjoy home-made soup by the open fire in winter.

Savour breath-taking panoramic views of the coast from Raven Hall Country House Hotel at Ravenscar, 'twixt moors and sea'. Take tea on the lawn, play croquet or perhaps a round of golf on the bracing clifftop course. Look out for the ancient carved rock set into the wall; it's thought to be Bronze Age.

Sea breezes transport the waft of fireplace smoke from the huddle of cottages below. From the windswept clifftop, the village seems sheltered and inviting.

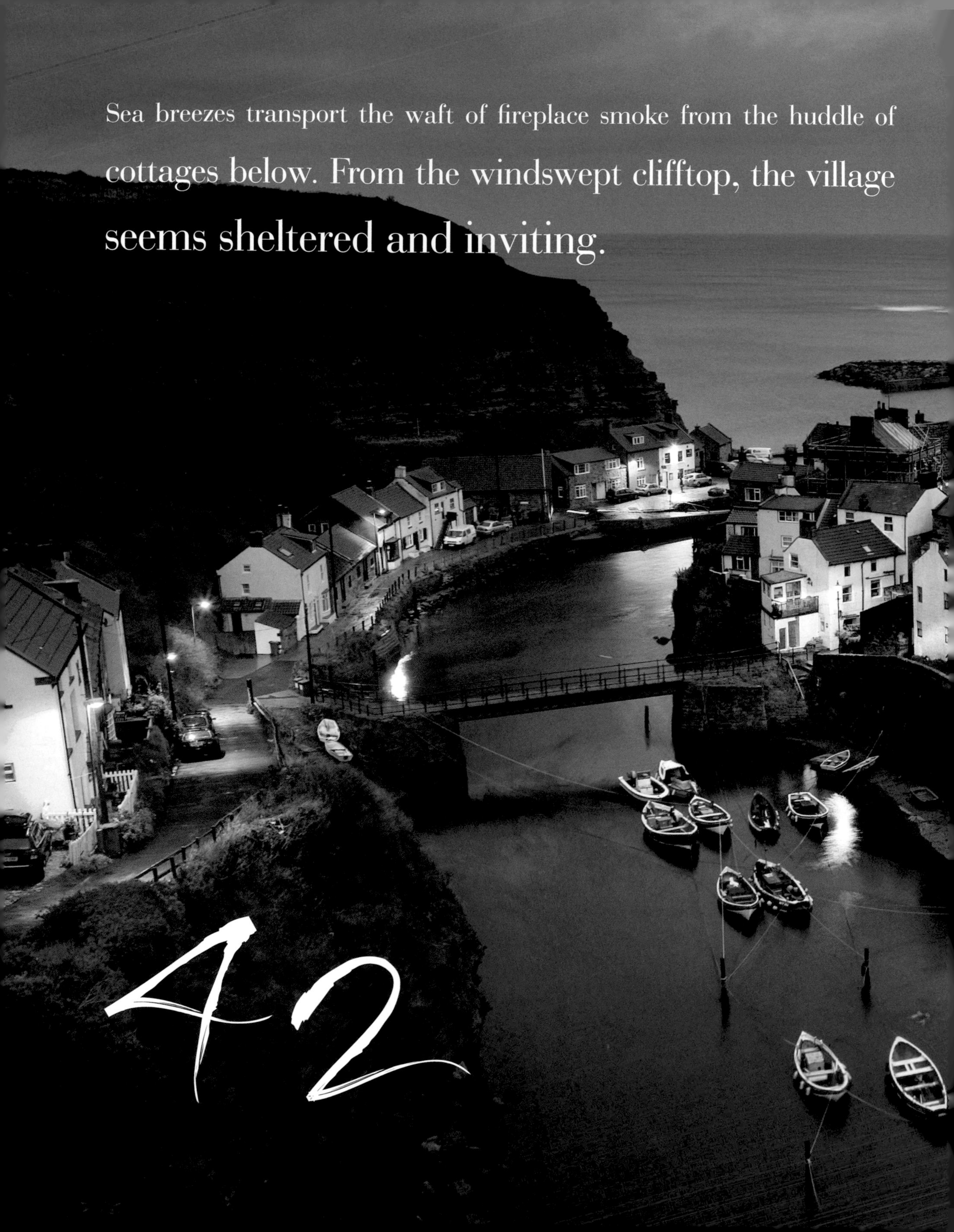

42

Downtime

Fishing villages   Fossils   Smoke signals

Jumbled cottages tumbling to the sea, cobbled streets snaking up and down hill and winter waves pounding on sandy beaches make North Yorkshire's fishing villages completely irresistible.

One of the loveliest views over Staithes (pronounced locally as 'Steers') is from the towering cliffs at Cowbar Nab. Sea breezes transport the waft of fireplace smoke from the huddle of cottages below. From the windswept clifftop, the village seems sheltered and inviting. Steep Cowbar Bank takes you quickly downhill to Roxby Beck, where ducks dabble and traditional fishing boats, known as cobles, are lashed tightly to their mooring posts.

The beck runs to the sea and lifeboat station at Cowbar Wharf. Cross the bridge, from where fishermen used to drape nets to dry, and you enter a maze of streets with colourful names like 'Slippery Hill', 'Barbers Yard', where the stonemason turned his hand to haircuts, and 'Dog Loup', wide enough for a hound, dangerously tight for adults.

Anchors in front gardens, lobster pots on ledges, the charming scene fascinated 'The Staithes Group' of Impressionist painters in the early 1900s. Dame Laura Knight, one of the first female members of

the Royal Academy was among them.

As a young man, James Cook came to work at Staithes' grocery store. To get a sense of his time there, visit the wonderfully idiosyncratic Captain Cook and Staithes Heritage Centre, a privately owned collection in the old Methodist chapel.

Staithes' sandy beach is good for fossil hunting, especially after stormy weather. Fossil fiends should follow the coast south for more rich pickings at Port Mulgrave. Dangerously steep and slippery steps, which are unsuitable for children, lead to the quiet beach. The now redundant harbour was built in 1857 to load iron ore from Grinkle mine on to steamers bound for blast furnaces and shipbuilders in Jarrow.

Follow the coast south from here to Runswick Bay's impossibly pretty fishing village at the bottom of a very steep hill. In immaculate cottages clinging to the slopes, holidaymakers have replaced permanent residents and so the village's mood changes dramatically with the seasons. The hum of activity in summer falls silent in winter when holiday houses are abandoned and upturned boats are stranded on grassy slopes.

The horseshoe-shaped bay is popular with experienced surfers who can handle the rocky slabs and boulders. In the distance, the lonely hamlet of Kettleness perches on the cliffs. Only ghost trains stop here now; the tracks are gone but the station house and platform remain,

surrounded by farmland. On a clear day, it's possible to see Boulby Cliffs; at 200 metres high, they are among the highest sea cliffs on the British mainland.

In fields on the headland between Kettleness and Goldsborough is the site of a fourth-century Roman signal station designed to warn forts on the Tyne and Humber estuaries of Scottish or Saxon invaders. An information board marks the spot.

Quarrying for alum, used in medicine and to fix the colour of dyes, led to the growth of Sandsend village, close to Whitby. Popular with bucket-and-spade holidaymakers, the seaside village offers good stops for tea, cake and ice cream.

The lush garden of the Wits End café makes an exotic hideaway on sunny days. Take afternoon tea at sixteenth-century Bridge Cottage Café, after a walk around Mulgrave Woods, open to the public on Wednesday, Saturday and Sunday, all year except May. Enjoy homemade cake, great beach views and a chat with the locals on the sheltered terrace of Sandside Café in a Cabin.

...hungry?

Book well in advance to enjoy a special evening meal at Staithes' celebrated Endeavour Restaurant, named after the ship Captain Cook sailed around the world. The restaurant's signature dish is the 'Staithes Plate', a starter of smoked, soused and salted line-caught fish.

For great food and rural views off the beaten track, book a table at the cosy Fox and Hounds restaurant in Goldsborough. Reservations strongly advised.

GOOD TO KNOW

Walkers following this section of the Cleveland Way can park at Staithes and follow the coast path over 9 miles to Sandsend. Here the regular Arriva X56 bus stops outside the Wits End café to take you back to Staithes.

There's excellent winter cod fishing along the coast from Staithes to Sandsend. Charter boats are available for hire. Beware tides and stormy weather.

...tired?

The cosy Staithes studio of Dame Laura Knight, one of the oldest buildings in Staithes, is the perfect holiday let for contemporary artists.
  Georgian Estbek House is a smart restaurant with a stylish seafood menu and luxurious rooms in Sandside.

43

And They're Off!

Seaside races   Teesside squaddies   Victorian vision

For a grand day out, take a trip to the north-east coast of England where Redcar's seaside racecourse extends a warm welcome to everyone from canny tipsters to racing rookies and young families. Hugged by terraced houses, a stone's throw from the shore, the red-painted racetrack is at the heart of the resort. The intimacy creates a friendly atmosphere and salty gusts and seagulls don't seem to bother the punters or the horses.

Before the course was built in 1875, races were run on the long firm beach at Coatham Sands, where many riders still exercise their mounts. Ropes marked out the route, judges observed from a bathing machine and the crowds enjoyed the free show until it was decided to make things more permanent and build a fashionable racetrack and grandstand.

For the cognoscenti, Redcar Racecourse is 'a left-handed oval of just over 1.5 miles. The key feature is a straight mile with a three-furlong "chute" joining the track at the point where the top bend meets the straight.' The cost of admission depends on where you want to go. To soak up the atmosphere of the parade ring, winner's enclosure and grandstand, tickets cost up to £15 per adult. Tickets for the course enclosure cost up to £5 per adult. Entry to either is free for children under sixteen accompanied by an adult.

Pre-race atmosphere is lively, with a jazz band in the Zetland Bar, families and birthday parties in the restaurants and tipsters casting an eye over meticulously groomed horses making circuits of the parade ring. Owners admire their four-legged investments and helicopters buzz overhead delivering jockeys to work. Bedecked with flowers and pink water buckets for thirsty horses, the hallowed confines of the winner's enclosure make a pretty scene.

At the old-fashioned sweet stall vendors do a roaring trade with cries of 'It's the only place you can be sure of getting something for your money!' Yet punters with Uncle Joe's Mint Balls still stop by the tic-tac men.

Steward Margaret Wilson told me that men and women place their bets quite differently. 'Most women choose a horse by its colour, and grey is always the favourite, or they go by its name or the jockey's colours. Men follow form and that doesn't always pay off.'

Unable to make head or tail of form after a moment's study, I went with beginner's luck and plumped for Striker Torres, wearing number nine, which seemed most auspicious to me. Last of the big spenders, I

…hungry?

The cheery Stray Café is a favourite local venue for chat, cake, brunch and concerts on the coast road between Redcar and Marske-by-the-Sea. The seaside rendezvous was long associated with the family of singer songwriter Chris Rea who wrote 'On the Beach'.

Take a table at stylish Vista Mar restaurant and bar for North Sea views by Saltburn pier, or traditional fish and chips from Seaview takeaway on the lower promenade.

It's more of a long walk over the sea than a kiss-me-quick affair but it is charming all the same.

backed the handsome Spaniard with the princely sum of £2.

Having been informed that the going was 'good to firm in places', I joined the crowd at the finishing post. Friendly locals suggested it was better to watch the start on the big screen opposite than peer down the track. Do this and you'll notice an extraordinary moment in the race when, with a mighty roar, the crowd switches its attention from the screen to real-life thundering horses. The sensation of sound, motion and colour surging towards the climax is thrilling. Striker Torres came second and I won £3. *Muy bien.*

...thirsty?

Ride Saltburn's miniature railway from the shore to the shelter of Valley Gardens, where you can take tea by vibrant Victorian flowerbeds all year round.

Before leaving Redcar, explore the promenade where the lovely one- screen Regent cinema sits above the waves, close by Lewis Robinson's movie sculpture, *Left Luggage*. The director's chair and kit recall 1,000 Teessiders playing their part on Redcar sands as Second World War squaddies in the re-enactment of the evacuation of Dunkirk for the 2007 film *Atonement*. Nearby is the RNLI museum, home of *Zetland*, built in 1802, and the oldest surviving lifeboat in the world.

You can hop on a train or bus for the short trip from Redcar to Saltburn or keep the sea to your left and cycle. It is around fourteen miles there and back. Stop to visit Winkies Castle, Teesside's smallest museum at Marske-by-the-Sea where, in a cottage named after his black cat, cobbler Jack Anderson collected thousands of Marske-related artefacts.

Saltburn-by-the-Sea sprang up after entrepreneur Henry Pease had visions in 1859 of a smart new town on the edge of a cliff. Twenty years later the resort was constructed from bricks imprinted with his name. Fashionable tourists poured into the Zetland Hotel from an extraordinary station platform within the building, designed to keep first-class passengers and hoi polloi apart. The hotel has been converted to apartments and while the disused platform remains, the tracks are gone.

The oldest water-balanced tramway in Britain links the town with the most northerly surviving pleasure pier. It's more of a long walk over the sea than a kiss-me-quick affair but it is charming all the same. Fishermen go for whiting on still winter nights and big cod in February and March. Enjoy panoramic views of the bay as you glide in the cliff lift, which is spectacularly illuminated at dusk.

North Sea surf rolling into the bay can be perfect for beginners and more experienced surfers. For lessons, equipment hire and the use of hot showers and changing rooms, visit the seafront surf school.

Dominating the hillside, Victorian grand designs look across the waves to the huge headland of Huntcliff Nab and its neighbour Cat Nab where the Ship Inn and a string of low-lying cottages cling to the shore like limpets. This isolated community of fishermen and smugglers was Saltburn before Henry Pease saw a bigger picture.

North and South

It's-all-here

There has been a light here since medieval times when monks built a chapel and graveyard to bury the victims of North Sea shipwrecks.

The sheer variety along this 7-mile stretch of the east coast makes for a fascinating weekend. From St Mary's lighthouse in the north to Souter lighthouse in the south, Tyneside may take you by surprise. Start at windswept St Mary's Island and Curry Point Local Nature Reserve, a wilderness just beyond suburbia. Take binoculars: this is an excellent place to watch bird migration in spring and autumn and an important winter roosting site for wading birds.

Cross the short causeway between tides to explore rock pools and visit the lighthouse, which was operational between 1898 and 1984. There has been a light here since medieval times when monks built a chapel and graveyard to bury the victims of North Sea shipwrecks.

The seaside resort of Whitley Bay is undergoing regeneration, without losing its character. The huge golden beach, wide promenade and open spaces of the grassy links make for an invigorating walk. Children will thank you for taking them to the magnificent Panama Skate Park, set in a dip by the beach. Inline skates, BMX bikes and skateboards are all welcome.

In 1880 Winslow Homer, one of America's leading artists, took a studio near the beach in Cullercoats. Impressed by the courage of the fishing community, he painted their lives. While much has changed, the fishermen's lookout, which appears in his work, still stands above the lifeboat station and sandy beach tinged black by underground coal.

The attractions of Tynemouth Park include cheery Longsands café – homemade specials seven days a week – the boating lake, bowling green

and beautifully planted adventure golf course where intrepid golfers negotiate the 'Lost World' of roaring dinosaurs. It's a long way from the tired crazy golf of so many seaside resorts.

Elegant lanterns announce the splendour of Tynemouth's Grand Hotel on the Grand Parade. Built as the summer residence of the Duchess of Northumberland, it oozes sumptuous seaside style. Call in for morning coffee on squashy sofas in the elegant drawing room and watch the surfers on Longsands Beach.

Tynemouth has a lively, urban village atmosphere; surf shops mingle with chic eateries. Brace yourself for a heart-breaking sight at the Turks Head Hotel where Wandering Willie, a winsome sheepdog, has been stuffed and displayed on a red velvet cushion since 1880. Willie and his master had been driving flocks of sheep from the Cheviots to town; in the noisy environment, the sheep scattered and dog and master were separated. The inconsolable hound awaited the return of his master in vain, only to be thrown from the Tyne ferry in a bizarre attempt at a mercy killing. He scrambled ashore but died later. Saluting his spirit, Wandering Willie was immortalised by the brewery.

The sandy beach of King Edward's Bay lies at the foot of Tynemouth Priory and Castle, managed by English Heritage and strategically positioned on a headland at the mouth of the River Tyne. Before crossing on the Shields Ferry, look out for daredevil surfers riding waves around cargo ships.

In the midst of South Shields' corner shops and terraced houses, a Unesco World Heritage Site is hidden from view. Follow signs to the extraordinary Roman fort of Arbeia, 'place of the Arabs'. Built around AD 160, this immense military supply base served seventeen forts along Hadrian's Wall. The imposing reconstruction of original buildings and

excavated remains make this a fascinating free visit.

From Arbeia, walk past Sandhaven beach and funfair to the grassy, wide-open spaces of the Leas where you'll find Europe's only cave bar and restaurant, the unmissable Marsden Grotto.

Ride the cliff lift down to the cavern where miner Blaster Jack resided. Huge windows overlooking seabirds on Marsden Rock make it especially atmospheric in stormy weather.

From the grotto, there's a short bracing walk along the coast to Lizard Point and Souter lighthouse, the first in the world to be powered by alternating electric current. The keepers are long gone from the National Trust tower; restless ghosts rule the roost now.

GETTING AROUND

Travel is easy; many locals walk or cycle and there's an efficient public transport network of metro, buses and ferries. Ferries have carried people from North and South Shields across the River Tyne since 1377. Still popular, the pedestrian ferry crossing takes seven minutes, cycles are transported free of charge and a regular service departs every half hour in each direction.

GREAT WORKS

There's inspired public art along this coast; have fun with *Conversation Piece*, Juan Muñoz's sculpture of twenty-two rounded women at Littlehaven beach.

Dolly Peel's statue stands on the hill above the landing stage in South Shields. Fishwife and smuggler, notorious Dolly hid fugitives from press gangs under her skirts.

...hungry?

Should a spooky sea fret creep in to Whitley Bay, or the North Sea air nip your ears, there's welcome refuge in the Rendezvous Café, built in the days when workers on holiday from Glasgow disrobed in beach bathing machines. The Arnone family have been serving ice-cream nut sundaes for fifty years. Huge arched windows gaze out to sea. Further along the prom, locals wrap up warm on breezy days to soak up sunshine and forget the bills at the Boardwalk Café.

Wash up with the surfers at Crusoe's friendly family-run café on Longsands Beach. Big picture windows mean you won't miss a wave.

Close to the Tynemouth Metro station, Sidney's Restaurant is renowned for award-winning seafood and there are tasty picnic treats at the Deli Around the Corner.

45

Amazing Grace

Lifeboats Castles Kippers

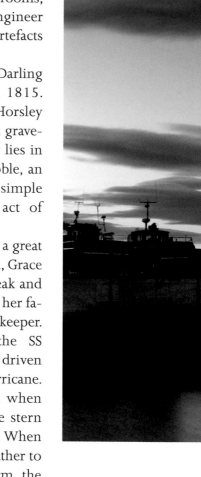

The pounding North Sea has shaped great swathes of beach along the Northumberland shore. From Bamburgh to Craster it is one magnificent stretch of sand after another. Whatever the season, a weekend exploring this spectacular coast is deeply invigorating.

Above the sea swell and dunes, mighty Bamburgh Castle dominates the skyline. Admire the fortress from the shore or visit the grand rooms, dungeons and Armstrong Museum, celebrating the work of engineer and inventor Lord Armstrong. The Aviation Artefacts Museum traces the history of flight.

Lifeboat heroine Grace Horsley Darling was born in Bamburgh village in 1815. Look out for the plaque on Horsley Cottage, opposite St Aidan's church graveyard, where she is buried. Her effigy lies in view of the sea, with the oar of a coble, an open rowing boat, in her hand, a simple reminder of an extraordinary act of heroism.

The Grace Darling Museum is a great visit. The seventh of nine children, Grace lived with her family on the bleak and isolated Longstone Rock where her father, William, was lighthouse keeper. On 7 September 1838, the SS Forfarshire paddle steamer was driven on to Big Harcar rock by a hurricane. Forty-three people drowned when the ship split in two and the stern was carried away by the storm. When Grace spied wreckage wedged on the rocks, she persuaded her father to attempt rescue in their small boat or coble. In the howling storm, the family launched the boat and saved nine survivors. The extraordinary events of that night unfold dramatically at the museum thanks to a spine-tingling audiovisual experience.

At the tender age of twenty-two, Grace earned the first RNLI Silver Medal for Gallantry to be awarded to a woman and became an instant, reluctant celebrity. Her story appeared on chocolate boxes and tea caddies and William Wordsworth wrote a poem about her. Just four years later she died of tuberculosis in her father's arms.

From the bustling harbour at Seahouses, boat trips leave for the

Darlings' Longstone lighthouse and the Farne Islands wildlife sanctuary. Wander around fishermen's squares, where clustered cottages shelter a large courtyard for mending nets and baiting lines. It's said that the world's first kipper came from Seahouses, thanks to someone accidentally leaving split herrings above a fire overnight. Local superstition dictates that kippers should be eaten from tail to head – approach them the wrong way round and the shoals leave the shores!

At Beadnell, black-tarred fishermen's huts, abandoned boats and broken benches illustrate how an old way of life has fallen apart. From the

sweeping sandy bay, popular with water sports enthusiasts, there are views to the Cheviot Hills, Newton Point and the ruins of mighty Dunstanburgh Castle. On the beach, the National Trust warden's hut stands guard over brave little terns nesting on the sand.

Football Hole is a secluded sandy bay on the way to Newton Point, a favourite spot for sea-watching, bird-watching, views to the Farne Islands and walks through organic hay meadows where wild flowers thrive. The tin church of St Mary the Virgin at Low Newton has a cosy timber interior that looks like an upturned boat. Fishing nets tumble from the ceiling and embroidered cloths in seawater colours drape around the altar and lectern.

On sunny days, tables and chairs from the Ship Inn pub and micro-brewery spill into the fishermen's square at Low Newton-by-the-Sea. If you fancy an evening meal of Newton Bay Lobster, freshly caught by Gary the fisherman in his boat *Sweet Promise*, you're advised to book ahead. The pub has an exciting range of distinctive beers: Sandcastles at Dawn, Sea Wheat, Ship Hot Ale and Sea Coal, the locals' favourite. Dolly Day Dream is a memorial to Dolly the dog, who beams happily from the holiday snap on the label.

Surfers meet golfers across the links at Embleton Bay, where quartz crystals on the beach are known as Dunstanburgh Diamonds. Towering above the waves on perpendicular cliffs, the ruins of Dunstanburgh Castle dominate the scene. There's no road to or from this

isolated fortress, one of the largest in Europe. To visit, follow footpaths along the shore from Embleton or Craster and savour the approach.

J. M. W. Turner's 1797 painting of the Lilburn Tower in the Tate Britain collection shows the castle at sunrise. But on a winter's day, lashed by surging seas, the atmosphere is quite different. Rocks are hurled around the Rumble Churn chasm by thunderous waves spewing white froth; the sensation can be terrifying.

...hungry?

Tuck into a bowl of crab soup at the Olde Ship in Seahouses. Cosily atmospheric with stained-glass windows and photographs of fishermen past and present. The nameplate of the SS *Forfarshire* hangs over the open fire.

Visit Patrick Wilkin for kippers from the Swallow Fish Smokehouse, just around the corner in South Street.

Call at the friendly takeaway van in Craster car park for a delicious kipper in a roll. And since the coast path cuts right through the beer garden of the Jolly Fisherman pub in Craster, it's always tempting to stop for chips and kipper pâté with harbour and sea views. You might find the waft of Craster kippers, smoked over oak sawdust at Robson and Sons opposite, hard to resist, so pop in to buy some.

In the pretty village of Craster, fishermen's cottage gardens tumble towards the sea and kippery clouds drift down Haven Hill and across the harbour from Robson & Sons smokehouse. Call in to artist Mick Oxley's airy studio to see inspirational paintings of the Northumberland coast in all its moods.

Sea Change

World-class diving   Surfing   Black Friday

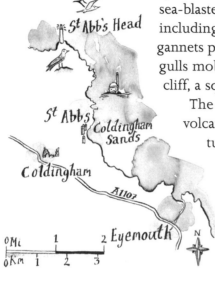

St Abb's Head

St Abbs

Coldingham
Sands

Coldingham

A1107

Eyemouth

0 Mi   1   2
0 Km 1   2   3

A weekend around the magnificent Berwickshire coast offers crystal clear waters, sandy beaches and surfing, awe-inspiring coastal scenery and the intense drama of fishermen's lives in shoreline villages.

St Abb's Head National Nature Reserve is a wild place to be buffeted by biting winds straight off the North Sea. Sheer cliffs, ninety metres high, are often swathed in fog but on a clear day they make a superb, sea-blasted vantage point. Offshore stacks and rocks throng with birds, including razorbills, kittiwakes, guillemots, fulmars and shags. White gannets plummet from sky to sea, spearing fish like darts and flocks of gulls mob fishing boats sailing to Eyemouth harbour. Tucked into the cliff, a squat lighthouse alerts ships to treacherous waters below.

The magnificent headland was formed by lava pouring from volcanoes around 400 million years ago, and in the seventh century, St Aebbe, or Ebba, established a monastery where nuns and monks lived in beehive huts of mud and branches. Separated from the outside world by turf walls three metres high, it seems the religious community enjoyed untoward hanky-panky. The monastery burned down and while some believe it was an accident, many regard it as divine punishment for disorderly behaviour.

The underwater world of the St Abbs and Eyemouth Voluntary Marine Reserve attracts around 25,000 divers every year. The combination of currents from the cold Arctic and warmer Gulf Stream creates an unusual combination of sea life: huge wolf-fish, up to one metre long, with fierce teeth and natural anti-freeze to keep their blood flowing, swim alongside tiny Devonshire Cup Corals, which grow up to three centimetres and are usually associated with warmer waters.

One of the best shore dives in Britain is just beyond St Abbs harbour.

The immense arch of Cathedral Rock rises magnificently from the seabed and attracts underwater explorers from around the world.

Before the decline of the fishing industry, village life revolved around a large fleet in the attractive harbour. Now there are just a few boats fishing for crab, lobster and prawns.

Led by Miss Jane Hay, locals campaigned for the unusual lifeboat station on the middle pier after seventeen sailors lost their lives in full view of the village when the *Alfred Erlandsen*

From 'Crossing the Bar'

Sunset and evening star,
    And one clear call for me!
And may there be no moaning of the bar,
    When I put out to sea

        Alfred Lord Tennyson

...thirsty?

Coldingham Sands'
pretty beach café
serves hot drinks and
snacks to hungry
surfers.

...hungry?

You might meet
dripping divers in
the harbourside tea
garden of Spring
Bank Cottage, St
Abbs. Freshly landed
crab sandwiches are
a real treat and the
McIntosh clan also
offer bed and break-
fast at the fisherman's
cottage.
    Try a Paradise
Slice, the locals'
favourite, at Lough's
traditional bakery in
Eyemouth.

cargo ship struck the treacherous Ebb Carrs rocks in 1907.

In Coldingham, peaceful ruins of an eleventh-century Benedictine priory surround the church and choice acts from the Edinburgh Fringe transfer from Scotland's capital city to the village hall for the annual 'Coldingham Fringe'.

Unearth second-hand bargains at the Coldingham Second-Hand Bookshop which raises funds for local projects.

When the weather's no good for diving, it can be great for surfing. For all the kit you need, visit farmer-turned-surfer Steve Powner at the surf shack within St Vedas hotel at Coldingham Sands. There's hourly hire of everything required to stay warm in North Sea swell as well as surf lessons and a repair service for damaged boards.

Patrolled by lifeguards in summer, Coldingham Sands is a great family beach overlooked by handsome Edwardian villas on the hill. A parade of brightly painted bathing huts stands to attention around the shore and the mermaid's pool on Pebble Beach nearby is great for leaping and sploshing.

There's good fishing for plaice and flounder from the rocks too. For an easy seaside walk, follow the Creel Path taken by fishermen from Coldingham village to Coldingham Sands and St Abbs harbour. The path is way-marked and you can buy copies of the route in Coldingham village.

For a good read, browse the shelves of Susan Shepherd's cheery bookshop, Crossing the Bar, in Eyemouth where the words of Tennyson's poem are writ large around the walls.

THE EYEMOUTH DISASTER

Along the coast from St Abbs to Burnmouth, Jill Watson's miniature sculptures of women and children in immense distress are a poignant reminder of the horrific events of Black Friday, 14 October 1881.

On a sunny morning, a fleet of forty-five boats, crewed by 279 fishermen, sailed from Eyemouth. At midday they were hit by a storm so violent that vessels were first lifted clear of the water and then swamped by waves rising like mountains.

All along the coast, families raced to the shore, watching helplessly as the ships struggled to reach safe harbours. Lifeboats couldn't go out because most of the crews were caught in the storm.

Only 150 men and twenty six boats survived, having sailed ahead of the tempest, some as far as Norway. Seventy-three widows and 263 fatherless children were left behind.

The agony continued for days as incoming tides washed wreckage, bodies and personal effects ashore.

Shattered communities survived thanks to the courage of women who remained faithful to their villages; it took around eighty years before the population of Eyemouth returned to the levels of 1881.

Do not miss the deeply moving exhibition exploring the fateful day at the Eyemouth Museum. A detailed tapestry, stitched by descendants, records the names of the crews and boats caught in the storm. The first boat listed is the Forget-Me-Not.

GOOD TO KNOW

Combine a visit to Eyemouth's fascinating Auld Kirk Museum and the intriguing World of Boats to receive a discount of 50p. Use it to buy fish scraps from the quayside stall and feed fat seals in the harbour.

47

Birdland

Famous gannets   Sandy beaches   Fine wines

Bass Rock marks the spot where the Firth of Forth meets the North Sea. Rising steeply out of the water, the volcanic island has been a prison, a retreat and a garrison. Now it is the largest single rock gannetry in the world.

Shags and gulls nest on the Bass too, but it's the dense mob of 100,000 white gannets that give the island its distinctive snow-capped appearance through spring and summer.

You can watch the birds from the comfort of North Berwick's Scottish Seabird Centre, where cameras are trained on the Bass Rock and three other islands in the

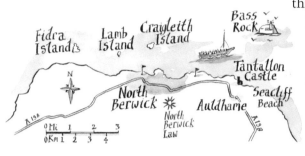

Forth: Craigleith, Lamb and Fidra. But nothing beats visiting the island in a beautiful boat with the seventh generation of a local fishing family. Pat Macaulay and her brother Chris Marr have taken generations of visitors to the island. Bass Rock and the gannets are in their blood. Even their boat, *Sula II*, takes its name from 'Sula Bassana', the name given to the birds by nineteenth-century ornithologists, which, in turn, comes from the island.

Before the lighthouse was demanned in 1988, the Marr family delivered letters, newspapers and even ice cream to the keepers. On special occasions they'd bring the men ashore for a swift pint.

Jumping aboard *Sula II* with Pat and Chris, I hardly expected to find a young gannet among the passengers. Several weeks ago the bird had tumbled from its nest to the lower ledges of the island where it had been dicing with death and would have been likely to expire from starvation, or end up as someone else's dinner, if brave Pat had not clambered out of the boat to rescue it.

Hugely familiar with the cliffs and ledges of the rock, Pat and Chris often retrieve birds that would otherwise perish. The pathetic creatures are taken to Pat's back garden, where they enjoy plenty of mackerel from her family of fishermen, but minimal contact in order to keep them safely untamed until, restored to good health, they are ready to be released.

It was a big day for the nineteen-week-old shipmate, who honked and hopped around, unaware that this was the chance of a lifetime. The strong westerly wind was just what the bird needed to get airborne from the sea.

...tired?

For a warm welcome, good night's sleep and breakfast with sea views, stay with Lorna Peressini at Seahome B&B on Melbourne Road.

As the handsome boat chugged out of the harbour, there were great views back to North Berwick and the North Berwick Law, crowned by a whalebone arch. Chris gave a running commentary, sharing his expert knowledge of seabirds and the coast.

Choosing her spot to release the bird, Pat flung the gannet towards the water with a cry of 'Good luck!' The youngster splashed down and then bobbed about on the waves. 'Hitting the water must be the strangest feeling,' said Pat, 'just like us putting *Sula* back in the sea after winter.' As the boat moved away, it was soon impossible to detect her

gannet in the crowd of young birds on the waves.

In the eighteenth century, Bass Mutton was a delicacy that commanded high prices in fashionable Edinburgh. The meat came from a small flock of sheep huddled on Bass Rock. The stink of ammonia is overwhelming on approaching the island. Gannets circle like snowflakes and the call of seabirds bounces off the cliffs. High above, dark young gannets teeter at the edge of the rock, summoning the courage to hit the water with a smack and a splash. To get this close is a memorable experience.

Back on shore, sandy beaches and renowned golf courses including the West Links, Gullane and Muirfield surround genteel North Berwick. Linking East Lothian with the city of Edinburgh and the Scottish borders, the John Muir Way long-distance path passes through Lodge Gardens where you can relax amid fragrant roses and lavender and visit the chirpy aviary.

Independent shops bring character to the high street. Handsome B&Bs on Melbourne Road have wonderful protected views out to sea; vehicles higher than seven feet and six inches are not permitted to park there. Designed as summerhouses for city workers, the elegant villas were traditionally boarded up in winter; now they are desirable homes all year round.

Four miles from the town, towards Dunbar, Seacliff Beach is something special off the beaten path. After the sharp bend at Auldhame, turn down a leafy lane where drivers need to feed an incongruous pay barrier with two £1 coins. There's adventurous swimming in the teeny extraordinary harbour and magnificent views towards mighty Tantallon Castle.

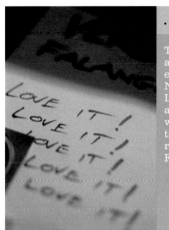

...thirsty?

There's a relaxed atmosphere at Lockett Bros. wine shop in North Berwick. Chris Lockett offers friendly advice and you're welcome to attend tastings in the backroom den on the last Friday of the month.

GANNETS

With a wingspan of up to two metres, gannets are the largest seabirds of the North Atlantic. They mate for life, up to forty years, and return to Bass Rock around February each year. Male birds adopt a nesting site as close as possible to where they were raised.

Gannets nest at height for vertical take-off; diving for fish from thirty metres they reach speeds of 62 miles per hour. Many break their wings on impact and 75 per cent of gannets die before becoming independent.

...hungry?

Award-winning rural chef Daniella Cocchina serves elegant food at the intimate Osteria restaurant in North Berwick.

After a walk on the beach at Tyninghame Links, refuel at Tyninghame Smithy, an excellent café and pretty shop on the green.

48

The Magic Kingdom

Village hopscotch   Fine dining   Award-winning fish & chips

In the East Neuk, or nook, of the Kingdom of Fife there's a string of distinctive fishing villages described by King James II of Scotland as 'a fringe of gold on a beggar's mantle'. The charm is still spellbinding: spend the weekend discovering delightful harbours, good food and ancient golf courses.

In medieval times, the Royal Burgh of Crail hosted one of the largest markets in Europe. Trading ships sailed to the Low Countries with cargoes of salted fish, linen and coal. They returned with European ideas that influenced Scottish architecture.

Wander around Crail's distinctively continental houses with steep fore stairs, crow-stepped gables and marriage lintels, bearing the initials and wedding date of the first owners. The sixteenth-century tollbooth, distinctly Dutch in design, sports a weathervane topped by a Crail capon, or smoked haddock.

Formed in 1786, the Crail Golfing Society is the seventh oldest golf club in the world. Legendary Old Tom Morris laid out the original windswept Balcomie course and Gil Hanse designed the later Craighead course in 1995. Golfing enthusiasts from all over the world come to play here. Visitors are welcome but booking ahead is advised. You can look at evocative photographs of the

game's early days at Crail Museum and Heritage Centre in Marketgate.

Meander along Castle Walk, close to the shore, for views of St Abb's Head and the Isle of May. Visit the overflowing courtyard of Crail Pottery, piled high with colourful creations. Buy fresh crab and lobster at the harbour; have them cooked while you wait.

From Crail, head south to the narrow lanes of Cellardyke. The name is a corruption of 'Silver Dyke', as the port was known to Dutch traders impressed by silver herrings drying on walls around the village. There are no herrings now, but catch the village on a drying day and you'll find bright billowing laundry on communal washing lines around the harbour.

Look out for divers from St Andrews University, surveying four nineteenth-century cast-iron cannons in the depths of the tidal bathing pool. Seawater protects them from deterioration.

Before storm damage, in 1898, Cellardyke was one of Scotland's most important ports. In the wake of the tempest, the fishing fleet shifted along the coast to Anstruther, pronounced 'Anster' by locals. Expansion came so quickly that both villages now rub shoulders; it's hard to see where one finishes and the other starts.

Anstruther was the capital of the Scottish herring industry. Allow several hours to visit the wonderful Scottish Fisheries Museum, which explores past and present life and work with the sea. 'It's bigger than you think' boasts the sign and they're not kidding. The museum is jam-packed with boats, captains' logs from whaling expeditions and stories of the herring girls who travelled from port to port to gut and

pack fish. Before a big night out, they'd pick the scales off their arms. Lovely.

There's no escaping the human cost of the fish we eat: every year twenty fishermen die at sea. The memorial room lists all Scottish fishermen, crews and individuals, who have lost their lives at sea since 1946.

East Neuk's last working harbour is in Pittenweem, which hosts a lively arts festival every August.

Visit St Fillan's cave, a dank and peaceful cavern in the village. Here the saint lived and worked by the mysterious light of his left arm. Today, fortunately, there's a light switch.

Take a stroll from the marketplace to the shore for a real sense of the community. Walk down steep Bruce's Wynd, past the uphill gardens of sea-captains' houses, to reach the harbour at West Shore. Follow the promenade, past fishermen's cottages, to the beach and tidal bathing pool, where locals have been baptised.

'Mare Vivimus' (we live by the sea) is the motto of whitewashed St Monans village, renowned for boatbuilding and fishing. Every June, the village celebrates Sea Queen Day, when a young St Monans 'Queen' sails from Anstruther to her home town on a traditional herring boat to bless fishermen and farmers.

Visit the Auld Kirk, closest to the sea in Scotland, where boats hang from the ceiling. Admission is free to St Monans Heritage Centre and windmill, used to pump seawater into saltpans along the shore.

United in 1929, the Burghs of Elie and Earlsferry overlook sweeping sandy beaches. Fringed with cowslips in spring, Ruby Bay is named after garnets, which wash up on the shore. Here Lady Janet Anstruther took to naked bathing from her Ladies Tower; a bell-ringer walked through town to announce the event and prevent any peeking.

Stout shoes are essential for the West Bay Chain Walk, reached from Earlsferry Golf Course. The unique coastal scramble uses horizontal and vertical chains to traverse rocks; attempt it only at low water and allow a couple of hours.

GETTING AROUND

The Millennium Cycle Way

Crail, Anstruther, Pittenweem, Kellie, Elie and Earlsferry are all on the Kingdom of Fife Millennium Cycle Way. This is a great way to explore the East Neuk. For routes and more information visit the website: www.fifedirect.org.

Fife Coastal Path

The fishing villages are also on the magnificent Fife Coastal Path, which offers walks for everyone. For more information visit: www.fifecoastalpath.co.uk.

...hungry? thirsty?

Crail
Relax in the courtyard café of Crail Harbour Gallery, a sheltered nook with heavenly views.

Anstruther
Stop for award-winning fish and chips at the Anstruther Fish Bar on the harbour. To avoid high summer's long queues, join locals at Flemings Fish Bar instead.

There's good beer, history and whisky at the cosy Dreel Tavern, one of East Neuk's oldest pubs.

Enjoy fine dining at the Cellar restaurant, one of the best seafood restaurants in Scotland. Book ahead.

Pittenweem
Plenty of foodie treats here, from the highly rated takeaways at Pittenweem Fish and Chip Bar, to bags of old-fashioned sweets from Nicholson's on the harbour.

Collect the keys to St Fillian's cave from the Cocoa Tree café. Let yourself in, then warm up with hot chocolate with chilli back at the café.

St Monans
Visit the Harbour Howff, community café, next to Feather Your Nest, a pretty homeware shop.

Enjoy fine dining al fresco at St Monans' Seafood Restaurant, superb views over the Firth of Forth to North Berwick Law and Edinburgh.

Elie & Earlsferry
In Elie, Sangster's Restaurant boasts a Michelin Star. There's a friendly welcome at the award-winning Station Buffet and you can watch cricket on the beach at the Ship Inn.

In Earlsferry, try Sunday morning brunch at the Golf Tavern, known locally as the nineteenth hole.

If you love to swim, take yourself to Stonehaven; if you don't love to swim, take someone who does, they will be eternally grateful.

Making a Splash

Unique swimming pool   Decadent art deco   Monumental fortress

Abandon the car and spend a weekend in the lovely east coast resort of Stonehaven, on the London to Aberdeen railway line. One of the town's main attractions is a summer swim in the one and only heated open-air, salt-water, Olympic-sized, art deco pool in Great Britain.

The stylish pool opened in 1934 with the aim of attracting holiday-makers to the resort. It was a huge success. Resident poolside musicians entertained the crowds with tunes like 'Doggy in the Window'; there were galas, famous exhibition swimmers, bathtub races and diving contests for prizes of canned fruit and lemonade.

The success continued until 1994 when the number of swimmers dwindled and the cost of repairs increased. The threat of closure spurred a group of enthusiastic volunteers into action. Thanks to their immense efforts, the pool has been kept open in partnership with Aberdeenshire Council and, although some necessary changes have been made, it retains the fabulous art deco style.

The pool's Splash Café is a favourite place for bathers to meet over hot chocolate and chips. Look out for the picture of 'pond-master' Bill Morrison taking swimming lessons in 1953 – fully clothed and wearing waders.

Recent entries in the visitors' book included 'Just how I remembered it 40 years ago', 'Worth the trip from Germany, excellent pool, great staff' and 'Enjoying my 70th year here'.

Original cubicles line the changing-room walls, each with a neat bench. Over the years, thousands of women must have painted their lips, rouged their cheeks and powdered their noses in the small mirror on the back of each disconcertingly tiny cubicle door, offering little protection for long-limbed females.

By the poolside, the air is often nippy. Sea breezes toy with bunting suspended across the water and the saltire on the flagpole. In sunny yellow sweatshirts, lifeguards survey the scene from high chairs. On cold, rainy days, they don high-visibility jackets and shelter under umbrellas.

At 28°C the clean, warm seawater comes as a surprise. Swimmers feel strangely buoyant, like children with new water wings. First strokes make even the most accomplished look ungainly. At the deep end, excited children climb up steps to shoot down a high slide into the water with delight. This kind of fun is priceless.

Having worked up an appetite in the art deco pool, dine in art deco

style at the Carron Restaurant, opened in 1937 by the Northern Cooperative Society for Stonehaven ladies who lunched. There are two entrances, the grander is on Cameron Street; go under the arch, through the pretty garden, across the original crazy paving and up the Hollywood steps to the sun terrace and dining room.

It's hard to believe this high temple of style fell into ruin before local man Jack Morrison stepped in to restore it in the 1990s. The detail is divine, much of it inspired by the *Queen Mary* liner. A fabulous clock must have counted down many a happy new year and an extraordinary etched mirror, known as 'The Mystic Lady', is said to be the work of Picasso.

Chef Robert Cleaver now owns the restaurant and regards himself a custodian, with a real responsibility to maintain it. The service is friendly and the food terrific.

Stonehaven's harbour is lovely, with seaside blue benches around the sheltered sandy beach. Look out for whirling model boats tucked away in Threadneedle Street. Based on real boats, they were handmade and

...tired?

For stylish interiors and comfortable bed and breakfast accommodation, stay with Janice and David at BayView in the heart of town, overlooking the sea.

...hungry?

Join the locals and gaze over Stonehaven Bay from the windows of the Boat House café tucked away on the old pier – it's well worth hunting down.

Home of the deep fried Mars bar, Stonehaven also promises fine dining at the Carron restaurant.

painted by a local fisherman. For Stella, who lives nearby, the speed at which they revolve indicates whether or not it's a good drying day.

From the harbour, follow signs for the steep walk uphill to extraordinary Dunnottar Castle, perched on dangerous cliffs above crashing waves. With its lion's den and turbulent history, this dramatic fortress truly has the wow factor.

Across the bay, on the headland, near the golf course, is the ruin of St Mary's church. Serried ranks of a tightly knit community are buried close to the sea: salmon fishers, white fishers, boat-builders, farmers and blacksmiths all sleep peacefully here.

GOOD TO KNOW

If you can possibly extend your weekend to enjoy midnight swims – on Wednesdays in summer – I can strongly recommend it. The sensation of swimming Olympic lengths under the stars is utterly delicious. In the dark sky, white seagulls fly overhead, probably off to bed.

...thirsty?

Visit the friendly bar at the Marine Hotel where they serve locally sourced food, including a signature dish of hot smoked salmon skink. Stylish accommodation too.

Sit out on the quayside benches at the handsome Ship Inn, built in 1771.

50

Fishy Business

Traditional boats   Wild salmon   Cullen skink

The extraordinary Bow Fiddle Rock is a favourite haunt of dolphins.

There's a rich vein of marble and maritime history in the handsome town of Portsoy on the Aberdeenshire coast between Cullen and Banff. Combining this with dolphins, clifftop castle ruins, ice cream and famous fish soup makes a great weekend on the east coast.

The beautiful harbour, one of the earliest on the Moray Firth, was built in 1693. In the heyday of salmon and herring fishing, Portsoy became a major port and in 1825 a second, larger harbour was built to accommodate the growing fleet.

Although all is quiet now, Portsoy was once at the centre of bustling trade with Scandinavia and the Low Countries. The architecture of buildings around the harbour shows European influences, reflecting a time when Portsoy imported coal, bones (for fertiliser) and flax and exported fish, grain, soapstone and Portsoy marble, or polished serpentine. The red, green and black stone from the quarry to the west of the harbour was so fashionable that it was used in two magnificent chimneypieces in the opulent palace of Louis XIV at Versailles.

One of the great Scots of his age, geologist Hugh Miller, visited the Portsoy lapidary, Mr Clark, at work on the stones in his studio. Miller was much impressed but couldn't tolerate the weather. In *The Cruise of the Betsey* (1858) he wrote: 'With better weather I could have spent a day or

two very agreeably in Portsoy and its neighbourhood.' Call into the Portsoy Marble Shop on the harbour to see the work of Tom Burnett-Stuart, a contemporary lapidary; there's no demand for grand fireplaces now but there are smaller polished items of red and green serpentine.

When Scottish salmon was more important and valuable than white fish, Portsoy was one of the main salmon fishing stations on the northeast coast. Fishermen worked from the salmon house or bothy, built on the harbour in 1834 and in use until 1990.

Between February and September, salmon were caught in bags or entangled in sheets of net stretched on stakes driven into sandy shores. Fish were removed and killed when the tide receded. Packed in ice from the local loch, the valuable catch was transported to markets in London and the near continent.

Visit Portsoy's sensitively restored salmon bothy to trace the town's fishing heritage. On the third Friday of every month, there's live music at the family-friendly folk club there.

...thirsty?

The Shore Inn on the quayside at Portsoy is a friendly pub awash with maritime character, low ceilings, great atmosphere and hotly contested darts games.

...hungry?

The staple industry of Cullen Bay was the catching and curing of fish. Cullen skink is a delicious broth of smoked haddock, potatoes, onions and milk or cream. Order it for supper at the Cullen Bay Hotel, where a distinct air of old-fashioned hospitality adds to the charm. The restaurant has panoramic views over the bay and Cullen's curiously small links golf course. Designed by Old Tom Morris, it is short on length but with more par threes than many others.

Portsoy Ice Cream on Seafield Street invites you to 'the ultimate ice cream experience'. Take sunglasses to choose from seventy flavours in glorious Technicolor, including 'Fudgy Wudgy' and 'Jammy Dodger', piled precariously high with psychedelic toppings. Take a taste test to compare Portsoy's ice cream with that of the Ice Cream Shop on Cullen's Seafield Street: locals insist that *theirs* is the best in Scotland.

On the first weekend in July, Portsoy hosts the Scottish Traditional Boat Festival, acclaimed as the best maritime event in Scotland. It is a colourful gathering, with music stages around the harbour, the Herring Road Run, a food festival in Loch Soy Park and a flotilla of traditional craft.

Wilma Woodin's bookshop is on Seafield Street at the top of the town. Double-fronted plate-glass windows display curious titles to lure you in, mostly with maritime, hunting and shooting connections. Once inside, it smells just as a bookshop should.

The Curiosity Shoppe next door is a den of treasure. 'Pre-loved' stags' heads, crystal chandeliers and chiming clocks are all part of the scene. Further along the road, Moira George makes traditionally crafted kilts, each one eight yards long and sewn by hand.

From Portsoy there's a coastal walk to the dramatic ruins of Findlater Castle: see them before they tumble into the North Sea. Take binoculars to spot dolphins, harbour porpoise and minke whales offshore and, as you pass the high-security bonded warehouses of revived Glenglassaugh distillery, twitch your nose to catch the distinct aroma of maturing whisky.

Mooch around the tiny harbour at Sandend Bay where rows of neat low houses are end-on to the sea. Traditional homes of fishermen crofters, many have smokehouse sheds in uphill gardens. Few people are resident now; most of the pretty cottages are holiday houses.

As the wind whips around the ruins of the spectacularly situated Findlater Castle, you can understand why Portsoy's wealthy Ogilvie family abandoned it in favour of the less draughty Cullen House. From the crumbling castle, walk back to Portsoy, along the coast or inland, or continue to Cullen for a warming bowl of the eponymous fish broth. Alternatively, from the car park next to Cullen Golf Club, enjoy a circular walk of 4 miles past caves and sea stacks to the extraordinary Bow Fiddle Rock at Portknockie.

...tired?

Watch Moray Firth dolphins from the shore at Portsoy campsite. Take surfboards and wetsuits to Sandend caravan park on the beach.

51

On the Black Isle

Famous Scotsmen Pictish stones Dolphin-watch

The slim, fertile peninsula is around 23 miles long and 8.5 miles wide.
The origin of its dark name is a mystery, linked perhaps with
witchcraft or maybe with the rich earth of the fields.

Not quite an island but certainly a place apart. Resident dolphins, mysterious Pictish stones and handsome eighteenth-century architecture make the Black Isle on the east coast of the Scottish Highlands a perfect place for a weekend visit.

The slim, fertile peninsula is around 23 miles long and 8.5 miles wide. The origin of its dark name is a mystery, linked perhaps with witchcraft or maybe the rich earth of the fields.

Agriculture and fishing were traditionally the main business of the Black Isle, which is surrounded by three firths, or narrow sea inlets: the deep natural harbour of the Cromarty Firth; the Moray Firth with resident bottlenose dolphins and the Beauly Firth, a sheltered sea loch.

At the heart of the Black Isle, the late eighteenth-century burgh of Cromarty is protected by two giant headlands known as the Sutors of Cromarty. In the shelter of the Sutors and spilling towards the shore, Fishertown is a gorgeous jumble of whitewashed cottages, flowerpots, vegetable gardens and narrow cobbled streets known as 'vennels'. This is where Cromarty's fisher folk lived, heaped on top of each other, just like the barrels, baskets and nets all around them.

To catch a glimpse of the sea, oddly shaped windows protrude from the houses at jaunty angles.

Two names are synonymous with Cromarty: George Ross and Hugh Miller.

Born in Cromarty in 1802, Hugh Miller was a self-taught geologist and naturalist, writer and folklorist, who became one of the most

...thirsty?

Mooching around Cromarty is a delightful way to spend a day. Explore the cobbled vennels of Fishertown to find Barbel Dister's Cromarty Pottery shop on Shore Street; look out for her flowerpots on sale in the lane. Cocoon yourself with coffee, good books and pretty things in the Emporium.

As you walk around the bay to see the dolphins, Crofters Bistro on Marine Terrace in Rosemarkie makes a good stop for tea.

The independent organic Black Isle Brewery at Munlochy offers visitors a free tour that starts with a grain of malted barley and is polished off with a taste of award-winning beer.

Tour the single malt Glen Ord Distillery on the edge of the Black Isle at Muir of Ord, west of Inverness.

influential Scotsmen of his age. Visit the Hugh Miller Museum and Birthplace Cottage, in the care of the National Trust for Scotland.

George Ross was 'Mr Cromarty', a businessman who saw the potential of the town and liked it so much that he bought it in 1722. The new laird invested heavily, building a harbour, hemp works, brewery, nail works, lace-making school, stables and a hog yard for breeding pigs. In hot weather the sweltering swine were walked to the sea for a cooling dip.

Cromarty enjoyed great prosperity between 1770 and 1840 and an influx of Gaelic speaking Highlanders sought work in the hemp factory of the English-speaking town. For them, Ross built the Gaelic chapel in 1784.

The endeavours of George Ross are recorded in the Cromarty Courthouse. Imaginatively run by the local community, this is one of my favourite quirky museums. Attend the trial of Cuthbert Mackenzie, a gardener from the Highlands, on a charge of 'notorious conduct last Saturday night'. It's great fun, if a little spooky. The exhibition exploring the town's connection with the colonial slave trade has provoked uncomfortable reactions; much of the prosperity that funded the growth

of the burgh was dependent on slave labour in the Caribbean, which was rarely spoken of.

From the Black Isle you can observe the only resident bottlenose dolphin population in the North Sea. Watch them from the Whale and Dolphin Conservation Society visitor centre in North Kessock, or, if you'd rather see them from the water, take a boat trip with an accredited operator who has signed up to a code of conduct under the Dolphin Space Programme. This respects the dolphins' need for space, allowing them to choose to interact with the boat rather than the boat pursuing and harassing them.

There's every chance of seeing dolphins and porpoise from the shore too. Walk around the bay from the café at Rosemarkie beach to the lighthouse at Chanonry Point. The gentle stroll takes around an hour, allowing time to stop and scan the sea for marine mammal activity, which tends to peak on an incoming tide.

At Fortrose and Rosemarkie golf course, on the approach to the lighthouse, there's a memorial to the seventeenth-century Brahan Seer who consulted a stone with a hole through the middle to make prophecies. Regarded as a witch, he was burned to death in a barrel of tar at Chanonry Point.

All around the lighthouse expectation hangs in the air as people of all ages and nationalities gather, binoculars fixed to their faces, waiting for the magic of the dolphins. It's a great way to spend the weekend.

GOOD TO KNOW

Dolphin-watching football fans might want to take a ball to Rosemarkie, there's a lovely football field near the Beach Café. Not far from the shore is an outstanding collection of Pictish and Celtic art at the Groam House Museum. Admission is free and you are invited to make rubbings of mysterious Pictish symbols and play a Pictish harp.

...hungry?

Have lunch in Cromarty's bright and breezy Sutor Creek restaurant – local seafood and wood-fired pizzas are a speciality.

For a great night out in the intimate setting of a restored, converted eighteenth-century brewery, book a meal with your ticket for a performance at Cromarty Arts Centre.

The Anderson bar and restaurant with rooms in Fortrose has been voted one of the top ten best traditional Scottish pubs. West coast seafood, Aberdeen Scotch beef and wild game are on the menu. Choose from 200 single malt whiskies and real ale from independent breweries. Cosy rooms and a roaring fire in the bar make this a great place to unwind.

52

Royal and Ancient

Majestic pilgrims   Championship golf   Famous whisky

For stunning Highland scenery, world-class golf links, award-winning beaches and Scotland's most popular single malt whisky, take a trip to the historic Royal Burghs of Tain and Dornoch.

At least once a year between 1493 and 1513, James IV of Scotland made pilgrimages to Tain for political and spiritual reasons. His visits to the shrine of St Duthac presented an opportunity to exert his influence in the remote and unsettled Highlands. Accompanied by astrologers, minstrels and falconers, the king set out to seek the saint's favour and enjoyed those of his mistress, Janet Kennedy, along the way.

James worshipped at the Collegiate Church of St Duthac in Tain, one of the finest medieval buildings in the Highlands. It's a pity he missed the Arts and Crafts windows; installed in the 1870s, they are magnificent.

In the church grounds, the Tain Through Time exhibition evokes the experience of the monarch's flamboyant cavalcade riding into town. The entrance fee includes a gentle walking tour of the town, on CD, with scene-setting commentary by Hannah Gordon and Bill Paterson.

Tain, Scotland's oldest Royal Burgh, maintains the tradition of ringing the curfew bell every night at eight. In Lamington Street, the long-established family business of R. Macleod & Son caters for the traditional Highland pursuits of hunting, shooting and fishing. This is the place to go for guns, rods, rifles and reels, posh wellies, midge protection, binoculars and even a smoker to cook up your catch of the day.

But there's more than country pursuits – prepare to be blown away by the extraordinary contemporary glass creations of Nichola Burns and Brodie Nairn. Their Glasstorm studio and gallery is a showcase of ground-breaking style. Nicola's pieces are exuberant; Brodie's are minimal. Sign up for a workshop to experience the wonder of glass-blowing for yourself.

Laid out by golfing pioneer Old Tom Morris, Tain's championship-length links is described as his 'northern jewel'. The seventeenth hole, Black Bridge, is considered the finest of all his short holes. The club welcomes visitors, though you are advised to book ahead.

Spring is a great time to go: fragrant yellow gorse erupts along both sides of the fairway and views of the Dornoch Firth, open sea and Sutherland's coastline are enough to put anyone off their stroke.

You won't regret a visit to a small rural industrial estate off the beaten track. At ANTA interiors and architecture outlet, delicious homemade soup is served at a handful of tables, surrounded by gorgeous stoneware, fabric and furniture designed by Annie and Lachlan Stewart and inspired by the Scottish landscape.

Close to the Pictish stones at Portmahomack, the Oystercatcher restaurant serves fresh local seafood in an idyllic spot overlooking the sheltered harbour.

Visit the serene coastal village of Portmahomack on the nearby Tarbat peninsula, where the mysterious Picts left fascinating marks on carved stones. Their extraordinary work is on display at the Tarbat Discovery Centre.

The lighthouse at Tarbat Ness headland is a great vantage point for dolphin-watching in summer and seabird migration in autumn, but take care, there's witchcraft in the air: according to legend, this was the meeting place of the local coven.

At Glenmorangie, the 'Sixteen men of Tain' craft a delicate malt that is exported worldwide. Visit the famous distillery to see unique stills, the tallest in Scotland and as long as a giraffe's neck. Reward yourself with a wee dram of Scotland's most popular single malt whisky in the tasting room but do the right thing: first try it neat, then add no more than a teaspoon of water, a drop at a time, to soften the spirit.

Exciting changes in the world of whisky are taking place at the Balblair distillery near Edderton. Award-winning Balblair single malt distinguishes itself from other whiskies by the use of vintages, like wine. Whisky to be bottled is selected carefully – any casks still to reach 'optimum maturation' are passed over and left to get on with it quietly.

Taking the A9 over the Firth, one of the first things I noticed in Dornoch was a steady procession of pilgrim golfers heading past the cathedral to worship at the golf course. Surrounded by purple hills and blue-flag beaches, Royal Dornoch Championship links are the work of Old Tom Morris and come highly recommended: 'the most fun I've ever had on a golf course' is how five-times Open Champion, Tom Watson described them.

Visitors are most welcome; there are handicap limits on the Championship course and it is wise to book ahead. Because the links dry out quickly after rain, there's rarely a day you can't play. In 1899 the Club invited ladies to play on the Struie, a separate course of twelve holes designed especially for them. Children of the parish of Dornoch could play too, free of charge.

If golf's not your thing, there are further delights around the small country town, not least the compact cathedral, founded by St Gilbert in the thirteenth century. For retail therapy and gorgeous things, visit Country Interiors and Jail in the square.

Vast sandy beaches between Embo Beach to the north and Dornoch Point to the south are perfect for long walks, picnics and observing seal colonies hauled out on the sandbanks of the Firth.

HEART-STOPPING SCENERY

Combine a forest walk with fabulous views from Tain over the Moray, Cromarty and Dornoch Firths. Follow the signposted 4 mile circular route from Jubilee Drive on the town bypass. Allow two and a half hours for the rewarding round trip.

Stop at the Struie Hill viewpoint on the B9176 for panoramic vistas of the immensely beautiful Kyle of Sutherland, known as Scotland's 'Million Dollar View'.

...tired?

Contemporary style and sumptuous soft furnishings from ANTA make Kyleview House one of my favourite places to stay by the sea. You can also snuggle down in the former palace of the Bishops of Caithness, now known as Dornoch Castle Hotel.

Directory

Please note — some businesses and services shut during the low season, while others operate reduced hours. We recommend calling ahead to avoid disappointment

1. Places to Remember

OS Landranger Map Sheet 9, Cape Wrath
OS Explorer Map Sheet 446, Durness and Cape Wrath

Durness Youth Hostel
Smoo
Lairg
IV27 4QA
Tel: 01971 511 244
www.syha.org.uk

Mackay's Rooms and Restaurant
Durness
IV27 4PN
Tel: 01971 511 202
www.visitmackays.com

Sango Sands Caravan and Camping
Sango Sands
Durness
IV27 4PP
Tel: 01971 511 262 / 01971 511 726 / 01971 511 222
www.scottishcampingguide.com

Loch Croispol Bookshop, Restaurant and Gallery
2 Balnakeil Craft Village
Durness
IV27 4PT
Tel: 01971 511 777
www.scottish-books.net

Cocoa Mountain Ltd
8 Balnakeil Craft Village
Durness
Lairg
IV27 4PT
Tel: 01971 511 233
www.cocoamountain.co.uk

Lotte Glob, Ceramic Artist
Sculpture Garden
105 Laid
Loch Eriboll
IV27 4UN
Tel: 01971 511 727
www.lotteglob.co.uk

Kyle of Durness Ferry
Tel: J. Morrison 07719 678 729

Cape Wrath Lighthouse visits
Mrs I. P. Mackay
Tel: 01971 511 343 or 511 287

Mobile: 07751 789 048
www.capewrath.org.uk

2. The Necessity of Wilderness

OS Landranger Map Sheet 9, Cape Wrath
OS Explorer Map Sheet 446, Durness and Cape Wrath

Old School Restaurant & Rooms
Inshegra
Kinlochbervie
Lairg
IV27 4RH
Tel: 01971 521 383
www.oldschoolklb.co.uk

Sandwood Estate
Contact the John Muir Trust:
Tower House
Station Road
Pitlochry PH16 5AN
Tel: 01796 470 080
www.jmt.org

London Stores
Badcall Inchard
Kinlochbervie
Lairg
IV27 4RQ
Tel: 01971 521 273

For information on fishing and permits at Rhiconich contact:
Rhiconich Hotel
Rhiconich
Lairg
IV27 4RN
Tel: 01971 521 224
Be sure to phone ahead to avoid disappointment.
www.rhiconichhotel.co.uk

For information on fishing and permits at Kinlochbervie contact:
Kinlochbervie Hotel
Kinlochbervie
Lairg
IV27 4RP
Tel: 01971 521 275
www.kinlochberviehotel.com

3. Highland Fling

OS Landranger Map Sheet 15, Loch Assynt
OS Explorer Map Sheet 439, Coigach and Summer Isles

Summer Isles Foods Smokehouse
Achiltibuie
Nr Ullapool
IV26 2YG
Tel: 01854 622 353
www.summerislesfoods.co.uk

Polbain Stores
Achiltibuie
Nr Ullapool
IV26 2YW
Tel: 01854 622 330
www.polbainstores.com

Knockan Crag National Nature Reserve
Tel: 01854 613 418
www.knockan-crag.co.uk

Achiltibuie Stores
Licensed Grocer: Petrol: Calor Gas
Achiltibuie
Nr Ullapool
IV26 2YG
Tel: 01854 622 496
www.achiltibuiestores.com

Coigach Craft and Gift Shop
Polbain
Nr Ullapool
IV26 2YW
Loch and river fishing permits available.
Tel: 01854 622 346

The Achiltibuie Garden
213 Altandhu
Achiltibuie
Nr Ullapool
IV26 2YR
Tel: 01854 622 202
www.thehydroponicum.com
At the time of going to press the gardens are welcoming visitors by prior arrangement only. They are due to re-open to the general public in Summer 2010. Please call for up-to-date information.

Summer Isles Hotel
Achiltibuie
Nr Ullapool
IV26 2YG
Tel: 01854 622 282
www.summerisleshotel.com

Am Fuaran Bar
Altandhu
Achiltibuie
Nr Ullapool
IV26 2YR
Tel: 01854 622 339

Summer Isles Cruises
Tel: 01854 622 200
www.summer-isles-cruises.co.uk

Achininver Youth Hostel
Achiltibuie
Nr Ullapool
IV26 2YL
Tel: 01854 622 482
www.syha.org.uk

Achiltibuie Piping School and Café
Achiltibuie
Nr Ullapool
IV26 2YG

Summer Isles Sailing School
Dinghy and powerboat courses
(R.Y.A recognised)
Tel: 01854 622 252 / 01854 622 272
www.summer-isles.com

4. Take the High Road

OS Landranger Map Sheet 24, Raasay & Applecross
OS Explorer Map Sheet 428, Kyle of Lochalsh, Plockton & Applecross

Kishorn Seafood Bar
Kishorn
Strathcarron
IV54 8XA
Tel: 01520 733 240
www.kishornseafoodbar.co.uk

Lochcarron Golf Club
Lochcarron
Strathcarron
IV54 8YS
Tel: 01599 577 219
www.lochcarrongolf.co.uk

The Applecross Inn
Shore Street
Applecross
IV54 8LR
Tel: 01520 744 262
www.applecross.uk.com/inn

Applecross Heritage Centre
Applecross
Strathcarron
IV54 8ND
Tel: 01520 744 478
www.applecrossheritage.org.uk

Applecross Campsite, Flower Tunnel Café and Broch Bar
Applecross
Strathcarron
IV54 8ND
Tel: 01520 744 268
www.applecross.uk.com/campsite

The Potting Shed Café
Applecross Walled Garden
Applecross
Strathcarron
IV54 8ND
Tel: 01520 744 440
www.eatinthewalledgarden.co.uk

Shieldaig Bar and Coastal Kitchen
Shieldaig
IV54 8XN
Tel: 01520 755 251

5. Between Heaven and Hell

OS Landranger Map Sheet 33, Loch Alsh, Glen Shiel & Loch Hourn
OS Explorer Map Sheet 413, Knoydart, Loch Hourn & Loch Duich

TSMV Western Isles Ferry
Mallaig to Inverie
Tel: 01687 462 320
www.knoydart-ferry.co.uk

Knoydart Foundation, Bunkhouse and Long Beach campsite
Inverie
Knoydart by Mallaig
PH41 4PL
Tel: 01687 462 242
www.knoydart-foundation.com

Kilchoan-Knoydart Estate
Tel: 01687 462 133
www.kilchoan-knoydart.com

The Old Forge
Inverie
Knoydart by Mallaig
PH41 4PL
Tel: 01687 462 267
www.theoldforge.co.uk

Knoydart Pottery and Tearoom
The Pier Stores
Inverie
Knoydart by Mallaig
PH41 4PL
Tel: 01687 460 191

Doune
Inverie
Knoydart by Mallaig
PH41 4PL
Tel: 01687 462 667
www.doune-knoydart.co.uk

6. The Train Now Arriving At Platform 9¾ …

OS Landranger Map Sheet 40, Mallaig and Glenfinnan
OS Explorer Map Sheet 398, Loch Morar and Mallaig

West Coast Railways
The Jacobite
Tel: 0845 128 4681
www.steamtrain.info

Off Beat Bikes
117 High Street
Fort William
PH33 6DG
Tel: 01397 704 008
www.offbeatbikes.co.uk

Fort William Train Station
Tom-na-Faire
Station Square
Fort William

PH33 6TQ
0845 748 4950
www.nationalrail.co.uk

Glenfinnan Station Museum and Dining Car
Station Cottage
Glenfinnan
PH37 4LT
Tel: 01397 722 295 (Museum) and 01397 722 300 (Dining Car)
www.glenfinnanstationmuseum.co.uk

Mallaig Heritage Centre
Station Road
Mallaig
PH41 4PY
Tel: 01687 462 085
www.mallaigheritage.org.uk

Fishermen's Mission Café
Harbour Road
Mallaig
PH41 4QB
Tel: 01687 462 086

The Cabin
Davies Brae
Mallaig
PH41 4PU
Tel: 01687 462 207

The Fish Market Restaurant
Station Road
Mallaig
PH41 4QS
Tel: 01687 462 299

Sheena's Backpackers Lodge
Station Road
Mallaig
PH41 4PU
Tel: 01687 462 764
www.mallaigbackpackers.co.uk

Seaview Guest House
Main Street
Mallaig
PH41 4QS
Tel: 01687 462 059
www.seaviewguesthousemallaig.com

Café Rhu
The Harbour
Arisaig
PH39 4NH
Tel: 01687 450 707
www.caferhu.com

7. Go West!

OS Landranger Map Sheet 47, Tobermory and North Mull
OS Explorer Map Sheet 390, Ardnamurchan

Corran Ferry
Ardgour
Tel: 01855 841 243
www.lochabertransport.org.uk/corranferry
The ferry crossing from Corran to Ardgour on Loch Linnhe runs every half hour. No booking required.

The Inn at Ardgour
Ardgour
Fort William
PH33 7AA
Tel: 01855 841 225
www.ardgour.biz

The Sunart Centre
Strontian
Acharacle
Argyll PH36 4JA
Tel: 01397 709 228
www.sunartcentre.org

Ardery Ard Airigh, Sunart
Oakwoods
OS Grid Reference: NM 748 618
www.forestry.gov.uk

RSPB Glenborrodale
Fort William
Tel: 01463 715 000
www.rspb.org.uk

Glenborrodale Nursery
Creag Darach
Glenborrodale
Acharacle
PH36 4JP
Tel: 01972 500 205

Ardnamurchan Natural History Centre
Glenmore
Acharacle
PH36 4JG
Tel: 01972 500 209
www.ardnamurchannatural historycentre.co.uk

Kilchoan Community Centre
Pier Road
Kilchoan
Acharacle
PH36 4LJ
Tel: 01972 510 711
www.kilchoan.org

Kilchoan House Hotel
Kilchoan
Ardnamurchan
PH36 4LH
Tel: 01972 510 200
www.kilchoanhousehotel.co.uk

Caledonian Macbrayne (ferry to Tobermory/Isle of Mull)
Tel: 01475 650 100
www.calmac.co.uk

The Ferry Stores and Filling Station and Post Office
Kilchoan
Acharacle
PH36 4LH
Tel: 01972 510 201

Sonachan Hotel
Kilchoan
Acharacle
PH36 4LN
Tel: 01972 510 211
www.sonachan.com

Ardnamurchan Lighthouse Visitor Centre and Stables Coffee Shop
The Lighthouse
Ardnamurchan Point
Kilchoan
Acharacle
PH36 4LN
01972 510 210
www.ardnamurchanlighthouse.com

8. Seaward

OS Landranger Map Sheet 55, Lochgilphead & Loch Awe
OS Explorer Map Sheet 358, Lochgilphead & Knapdale North

Crinan Cycles
34 Argyll Street
Lochgilphead
PA31 8NE
Tel: 01546 603 511
www.crinancycles.co.uk

Cockles Fishmonger and Delicatessen
11 Argyll Street
Lochgilphead
PA31 8LZ
Tel: 01546 606 292
www.cocklesfinefoods.co.uk

The Comm (Commercial) Pub
Lochnell Street
Lochgilphead
PA31 8JI
Tel: 00721 077 077

Empire Travel Lodge
Union St
Lochgilphead
PA31 8JS
Tel: 01546 602 381
www.empirelodge.co.uk

Frances Macdonald and Ross Ryan
Crinan Hotel
Lochgilphead
PA31 8SR
Tel: 01546 830 261
www.crinanhotel.com

Cairnbaan Hotel
Cairnbaan
Lochgilphead
PA31 8SJ
Tel: 01546 603 668
www.cairnbaan.com

Fraser MacIver at the Wagon Press
Crinan Wood
Crinan
Lochgilphead
PA31 8SW
Tel: 07795 186 698
www.frasermaciver.com

Crinan Classic Boat Festival
Held annually in early July
Tel: 01546 830 261
www.crinanclassic.com

9. Let's Get Away From It All

OS Landranger Map Sheet 82,
Stranraer and Glenluce
OS Explorer Map Sheet 309,
Stranraer and the Rhins

Dunskey Estate
Portpatrick
Stranraer
Wigtownshire
DG9 8TJ
Tel: 01776 810 211
www.dunskey.com

Portpatrick Dunskey Golf Club
Golf Course Road
Portpatrick
DG9 8TB
Tel: 01776 810 273
www.portpatrickgolfclub.com

Campbell's Restaurant
1 South Crescent
Portpatrick
Wigtownshire
DG9 8JR
Tel: 01776 810 314
www.campbellsrestaurant.co.uk

Knockinaam Lodge
Portpatrick
DG9 9AD
Tel: 01776 810 471
www.knockinaamlodge.com

Logan Botanic Garden
Port Logan
Stranraer
DG9 9ND
Tel: 01776 860 231
www.rbge.org.uk

The Old School House
Market Garden
Port Logan

RSPB Visitor Centre
Mull of Galloway

Tel: 01556 670 464
www.rspb.org.uk

Mull of Galloway Lighthouse
Stranraer
www.mull-of-galloway.co.uk

Gallie Craig Coffee House
Mull of Galloway
Drummore
Stranraer
DG9 9HP
Tel: 01776 840 558
www.galliecraig.co.uk

Corsewall Lighthouse Hotel
Corsewall Point
Kirkcolm
Stranraer
DG9 0QG
Tel: 01776 853 220
www.lighthousehotel.co.uk

Glenwhan Gardens
Dunragit
Stranraer
Wigtownshire
DG9 8PH
Tel: 01581 400 222
www.glenwhangardens.co.uk

10. Fish and Paint

OS Landranger Map Sheet 83,
Newton Stewart & Kirkcudbright
OS Explorer Map Sheet 312,
Kirkcudbright & Castle Douglas

Tolbooth Arts Centre
High Street
Kirkcudbright
DG6 4JL
Tel: 01557 331 556

Broughton House
National Trust for Scotland
12 High Street
Kirkcudbright
DG6 4JX
Tel: 08444 932 246
www.nts.org.uk

MacLellan's Castle
Castle Street
Kirkcudbright
DG6 4JD
Tel: 01557 331 856

The Greengate B&B and Studio
46 High Street
Kirkcudbright
DG6 4JX
Tel: 01557 331 895
www.thegreengate.co.uk

The Masonic Arms
10 Ann Street
Gatehouse of Fleet
DG7 2HU

Tel: 01557 814 335
www.themasonic-arms.co.uk

Polarbites Fish & Chips
Harbour Square
Kirkcudbright
DG6 4HY
Tel: 01557 339 050

Elizabeth MacGregor Nursery
Ellenbank
Tongland Road
Kirkcudbright
DG6 4UU
Tel: 01557 330 620
elizabethmacgregornursery.co.uk

Buckland Plants
Whinnieliggate
Kirkcudbright
DG6 4XP
Tel: 01557 331 323
www.bucklandplants.co.uk

Cally Gardens
Gatehouse of Fleet
Castle Douglas
Kirkcudbrightshire
DG7 2DJ
Tel: 01557 815 029
www.callygardens.co.uk

The David Coulthard Museum and
Pitstop Diner
Burn Brae
Twynholm
DG6 4NU
Tel: 01557 860 050
www.dcmuseum.co.uk

11. The Crossing Place

OS Landranger Map Sheet 85,
Carlisle and Solway Firth
OS Explorer Map Sheet 314, Solway
Firth

Drumbrugh Moss
Cumbria Wildlife Trust
Plumgarths
Crook Road
Kendal
LA8 8LX
Tel: 01539 816 300
www.cumbriawildlifetrust.org.uk

The Greyhound Inn
Burgh-by-Sands
Carlisle
CA5 6AN
Tel: 01228 576 579
www.greyhoundcatering.com

The Grange and Laal Bite Tuckshop
Drumburgh
Carlisle
CA7 5DW
Tel: 01228 576 551
www.thegrangecottage.co.uk

The Hope and Anchor Inn
Port Carlisle
Wigton
CA7 5BU
Tel: 01697 351460
www.hopeandanchorinn.com

Kings Arms
Bowness-on-Solway
Wigton
CA7 5AF
Tel: 01697 351 426
www.kingsarmsbowness.co.uk

Highland Laddie
Glasson
Wigton
CA7 5DT
Tel: 01697 351 839

RSPB Campfield Marsh Nature
Reserve
Wigton
CA7 5AG
Tel: 01697 351 330
www.rspb.org.uk

Hesket House B&B
Port Carlisle
Wigton
Tel: 01697 351876
www.heskethouse.com

12. See Red

OS Landranger Map Sheet 89, West
Cumbria
OS Explorer Map Sheet 303,
Whitehaven and Workington

St Bees Priory
The Priory
St Bees
CA27 0DR
stbeespriory.org.uk

Coast to Coast walk information
can be found at:
www.thecoasttocoastwalk.info

Cycle Route 72
www.sustrans.org.uk

Cycling routes:
www.virtualegremont.co.uk

The Manor House Hotel
10–12 Main Street
St Bees
Whitehaven
CA27 0DE
Tel: 01946 820587
www.manorhousestbees.com

The Oddfellows Arms
92 Main St
St Bees
CA27 0AD
Tel: 01946 822317

Hartleys Beach Shop & Café
Beach Rd
St. Bees
CA27 0ES
Tel: 01946 820175

The Beacon Museum
West Strand
Whitehaven
CA28 7LY
Tel: 01946 592302
www.thebeacon-whitehaven.co.uk

Haig Colliery Mining Museum
Solway Road
Kells
Whitehaven
CA28 9BG
Tel: 01946 599949
www.haigpit.com

13. Another Place

OS Landranger Map Sheet 108,
Liverpool
OS Explorer Map Sheet 285,
Southport and Chorley

Mersey Travel
Tel: 0151 227 5181
www.merseytravel.gov.uk

The Volunteer Canteen
45 East Street
Waterloo
Liverpool
L22 8QR
Tel: 0151 928 1676

The Crows Nest
63–65 Victoria Road
Crosby
Liverpool
L23 7XY
Tel: 0151 924 6953

The Edinburgh
119 College Road
Crosby
Liverpool
L23 3AS
Tel: 0151 924 5822

Blundellsands Sailing Club
The Forshore
Hightown
Liverpool
L38 9EY
Tel: 0151 929 2101
www.homepages.rya-
online.net/blundellsands
sailingclub

Formby Point
The National Trust
Victoria Road
Freshfield
Formby
Liverpool

L37 1LJ
Tel: 01704 878591
www.nationaltrust.org.uk

Cabin Hill National Nature Reserve
Range Lane
Formby
Liverpool
Tel: 01704 578774
www.naturalengland.org.uk

Larkhill Farm
Wicks Lane
Formby
Liverpool
L37 1PJ
Tel: 01704 872315

Marsh Farm
Range Lane
Formby
Liverpool
Tel: 01704 872948

The Courtyard Eatery & Gift Shop
Delph Road
Little Crosby
L23 4TU
Tel: 0151 932 9333

Warehouse Brasserie
30 West Street
Southport
PR8 1QN
Tel: 01704 544662
www.warehouse-brasserie.co.uk

14. Where the Dee Meets the Sea

OS Landranger Map Sheet 108,
Liverpool
OS Explorer Map Sheet 266, Wirral
and Chester

Wirral Country Park Visitor Centre
Station Road
Thurstaston
Wirral
CH61 0HN
Tel: 0151 648 4371
www.wirral.gov.uk

West Kirby Sailing Club
Sandy Lane
West Kirby
Wirral
CH48 3HZ
Tel: 0151 625 5579
www.wksc.net

Wirral Country Park Caravan Club
Site
Station Road
Thurstaston
Wirral
CH61 0HN
Tel: 01342 326944

Royal Liverpool Golf Club
Meols Drive
Hoylake
Wirral
CH47 4AL
Tel: 0151 632 7772
www.royal-liverpool-golf.com

Roses Tea Rooms
23 Milner Road
Heswall
Wirral
CH60 5RT
Tel: 0151 342 9912
www.rosestearooms.co.uk

Linghams Booksellers
248 Telegraph Road
Heswall
Wirral
CH60 7SG
Tel: 0151 342 7290
www.linghams.co.uk

Emma's Coffee Shop
21 Village Road
Lower Heswall
Wirral
CH60 0DX
Tel: 0151 342 8771

Sheldrakes Bistro
Banks Road
Lower Heswall
Wirral
CH60 9JS
Tel: 0151 342 1556
www.sheldrakesrestaurant.co.uk

Church Farm Organics
Church Lane
Thurstaston
Wirral
CH61 0HW
Tel: 0151 648 7838
www.churchfarm.org.uk

Palms Fine Foods
22 Banks Road
West Kirby
Wirral
CH48 0RD
Tel: 0151 625 6776

GJ's Cafe
Station Road
Thurstaston
Wirral
CH61 0HN
Tel: 0151 648 4959

Sands Café Bar
8a Dee Lane
West Kirby
Wirral
CH48 0QA
Tel: 0151 625 3986
www.sandswestkirby.co.uk

Marigolds Fish & Chip Takeaway &
Restaurant
14 Banks Road
West Kirby
Wirral
CH48 0RD
Tel: 0151 625 8693

Ness Botanic Gardens
Ness
Neston
South Wirral
CH64 4AY
Tel: 0151 353 0123
www.nessgardens.org.uk

Harp Inn
19 Quayside
Little Neston
CH64 0TB
Tel: 0151 336 6980
www.harpinn.co.uk

15. A Touch of Class

OS Landranger Map Sheet 115,
Snowdon and 116, Denbigh and
Colwyn Bay
OS Explorer Map Sheet OL17,
Snowdon

Camera Obscura
Happy Valley
Llandudno
LL30 2LS
Tel: 01492 876922 / 07788 450
445
www.visitllandudno.org.uk

Llandudno Cable Car
Happy Valley
Great Orme
Llandudno
Tel: 01492 877 205

Llandudno Great Orme Tramway
Victoria Station
Church Walks
Llandudno
LL30 2NB
Tel: 01492 879306
www.greatormetramway.co.uk

Haulfre Gardens Cafe
Haulfre Gardens
Cwlach Road
Llandudno
LL30 2HT
Tel: 01492 876731

Nineteen Café
19 Lloyd Street
Llandudno
LL30 2UU
Tel: 01492 873333

Fish Tram Chips
Old Road

Llandudno
LL30 2NB
Tel: 01492 872673

Kings Head
Old Road
Llandudno
LL30 2NB
Tel: 01492 877993

Llandudno Ski Centre
John Nike Leisuresport Complex
Great Orme
Llandudno
LL30 2QL
Tel: 01492 874707
www.llandudnoskislope.co.uk

Great Orme Mines
Great Orme
Llandudno
LL30 2XG
01492 870447
www.greatormemines.info

The Empire Hotel
Church Walks
Llandudno
LL30 2HE
Tel: 01492 860555
www.empirehotel.co.uk

Osborne House Hotel
Promenade
17 North Parade
Llandudno
LL30 2LP
Tel: 01492 860330
www.osbornehouse.com

The Cliffbury Guest House
34 St David's Road
Llandudno
LL30 2UH
Tel: 01492 877224
www.thecliffbury.co.uk

16. Secrets of Wild West Wales

OS Landranger Map Sheet 123,
Llyn Peninsula
OS Explorer Map Sheet 253, Llyn
Peninsula West

Tŷ Coch Inn
Porthdinllaen
Tel: 01758 720498
www.tycoch.co.uk

Caffi Porthdinllaen
Golf Road
Morfa Nefyn
Tel: 01758 721244
www.walesdirectory.co.uk

Nefyn & District Golf Club
Lon Golff
Morfa Nefyn

Pwllheli
LL53 6DA
Tel: 01758 720966
www.nefyn-golf-club.com

Cwt Tatws
Towyn
Tudweiliog
Pwllheli
LL53 8PD

Selective Seafoods
Ffridd Wen
Tudweiliog
Pwllheli
LL53 8BJ
Tel: 01758 770397
www.selectiveseafoods.com

Lion Hotel
Tudweiliog
Pwllheli
LL53 8ND
Tel: 01758 770244

Sion Williams
Wildlife and Fishing Trips
Tel: 01758 730231/07817 312
576
www.selectiveseafoods.com

Enlli Charters
Day trips to Bardsey Island from
Hafan Pwllheli Marina and Porth
Meudwy. It is wise to pre-book.
Tel: 0845 811 3655 or 07836
293146
www.enllicharter.co.uk

Hen Blas
Café, crafts, fish & chips
Aberdaron
Tel: 01758 760209

Eleri Stores
Aberdaron
Pwllheli
LL53 8BE
Tel: 01758 760233

The Ship Hotel
Aberdaron
Pwllheli
LL53 8BE
Tel: 01758 760204
www.theshiphotelaberdaron.co.uk

Gwesty Tŷ Newydd
Aberdaron
Pwllheli
LL53 8BE
Tel: 01758 760207
www.gwesty-tynewydd.co.uk

17. Colour Therapy

OS Landranger Map Sheet 146,
Lampeter & Llandovery
OS Explorer Map Sheet 198,
Cardigan and New Quay

Harbour Master Hotel
Pen Cei
Aberaeron
SA46 OBT
Tel: 01545 570755
www.harbour-master.com

Hive on the Quay
Cadwgan Place
Aberaeron
SA46 OBU
Tel: 01545 570445
www.hiveonthequay.co.uk

Llanerchaeron,
The National Trust
Ciliau Aeron
Aberaeron
SA48 8DG
Tel: 01545 570200
www.nationaltrust.org.uk

The Black Lion Hotel
New Quay
SA45 9PT
Tel: 01545 560209
www.blacklionnewquay.co.uk

Queens Hotel
Church Street
New Quay
SA45 9NZ
Tel: 01545 560650

Cardigan Bay Boat Place
Cardigan Bay
New Quay Harbour
Tel: 01545 561074
www.cardiganbaysac.org.uk

Cardigan Bay Watersports Centre
Sandy Slip
Glanmore Terrace
New Quay
SA45 9PS
Tel: 01545 561257
www.cardiganbaywatersports.org.
uk

Cardigan Bay Marine Wildlife
Centre
Patent Slip Building
Glanmor Terrace
New Quay
SA45 9PS
Tel: 01545 560032
www.cbmwc.org

The Fresh Fish Shop
New Quay
Tel: 01545 560375

18. Splashdown

OS Landranger Map Sheet 157, St
David's & Haverfordwest
OS Explorer Map Sheet OL35,
North Pembrokeshire

Pembrokeshire Coastal Bus Services
www.pembrokeshire.gov.uk/coast
bus

The Sloop Inn
Porthgain
SA62 5BN
Tel: 01348 831449
www.sloop.co.uk

The Shed Wine Bar and Bistro
Porthgain
Haverfordwest
SA62 5BN
Tel: 01348 831518
www.theshedporthgain.co.uk

The Old School Hostel
Ffordd-yr-Afon
Trefin
Haverfordwest
SA62 5AU
Tel: 01348 831800
www.theoldschoolhostel.co.uk

Melin Tregwynt Mill, Shop and
Café
Castlemorris
Haverfordwest
SA62 5UX
Tel: 01348 891225
www.melintregwynt.co.uk

Trellyn Woodland Camping
Abercastle
Haverfordwest
SA62 5HJ
Tel: 01348 837762
www.trellyn.co.uk

Pwll Deri Youth Hostel
Castell Mawr
Tref Asser
Goodwick
SA64 0LR
Tel: 01348 891385
www.yha.org.uk

19. Headspace

OS Landranger Map Sheet 157, St
David's & Haverfordwest
OS Explorer Map Sheet OL36,
South Pembrokeshire

Pembrokeshire Coastal Bus Services
www.pembrokeshire.gov.uk/coast
bus

YHA Marloes Sands
Runwayskiln
Marloes

Haverfordwest
SA62 3BH
Tel: 01646 636667
www.yha.org.uk

The Clock House
Marloes
Haverfordwest
SA62 3AZ
Tel: 01646 636527
www.clockhousemarloes.co.uk

The Lobster Pot & Inn
Marloes
Haverfordwest
SA62 3AZ
Tel: 01646 636233

Skomer Island
Boats from Martins Haven
www.welshwildlife.org

The Wildlife Trust of South and
West Wales
Lockley Lodge Visitor Centre
Martin's Haven
SA62 3BJ
Tel: 01646 636800
www.welshwildlife.org

Skomer Marine Nature Reserve
Visitor Centre
Located down the steep hill from
Lockley Lodge, next to the Marine
Nature Reserve office.
www.welshwildlife.org

Griffin Inn
Dale
Haverfordwest
SA62 3RB
Tel: 01646 636227
www.griffininndale.co.uk

20. Circle of Friends

OS Landranger Map Sheet 158,
Tenby and Pembroke
OS Explorer Map Sheet OL36,
South Pembrokeshire

Coastal Cruiser
For timetable, see
www.pembrokeshire.gov.uk

Ye Olde Worlde Café
Bosherston
Pembroke
SA71 5DN
Tel: 01646 661216

National Trust Estate Office
Old Home Farm
Stackpole
SA71 5DQ
Tel: 01646 661359 (Estate Office)
01646 661464 (Stackpole for Out-
door Learning)
01646 661425 (Stackpole Centre)

01646 661442 (Mencap Walled
Garden)
01646 672672 (Stackpole Quay
Boathouse Tearoom)
www.nationaltrust.org.uk

The Stackpole Inn
Jasons Corner
Stackpole
SA71 5DF
Tel: 01646 672324
www.stackpoleinn.co.uk

Castlemartin Range Firing Notices
www.pembrokeshireranges.com

21. Saddle Up

OS Landranger Map Sheet 159,
Swansea and Gower
OS Explorer Map Sheet 164, Gower

Parc-le-Breos pony trekking
Parc-Le-Breos House
Parkmill
SA3 2HA
Tel: 01792 371636
www.parc-le-breos.co.uk

Broad Pool and Bog
Abot 2 miles northeast of
Reynoldston. The reserve may be
approached from the north Gower
Road (B4271) via Cilibion or from
the south Gower Road (A4118) via
Reynoldston. The reserve lies on
both sides of the road between
Reynoldston and Cilibion.

Pennard Golf Club
2 Southgate Road
Southgate
Swansea
SA3 2BT
Tel: 01792 233131
www.pennardgolfclub.com

Pennard Castle
Three Cliffs Bay
Gower Peninsula
For further information: Swansea
Tourist Information Centre
Tel: 01792 468321
www.visitswanseabay.com

Three Cliffs Coffee Shop
68 Southgate Road
Southgate
SA3 2DH
Tel: 01792 233230
www.threecliffs.com

The King Arthur Hotel
Higher Green
Reynoldston
Swansea
SA3 1AD
Tel: 01792 390775
www.kingarthurhotel.co.uk

Dolphin Inn
Mill Lane
Llanrhidian
SA3 1FH
01792 391069

Joiners Arms
50 Bishopston Road
Bishopston
Swansea
SA3 3EJ
Tel: 01792 232658

22. Shiver Me Timbers!

OS Landranger Map Sheet 170, Vale
of Glamorgan
OS Explorer Map Sheet 151, Cardiff
and Bridgend

Old Swan Inn
Church Street
Llantwit Major
CF61 1SB
Tel: 01446 792230

The Beach Cafe
Colhugh Street
Llantwit Major
CF61 1RF
Tel: 01446 792665

St Donat's Arts Centre
St Donat's Castle
Llantwit Major
CF61 1WF
Box Office: 01446 799100
www.stdonats.com

The Plough and Harrow
Monknash
Nr Cowbridge
CF71 7QQ
Tel: 01656 890209
www.theploughmonknash.com

Glamorgan Heritage Coast Centre
Dunraven Park
Southerndown
CF32 0RP
Tel: 01656 880157
www.valeofglamorgan.gov.uk

Ogmore Farm Tea Room
Ogmore-by-Sea
Wales
Tel: 01656 656878

Ogmore Castle
In the care of CADW
www.cadw.wales.gov.uk

Ogmore Farm Riding Centre
Ogmore-by-Sea
Bridgend
CF32 0QP
Tel: 01656 880856
www.rideonthebeach.co.uk

Tipi Wales
8 Main Road
Ogmore-by-Sea
CF32 0PD
Tel: 0845 409 0771
www.tipiwales.co.uk

23. The Wreckers' Coast

OS Landranger Map Sheet 190,
Bude and Clovelly
OS Explorer Map Sheet 126,
Clovelly and Hartland

Rectory Farm and Tea Rooms
Crosstown
Morwenstow
Nr Bude
EX23 9SR
Tel: 01288 331251
www.rectory-tearooms.co.uk

The Old Vicarage B&B
Morwenstow
Bude
EX23 9SR
Tel: 01288 331369
www.rshawker.co.uk

The Bush Inn
Morwenstow
EX23 9SR
Tel: 01288 331242
www.bushinn-morwenstow.co.uk

Docton Mill
Lymebridge
Hartland
EX39 6EA
Tel: 01237 441369
www.doctonmill.co.uk

Hartland Quay Shipwreck Museum
Hartland
Bideford
EX39 6DU
Tel: 01288 331353

Hartland Abbey
Hartland
Bideford
EX39 6DT
Tel: 01237 441264/234
www.hartlandabbey.com

Hartland Point
Refreshment kiosk
www.thenorthdevonfocus.co.uk

Elmscott Youth Hostel
Elmscott
Hartland
Bideford
EX39 6ES
Tel: 01273 441276
www.yha.org.uk

24. Beach Break

OS Landranger Map Sheet 200,
Newquay and Bodmin
OS Explorer Map Sheet 106,
Newquay and Padstow

Constantine Bay Surf School
Constantine Bay
Padstow
PL28 8JJ
Tel: 01841 520250/07837
488083
constantinebaysurfschool.co.uk

Food For Thought Mobile Takeaway
Upper Beach Car Park
Harlyn Bay

Padstow Farm Shop
Trethillick Farm
Padstow
PL28 8HJ
Tel: 01841 533060
www.padstowfarmshop.co.uk

The Seafood Restaurant
Riverside
Padstow
PL28 8BY
Tel: 01841 532700
www.rickstein.com

Treyarnon Youth Hostel
Tregonnan
Treyarnon
Padstow
PL28 8JR
0845 371 9664
www.yha.org.uk

RNLI Padstow Lifeboat Station
Tel: 01841 520667
www.padstow-lifeboat.org.uk

Royal Cornwall Museum
River Street
Truro
TR1 2SJ
Tel: 01872 272205
www.royalcornwallmuseum.org.uk

Porthcothan Bay Stores
Porthcothan Bay
Padstow
PL28 8LW
Tel: 01841 520289
www.porthcothanbaystores.com

25. On the Towan

OS Landranger Map Sheet 203,
Land's End & Isles of Scilly
OS Explorer Map Sheet 102, Land's
End

RSPB Hayle Estuary
01736 711682
www.rspb.org.uk

Philps Bakery
1 East Quay
Hayle
TR27 4BJ
Tel: 01736 755661

Philps Shop and Bakery
1 Foundry Hill
Hayle
TR27 4HL
Tel: 01736 753302

Johnny's Café
50–51 Penpolol Terrace
Hayle
TR27 4BQ
Tel: 01736 755928

Sunset Surf Shop and Café
10 Gwithian Towans
Gwithian
TR27 5BT
Tel: 01736 752575
www.sunsetsurfshop.co.uk

The Jam Pot
Gwithian Towans
Gwithian
Nr Hayle
TR27 5BT

Godrevy Café
National Trust
Godrevy Towans
Gwithian
Hayle
TR27 5ED
Tel: 01736 757999
www.nationaltrust.org.uk

Sandsifter Bar and Restaurant
1 Godrevy Towans
Gwithian
Hayle
TR27 5ED
Tel: 01736 758384
www.sandsiftervenue.com

26. Ocean Drive

OS Landranger Map Sheet 203,
Land's End & Isles of Scilly
OS Explorer Map Sheet 102, Land's
End

Tinners Arms
Zennor
St Ives
TR26 3BY
Tel: 01736 796927
www.tinnersarms.com

Wayside Folk Museum
Zennor
St Ives
TR26 3DA
Tel: 01736 796945

Levant Mine and Beam Engine
National Trust
Trewellard
Pendeen, nr St Just
TR19 7SX
Tel: 01736 786156
www.nationaltrust.org.uk

Geevor Tin Mine
Pendeen
Land's End
TR19 7EW
Tel: 01736 788662
www.geevor.com

Plen-an-Gwary
St Just
Penzance
TR19 7LS
Tel: 01736 788906/01736
787189
www.plenproject.com

The Cook Book Café
4 Cape Cornwall Street
St Just
TR19 7JZ
Tel: 01736 787266
www.thecookbookstjust.co.uk

The Beach Restaurant
Sennen Cove
TR19 7BT
Tel: 01736 871191
www.thebeachrestaurant.com

27. Fish and Ships

OS Landranger Map Sheet 203,
Land's End & Isles of Scilly
OS Explorer Map Sheet 102, Land's
End

Newlyn Harbour Café
58 The Strand
Newlyn
TR18 5HW
Tel: 01736 363826

The Swordfish Inn
The Strand
Newlyn
TR18 5HN
Tel: 01736 362830
www.swordfishinn.co.uk

The Dolphin Inn
Jack Lane
Newlyn
TR18 5HZ
Tel: 01736 366253

The Star Inn
The Strand
Newlyn
TR18 5HW
Tel: 01736 368674

The Fishermen's Mission
Ship Institute
North Pier
Newlyn
TR18 5JB
Tel: 01736 363499
www.fishermensmission.org.uk

Newlyn Seafood Café
Newlyn
1 The Bridge
Penzance
TR18 5PZ
Tel: 01736 367199
www.newlynseafoodcafe.co.uk

Newlyn Art Gallery
New Road
Newlyn
TR18 5PZ
Tel: 01736 363715
www.newlynartgallery.co.uk

Jelberts Ices
New Road
Newlyn
TR18 5PZ

Penlee House Gallery and Museum
Morrab Road
Penzance
TR18 4HE
Tel: 01736 363625
www.penleehouse.org.uk

Porthcurno Telegraph Museum
Eastern House
Porthcurno
TR19 6JX
Tel: 01736 810966
www.porthcurno.org.uk

Minack Theatre and Visitor Centre
Porthcurno
TR19 6JU
Tel: 01736 810181
www.minack.com

The Cornish Range and Pender
Room
6 Chapel Street
Mousehole
TR19 6SB
Tel: 01736 731488
www.cornishrange.co.uk

The Ship Inn
South Cliff
Mousehole
Nr Penzance
TR19 6QX
Tel: 01736 731234
www.shipmousehole.co.uk

The Cove
Lamorna
Nr Penzance
TR19 6XH
Tel: 01736 731411
www.lamornacove.com

28. Getting to the Point

OS Landranger Map Sheet 203, Land's End & Isles of Scilly and 204, Truro and Falmouth
OS Explorer Map Sheet 103, The Lizard

Marconi Centre
Poldhu
Mullion
TR12 7JB
Tel: 01326 241656

The Polurrian Hotel
Mullion
TR12 7EN
Tel: 01326 240421
www.polurrianhotel.com

Kynance Cove Café and Cottage
Tregominion Barn
The Lizard
TR12 7PF
Tel: 01326 290436/01326 291117
www.kynancecovecafe.co.uk

The Lizard Lighthouse Heritage Centre
The Lizard
TR12 7NT
Tel: 01326 290202
www.lizardlighthouse.co.uk

Lizard Youth Hostel
Lizard Point
TR12 7NT
Tel: 0845 3719550
www.yha.org.uk

The National Seal Sanctuary
Gweek
TR12 6UG
Tel: 01326 221361
www.sealsanctuary.co.uk/corn1.html

Halzephron Inn
Gunwalloe
Helston
TR12 7QB
Tel: 01326 240406
www.halzephron-inn.co.uk

Cadgwith Cove Inn
Cadgwith
Nr Helston
TR12 7JX
Tel: 01326 290513
www.cadgwithcoveinn.com

29. Gardeners' Delight

OS Landranger Map Sheet 204, Truro and Falmouth
OS Explorer Map Sheet 103, The Lizard

Glendurgan Garden
National Trust
TR11 5JZ
Tel: 01326 250906
www.nationaltrust.org.uk

Trebah Garden
Mawnan Smith
Nr Falmouth
TR11 5JZ
Tel: 01326 252200
www.trebahgarden.co.uk

Trewithen Gardens
Grampound Road
Truro
TR2 4DD
Tel: 01726 883647
www.trewithengardens.co.uk.

Penjerrick Garden
Budock
Falmouth
TR11 5ED
Tel: 01872 870105
www.penjerrickgarden.co.uk

Carwinion House, Garden B&B
Carwinion Road
Mawnan Smith
TR11 5JA
Tel: 01326 250258
www.carwinion.co.uk

The Red Lion Inn
The Square
Mawnan Smith
Falmouth
TR11 5EP
Tel: 01326 250026

The Ferryboat Inn
Helford Passage
Nr Falmouth
TR11 5LB
Tel: 01326 250625
www.wrightbros.eu.com

Potager Garden and Glasshouse Café
High Cross
Constantine
Falmouth
TR11 5RF
Tel: 01326 341258
www.potagergardennursery.co.uk

30. Heads and Tails

OS Landranger Map Sheet 202, Torbay and South Dartmoor
OS Explorer Map Sheet OL20, South Devon

Prawle Point Lookout
Prawle Point
East Prawle
Tel: 01548 511259
www.nci-prawlepoint.org.uk

Pig's Nose Inn
East Prawle
Kingsbridge
TQ7 2BY
Tel: 01548 511209
www.pigsnose.co.uk

Start Point Lighthouse
Start Point is signposted from the village of Stokenham which is located on the A379 from Kingsbridge.
Tel: 01803 770606
www.trinityhouse.co.uk

The Fish Shack
Beesands
Kingsbridge
TQ7 2EH
Tel: 08450 550711/01548 581168
www.britanniashellfish.co.uk

Slapton Ley National Nature Reserve
Slapton
Kingsbridge
TQ7 2QP
Tel: 01548 580466
www.slnr.org.uk

South Allington House
Chivelstone
Kingsbridge
TQ7 2NB
Tel: 01548 511272
www.southallingtonhouse.co.uk

The Cricket Inn
Beesands
Kingsbridge
TQ7 2EN
Tel: 01548 580215
www.thecricketinn.com

Seabreeze Café
Torcross
Kingsbridge
TQ7 2TQ
Tel: 01548 580697
www.seabreezebreaks.com

Rocket House Café
Sea Front
Slapton Beach
Torcross
TQ7 2TQ
Tel: 01548 581096

Start Bay Inn
Torcross
Kingsbridge
TQ7 2TQ
Tel: 01548 580553
www.startbayinn.co.uk

The Tower Inn
Church Road
Slapton
TQ7 2PN

Tel: 01548 580216
www.thetowerinn.com

Mollie Tucker's Field
Marilyn Tucker
East Prawle
Kingsbridge
TQ7 2DF
Tel: 01548 511422

Anglican Community of the Glorious Ascension
The Priory
Lamacraft Farm
Start Point
Kingsbridge
TQ7 2NG
Visitors interested in staying at the Priory are asked to write to the brothers for details

31. Cliffhanger

OS Landranger Map Sheet 193, Taunton and Lyme Regis
OS Explorer Map Sheet 116, Lyme Regis and Bridport

The Jurassic Coast World Heritage Site
www.jurassiccoast.com

Bus service
CoastLINXX53
www.devon.gov.uk

Sladers Yard
West Bay
Bridport
DT6 4EL
Tel: 01308 459511
www.sladersyard.co.uk

Bridport Museum
The Coach House
Gundry Lane
Bridport
DT6 3RJ
Tel: 01308 458703
www.bridportmuseum.co.uk

Bridport Market
www.bridportmarket.co.uk

Girl's Own Store
30 South Street
Bridport
DT6 3NQ
01308 424474
www.girlsownstore.co.uk

Malabar Trading
33 South Street
Bridport
DT6 3NY
Tel: 01308 425734
www.malabartrading.com

The Riverside Restaurant
West Bay
Bridport
DT6 4EZ
Tel: 01308 422011
www.thefishrestaurant-westbay.co.uk

River Brit Rowing Boats
West Bay
Bridport
Tel: 01308 422998
www.cu4bnb.com

The Electric Palace
35 South Street
Bridport
DT6 3NY
Tel: 01308 428354
www.electricpalace.org.uk

Bridport Arts Centre
South Street
Bridport
DT6 3NR
Tel: 01308 424204
www.bridport-arts.com

Downhouse Farm Garden Café &
Working Organic Farm
Higher Eype
Bridport
DT6 6AH
Tel: 01308 421232
www.downhouse-farm.co.uk

The Bull Hotel
34 East Street
Bridport
DT6 3LF
Tel: 01308 422878
www.thebullhotel.co.uk

Hive Beach Café
Beach Road
Burton Bradstock
Nr Bridport
DT6 4RF
Tel: 01308 897070
www.hivebeachcafe.co.uk

Lyme Bay Rigid Inflatable Boat
Charter
Lyme Bay
Tel: 07971 258515
www.lymebayribcharter.co.uk

32. Set in Stone

OS Landranger Map Sheet 194,
Dorchester and Weymouth
OS Explorer Map Sheet OL15,
Purbeck and South Dorset

Portland Youth Hostel
Hardy House
Castletown
Portland
DT5 1AU

Tel: 0845 371 9339
www.yha.org.uk

Tout Quarry Sculpture Trust
The Drill Hall
Easton Lane
Isle of Portland
DT5 1BW
Tel: 01305 826736
www.learningstone.org

Portland Bird Observatory and
Field Centre
The Old Lower Light
Portland Bill
DT5 2JT
Tel: 01305 820553
www.portlandbirdobs.org.uk

Portland Museum
217 Wakeham
Portland
DT5 1HS
Tel: 01305 821804

Portland Castle
English Heritage
Castletown
Isle of Portland
DT5 1AZ
Tel: 01305 820539
www.english-heritage.org.uk

Quiddles Seafood Café
The Esplanade
Chesil Cove
Weymouth
DT5 1LN
Tel: 01305 820651

The Cove House Inn
91 Chiswell
Portland
DT5 1AW
Tel: 01305 820895
www.thecovehouseinn.co.uk

The Blue Fish Café and Restaurant
15-17a Chiswell
Portland
DT5 1AN
Tel: 08445 672359

The Lobster Pot
Portland Bill
Portland
DT5 2JT
Tel: 01305 820242
www.lobsterpotrestaurant
portland.co.uk

White Stones Café Gallery
13 Easton Street
Easton
Portland
DT5 1BS
Tel: 01305 860003
www.whitestonescafegallery.com

Chesil Beach Visitors Centre
Portland Beach Road
Portland
DT4 9XE
Tel: 01305 760579
www.chesilbeach.org

The Fleet Observer Ferry
Ferryman's Way
Wyke Regis
Weymouth
DT4 9YU
Tel: 01305 759692
Please visit the Chesil Visitors
Centre (www.chesilbeach.org) or
call to book.

Portland Bill Lighthouse tour and
visitor centre
Tel: 01305 820 495
www.trinityhouse.co.uk

33. Island of Adventure

OS Landranger Map Sheet 195,
Bournemouth and Purbeck
OS Explorer Map Sheet OL15,
Purbeck and South Dorset

The Art Hut
Pier Approach
Swanage
BH19 2LN
www.arthuts.co.uk

Purbeck House
91 High Street
Swanage
BH19 2LZ
Tel: 01929 422872
www.purbeckhousehotel.co.uk

Gee Whites Seafood Restaurant
1 The High Street
Swanage
BH19 2LN
Tel: 01929 425720
www.geewhites.co.uk

The Lookout Cafe
Durlston Country Park
Lighthouse Road
Swanage
BH19 2JL
Tel: 01929 424443
www.durlston.co.uk

Swanage Steam Railway
Station House
Swanage
BH19 1HB
Tel: 01929 425800
www.swanagerailway.co.uk

The Bird's Nest Buffet
Swanage Railway
Swanage Station
Swanage
BH19 1HB

Tel: 01929 475216
www.swanagerailway.co.uk

Corfe Castle
National Trust
Wareham
BH20 5EZ
Tel: 01929 481294
www.nationaltrust.org.uk

The Ginger Pop Shop
The Town House
The Square
Corfe Castle
BH20 5EZ
Tel: 01929 477214
www.gingerpop.co.uk

The Square and Compass Tavern
Worth Matravers
Swanage
BH19 3LF
Tel: 01929 439229

34. In Retreat

OS Landranger Map Sheet 199,
Eastbourne and Hastings
OS Explorer Map Sheet 123,
Eastbourne and Beachy Head

The Birling Gap Hotel and
Thatched Bar
Seven Sisters Cliffs
Birling Gap
East Dean
Eastbourne
BN20 0AB
Tel: 01323 423197
www.birlinggaphotel.co.uk

The Boathouse B&B
Birling Gap
East Dean
Eastbourne
BN20 0AB
Tel: 01323 423073

Countryside Centre
Beachy Head Road
Beachy Head
Eastbourne
BN20 7YA
Tel: 01323 737273
www.beachyhead.org

Frith & Little
The Green
East Dean
BN20 0BY
Tel: 01323 423631
www.frithandlittle.com

The Tiger Inn
The Green,
East Dean,
BN20 0DA
Tel: 01323 423209
beachhead.org.uk/the_tiger_inn_
info

The Hikers Rest Coffee and Gift
Shop
The Green
East Dean
BN20 0DR
Tel: 01323 423733
beachyhead.org.uk/hikers_rest

Seven Sisters Country Park Visitor
Centre
Exceat
Seaford
Tel: 01323 870280
www.sevensisters.org.uk

Seaford Head Local Nature Reserve
Seaford
Tel: 01323 871095

Seaford Museum and Heritage
Society
Martello Tower
Esplanade
Seaford
BN25 9BH
Tel: 01323 898222
www.seafordmuseum.co.uk

The Crypt Gallery
Church Street
Seaford
BN25 1HE
Tel: 01323 891461
www.cryptgallery.com

35. The Beach Boys

OS Landranger Map Sheet 199,
Eastbourne and Hastings
OS Explorer Map Sheet 124,
Hastings and Bexhill

West Hill Lift
George Street
Hastings
TN34 3EG
Tel: 01424 451113

East Hill Lift
Rock a Nore Road
Hastings
TN34 3AR
Tel: 01424 781040

Hastings Fishermen's Museum and
The Stade
Rock-a-Nore Road
Hastings
TN34 3DW
Tel: 01424 461446
www.hastingsfish.co.uk

Shirley Leaf and Petal Company
Working Leaf and Flower Museum
58a/b High Street
Hastings
TN34 3EN
Tel: 01424 427793

Electric Palace Cinema
39a High Street
Hastings
TN34 3ER
Tel: 01424 720393
www.electricpalacecinema.com

The White Rock Theatre
White Rock
Hastings
TN34 1JX
Tel: 01424 462280
www.whiterocktheatre.org.uk

Hastings Museum and Art Gallery
Johns Place
Bohemia Road
Hastings
TN34 1ET
Tel: 01424 451052
www.hmag.org.uk

St Leonards Gardens
South Lodge
Hastings

Judges Bakery
51 High Street
Hastings
TN34 3EN
Tel: 01424 722588
www.judgesbakery.com

Penbuckles Deli
50 High Street
Hastings
TN34 3EN
Tel: 01424 465050

First In Last Out Free House
14–15 High Street
Hastings
TN34 3EY
Tel: 01424 425079
www.thefilo.co.uk

Land of Green Ginger Café
45 High Street
Hastings
TN34 3EN
Tel: 01424 434191
www.landofgreenginger.org

West Hill Café
Castle Hill Road
Hastings
TN34 3RD
Tel: 01424 429636

QOL Café
39, Norman Road
St Leonards-on-Sea
TN38 0ED
www.thenormanroad.co.uk

St Clements Restaurant
3 Mercatoria
St Leonards-on-Sea
TN38 0EB
Tel: 01424 200355
www.stclementsrestaurant.co.uk

The Cavalier House
1 Pleasant Row
Hastings
TN34 3AS
Tel: 01424 428944
www.thecavalierhouse.webs.com

Black Rock House
10 Stanley Road
Hastings
TN34 1UE
Tel: 01424 438448
www.hastingsaccommodation.com

36. Go Native

OS Landranger Map Sheet 179,
Canterbury and East Kent
OS Explorer Map Sheet 150,
Canterbury & the Isle of Thanet

Old Neptune Pub
Marine Terrace
Whitstable
CT5 1EJ
Tel. 01227 272262
www.neppy.co.uk

Favourite Oyster Yawl
Island Wall
Whitstable
www.favourite.org.uk

The Tudor Tea Rooms
29 Harbour Street
Whitstable
CT5 1AH
Tel. 01227 273167
www.tudortearooms.co.uk

Whitstable Museum and Gallery
Oxford Street
Whitstable
CT5 1DB
Tel: 01227 276998
www.whitstable-museum.co.uk

The Royal Native Oyster Stores
Restaurant
(The Whitstable Oyster Company
Ltd)
Horsebridge
Whitstable
CT5 1BU
Tel: 01227 276856
www.oysterfishery.co.uk

Whitstable Fish Market
South Quay
The Harbour
Whitstable
CT5 1AB
Tel: 01227 771245

West Whelks
West Quay
Whitstable Harbour
CT5 1AB
Tel: 01227 266873
www.westwhelks.co.uk

Thames Barge, Greta
Tel: 07711 657919
www.greta1892.co.uk

Hotel Continental
29 Beach Walk
Whitstable
CT5 2BP
Tel: 01227 280280
www.hotelcontinental.co.uk

The Whitstable Brewery Bar
East Quay
The Harbour
Whitstable
CT5 2BP
Tel: 01622 851007
www.hotelcontinental.co.uk

Beach Huts
42c Southcote Road
Bournemouth
BH1 3SR
01202 315437
www.beach-huts.com

David Brown's Deli
28a Harbour Street
Whitstable
CT5 1AH
Tel: 01227 274507

Frank
65 Harbour Street
Whitstable
CT5 1AG
Tel: 01227 262500
www.frankworks.eu

Jane at Graham Greener
27 Harbour Street
Whitstable
CT5 1AH
Tel: 01227 277100
www.grahamgreener.com

The Pearson's Arms
The Horsebridge
Sea Wall
Whitstable
CT5 1BT
Tel: 01227 272005
www.pearsonsarms.com

The Cheese Box
60 Harbour Street
Whitstable
CT5 1AG
Tel: 01227 273711
www.thecheesebox.co.uk

Tea & Times
36A High Street
Whitstable
CT5 1BQ
Tel: 01227 262639

Wheelers Oyster Bar
8 High Street
Whitstable
CT5 1BQ
Tel: 01227 273311

The Sportsman Pub
Faversham Road
Seasalter
Whistable
CT5 4BP
Tel: 01227 273370
www.thesportsmanseasalter.co.uk

37. Yow Boys and Whoopers

OS Landranger Map Sheet 168,
Colchester
OS Explorer Map Sheet 176,
Blackwater Estuary and 184,
Colchester

For vital information on tides and
safe times to cross the Strood
Causeway to Mersea, see
www.mersea-island.com

Dengie Camra Beer Festival
www.dengiecamra.org.uk

Barge matches
www.sailingbargeassociation.co.uk

Maldon Carnival
www.maldon-carnival.co.uk

Maeldune Heritage Centre
Plume Building
Market Hill
Maldon
CM9 4RL
Tel: 01621 851628
www.aboutbritain.com/Maeldune-
HeritageCentre.htm

Basin Pleasure Boats
Located on the canal at
Daisy Meadow Car Park
Heybridge Basin
Maldon
For bookings or more information
please call Mark on 07835 657462
www.basinpleasureboats.co.uk

The Queens Head
The Hythe

Maldon
CM9 5HN
Tel: 01621 854 112
www.thequeensheadmaldon.co.uk

West Mersea Oyster Bar
Coast Road
West Mersea
Colchester
CO5 8LT
Tel: 01206 381600
www.westmerseaoysterbar.co.uk

The Company Shed
129 Coast Road
West Mersea
Colchester
CO5 8PA
Tel: 01206 382700

Mersea Island Vineyard, The
Courtyard Café and Vineyard Shop
Rewsalls Lane
East Mersea
Colchester
CO5 8SX
Tel: 01206 385900
www.merseawine.com

Cudmore Grove Country Park
Bromans Lane
East Mersea
CO5 8UE
Tel: 01206 383868
www.essexcc.gov.uk

Foot Ferry
www.brightlingseaharbour.org/
ferry.html

The Lock Tea Room
Basin Road
Heybridge Basin
Maldon
CM9 4RS
Tel: 01621 854466
www.trooms.com

The Coast Inn
108 Coast Road
Mersea Island
CO5 8NA
Tel: 01206 383568
The Jolly Sailor
Hythe Quay
Church St
Maldon
CM9 5HP
Tel: 01621 853463
www.jollysailor.com

38. Life and Sole

OS Landranger Map Sheet 156,
Saxmundham
OS Explorer Map Sheet 231,
Southwold and Bungay

Southwold Lighthouse Visitor
Centre
Tel: 01502 722576

Adnams Brewery
Adnams Cellar and Kitchen Store
4 Drayman Square
Victoria Street
Southwold
IP18 6GB
Tel: 01502 727244
www.adnams.co.uk

The Serena Hall Gallery
16 Queen Street
Southwold
IP18 6EQ
Tel: 01502 723887
www.serenahallgallery.co.uk

CRAFTCO
40a High Street
Southwold
IP18 6AE
Tel: 01502 723211
www.craftco.co.uk

Cornucopia Antiques
Blackmill Road
Town Centre
Southwold
IP18 6AQ
Tel: 01502 725146

Puritan Values Ltd
Dome Art and Antiques Centre
Southwold Business Centre
St Edmunds Road
Southwold
IP18 6BZ
Tel: 01502 722211
www.puritanvalues.co.uk

The Amber Shop & Museum
15 Market Place
Southwold
IP18 6EA
Tel: 01502 723394
www.ambershop.co.uk

Electric Picture Palace
Blackmill Road
Southwold
IP18 6AQ
Tel: 07815 769565

Southwold Pier
North Parade
Southwold
IP18 6BN
Tel: 01502 722105
www.southwoldpier.co.uk

Alfred Corry Museum
Ferry Road
Southwold
IP18 6NG
Tel: 01502 723200

Sailors' Reading Room
East Cliff
Southwold
IP18 6JJ

The Pit Stop Café and Tennis Courts
The Common
Southwold
IP18 6TB
Tel: 07887 901027
www.thepitstopcafe.com

Southwold to Walberswick Ferry
www.explorewalberswick.co.uk

Open Crabbing Championship
www.walberswick.ws/crabbing

Southwold Boating Lakes and Café
North Parade
Southwold
Tel: 07939 410182

Casa Mia Italian Piano Bar
53 Ferry Road
Southwold
IP18 6HQ
Tel: 01502 724416

The Swan Hotel
Market Place
Southwold
IP18 6EG
Tel: 01502 722186
www.hotels.adnams.co.uk/the-
swan

The Crown Hotel
High Street
Southwold
IP18 6DP
Tel: 01502 722275
www.hotels.adnams.co.uk/the-
crown

The Lord Nelson
East Street
Southwold
IP18 6EJ
Tel: 01502 722079
www.thelordnelsonsouthwold.co.uk

The Harbour Inn
Blackshore
Southwold
IP18 6TA
Tel: 01502 722381

Coastal Voyager
Southwold Harbour
Either visit the Coastal Voyager
Office at the Harbour or ring Mar-
cus Gladwell on Tel: 07887 525082
www.coastalvoyager.co.uk

Harbour Marine Services Ltd
Blackshore,
Southwold Harbour
Southwold
IP18 6TA
Tel: 01502 724721
www.southwoldharbour.co.uk

The Parish Lantern Tea Room
The Green
Walberswick
IP18 6TT
Tel: 01502 723173

The Bell
Ferry Road
Walberswick
IP18 6TN
Tel: 01502 723109
www.hotels.adnams.co.uk/the-bell

The Anchor
Walberswick
IP18 6UA
Tel: 01502 722112
www.anchoratwalberswick.com

Tinkers
The Green
Walberswick
IP18 6TT
Tel: 01502 722337

39. Wild Goose Chase

OS Landranger Map Sheet 132,
North West Norfolk and 133,
North East Norfolk
OS Explorer Map Sheet 251,
Norfolk Coast Central

Holkham National Nature Reserve
Tel: 01328 711183
www.holkham.co.uk/naturereserve

The Wells Harbour Railway
www.wellsharbourrailway.com

The Wells & Walsingham Light
Railway
Wells-next-the-Sea,
NR23 1QB
Tel: 01328 711630
www.wellswalsinghamrailway.co.uk

Big Blue Sky
Warham Road
Wells-next-the-Sea
NR23 1QA
Tel: 01328 712023
www.bigbluesky.uk.com

Blakeney National Nature Reserve
National Trust
Tel: 01263 740241
www.nationaltrust.org.uk

Cley Marshes Norfolk Wildlife Trust
Visitor Centre

Coast Road
Cley
NR25 7SA
Tel: 01263 740008
www.norfolkwildlifetrust.org.uk

Cookies Crab Shop
The Green
Salthouse
Holt
NR25 7AJ
Tel: 01263 740352
www.salthouse.org.uk

Dun Cow Inn
The Dun Cow
Coast Road
Salthouse
NR25 7XA
Tel: 01263 740467
www.theduncow-salthouse.co.uk

Weybourne station (Poppy Line)
www.nnrailway.co.uk/
weybourne_station.php

Sea
Watermill House
Beach Lane
Weybourne
Tel: 01263 588464

Holkham Hall
Wells-next-the-Sea
NR23 1AB
Tel: 01328 710227
www.holkham.co.uk

Marsh Larder and Tearooms
Park Road
Holkham
Wells-next-the-Sea
NR23 1RG
Tel: 01328 711285

Adnams Wine Cellar and Kitchen
Store
The Old Stable House
Park Road
Holkham
Wells-next-the-Sea
NR23 1AB
Tel: 01328 711714

The Real Ale Shop
Branthill Farm
Wells-next-the-Sea
NR23 1SB
Tel: 01328 710810
www.therealaleshop.co.uk/norfolk

Stiffkey Red Lion
44 Wells Road
Stiffkey
NR23 1AJ
Tel: 01328 830 552
www.stiffkey.com

Wiveton Hall Café
Holt
NR25 7TE
Tel: 01263 740525
www.wivetonhall.co.uk

Blakeney Hotel
Blakeney
Nr Holt
NR25 7NE
Tel: 01263 740797
www.blakeney-hotel.co.uk

Blakeney Deli
30 High Street
Blakeney
NR25 7AL
Tel: 01263 740939
www.blakeneydeli.co.uk

Cley Windmill and B&B
Cley-next-the-Sea
Holt
NR25 7RP
Tel: 01263 740209
www.cleymill.co.uk

West Cottage Café
New Road
Cley-next-the-Sea
NR25 7RA

Picnic Fayre Deli
The Old Forge
Cley-next-the-Sea
NR25 7AP
Tel: 01263 740587
www.picnic-fayre.co.uk

40. Take Flight

OS Landranger Map Sheet 101,
Scarborough
OS Explorer Map Sheet 301,
Scarborough, Bridlington &
Flamborough Head

Flamborough Head Lighthouse
Visitor Centre
Tel: 01262 673769

Sewerby Hall and Gardens
Church Lane
Sewerby
Bridlington
YO15 1EA
Tel: 01262 673769
www.eastriding.gov.uk/sewerby

Bempton Cliffs RSPB Bird Reserve
Tel: 01262 851179
www.rspb.org.uk

RSPB Seabird cruises
Tel: 01262 850959
bempton.cruises@rspb.org.uk

Ethical Catering Outdoors
In the car park at Bempton Cliffs

Thornwick Bay Café
Thornwick Bay
Flamborough
Bridlington
YO15 1BD

41. The Coast is Clear

OS Landranger Map Sheet 94,
Whitby and Esk Dale
OS Explorer Map Sheet OL27,
North York Moors

The Bay Hotel
The Dock
Robin Hood's Bay
YO22 4SJ
Tel: 01947 880278

Old Coastguard Station
Robin Hood's Bay
Whitby
YO22 4SJ
Tel: 01947 885900

Robin Hood's Bay Museum
Fisherhead
Whitby
YO22 4TQ
Tel: 01947 881252
museum.rhbay.co.uk

Swell Café Bar, Gift Shop and
Cinema
The Old Chapel
Chapel Street
Robin Hood's Bay
Whitby
YO22 4SQ
Tel: 01947 880180
www.swell.org.uk

Boggle Hole Youth Hostel
Mill Beck
Flyingthorpe
Whitby
YO22 4UQ
Tel: 01947 880 352
www.yha.org.uk

The Laurel Inn
Bay Bank
Robin Hood's Bay
Whitby
YO22 4SE
Tel: 01947 880400

Raven Hall Country House Hotel
Ravenscar
Scarborough
YO13 0ET
Tel: 01723 870353
www.ravenhall.co.uk

Wayfarer Bistro
Station Road
Robin Hood's Bay
Whitby
YO22 4RL
Tel: 01947 880240
www.wayfarerbistro.co.uk

42. Downtime

OS Landranger Map Sheet 94,
Whitby and Esk Dale
OS Explorer Map Sheet OL27,
North York Moors

Captain Cook and Staithes Heritage
Centre
High Street
Staithes
Near Whitby
TS13 5BQ
Tel: 01947 841454
www.captaincookatstaithes.co.uk

Sea Drift Café
Seaton Garth
Staithes
TS13 5DH
Tel: 01947 841345

Wits End Cafe
Lythe Bank Bottom
Sandsend
Whitby
YO21 3TG
Tel: 01947 893658
www.witsendcafe.co.uk

Bridge Cottage Café Tea Room
East Row
Sandsend
Whitby
YO21 3SU
Tel: 01947 893111
www.bridgecottagecafe.co.uk

Sandside Café
East Row
Sandsend
Whitby
YO21 3SU
Tel: 01947 893916
www.sandsidecafe.co.uk

Endeavour Restaurant
1 High Street
Staithes
TS13 5BH
Tel: 01947 840825
www.endeavour-restaurant.co.uk

The Fox and Hounds
Goldsborough
Whitby
YO21 3RX
Tel: 01947 893372
www.foxandhounds
goldsborough.co.uk

Sandside Beach Café
Runswick Bay
Sandside Café
Runswick Bay
Tel: 01947 840224
www.sandsidecafe.co.uk

Estbek House
East Row
Sandsend
Whitby
YO21 3SU
Tel: 01947 893424
www.estbekhouse.co.uk

For fishing trips out of Staithes,
contact Sean Baxter. Sean also offers
guided walks from Staithes to Port
Mulgrave.
Tel: 01947 840278
www.sea-angling-staithes.co.uk

For residential weekend courses
and Dame Laura Knight studio and
cottage:
Staithes Art School
Staithes Gallery
High Street
Staithes
TS13 5BH
01947 841840
www.staithesgallery.co.uk

43. And They're Off!

OS Landranger Map Sheet 93,
Middlesbrough and 94 Whitby and
Esk Dale
OS Explorer Map Sheet 306,
Middlesbrough and Hartlepool

Redcar Racecourse
Redcar
TS10 2BY
Tel: 01642 484068
www.redcarracing.co.uk

The Regent Cinema
Newcomen Terrace
Redcar
TS10 1AU
Tel: 01642 482094
www.regentredcar.co.uk

RNLI Zetland Museum
The Esplanade
Redcar
TS10 3AH
Tel: 01642 494311
www.rnli.org.uk

Winkies Castle
162 Marske High Street
Marske-by-the-Sea
TS11 7NB
Tel: 01642 775086
www.winkiescastle.co.uk

Ship Inn
Saltburn-by-the-Sea
Cleveland
TS12 1HF
Tel: 01287 622361

Stray Café
Coast Road
Redcar
TS10 3RA

Vista Mar
Saltburn Bank
Saltburn-by-the-Sea
TS12 1HH
Tel: 01287 623771
www.vista-mar.com

Seaview Takeaway
Lower Promenade
Saltburn-by-the-Sea

Saltburn Miniature Railway
Tel: 07813 153975
Ticket price information: 07977
384724

Saltburn Valley Gardens and
Woodland Centre
Valley Gardens
Saltburn-by-the-Sea
TS12 1GG
Tel: 01287 622408

44. North and South

OS Landranger Map Sheet 88,
Newcastle upon Tyne
OS Explorer Map Sheet 316,
Newcastle upon Tyne

St Mary's Island and Curry's Point
Nature Reserve
St Mary's Island
Whitley Bay
NE26 4RS
Tel: 0191 200 8650

St Mary's Lighthouse
St Mary's Island
Whitley Bay
NE26 4RS
Tel: 0191 200 8650

Tynemouth Park, Boating Lake and
Longsands Café
61 Front Street
Tynemouth
North Shields
NE30 4BT
Tel: 0191 258 7593
www.tynemouthpark.com

The Grand Hotel
Grand Parade
Tynemouth
North Shields
NE30 4ER
Tel: 0191 293 6666
www.grandhotel-uk.com

The Turks Head Hotel
41 Front Street
Tynemouth
North Shields
NE30 4DZ
Tel: 0191 257 6547

Tynemouth Priory and Castle
English Heritage
Benebalcrag
North Shields
NE30 4BZ
Tel: 0191 257 1090
www.english-heritage.org.uk

Shields Ferry
South Shields Ferry Landing
Ferry Street
Off River Drive
South Shields
NE33 1JR
Tel: 0191 454 8183
www.nexus.org.uk

Arbeia Fort and Museum
Baring Street
South Shields
NE33 2BB
Tel: 0191 456 1369
www.twmuseums.org.uk/arbeia

Marsden Grotto
Coast Road
South Shields
NE34 7BS
Tel: 0191 455 6060

Souter Lighthouse
National Trust
Coast Road
Whitburn
Sunderland
SR6 7NH
Tel: 0191 529 3161
www.nationaltrust.org.uk

Rendezvous Café
Dukes Walk
Northern Promenade
Whitley Bay
NE26 1TP
Tel: 0191 252 5548
www.rendezvouswhitleybay.com

Boardwalk Café
Watts Slope
Whitley Bay
NE26 1BQ
Tel: 0191 251 1988
theboardwalkwhitleybay.com

Longsands Café
www.tynemouthpark.com/cafe.
html

Crusoe's Café
Longsands Beach
Tynemouth
North Shields
NE30 4BY
Tel: 0191 296 4152
www.crusoescafe.co.uk

Sidney's Restaurant
Percy Park Road
North Shields
NE30 4LZ
Tel: 0191 257 8500

The Deli Around the Corner
61 Hotspur Street
Tynemouth
North Shields
NE30 4FF
Tel: 0191 259 0086
www.thedeliaroundthecorner.co.uk

45. Amazing Grace

OS Landranger Map Sheets 75,
Berwick upon-Tweed and 81,
Alnwick & Morpeth
OS Explorer Map Sheets 340, Holy
Island & Bamber and 332, Alnick &
Amble

Bamburgh Castle
Bamburgh
NE69 7DF
Tel: 01668 214515
www.bamburghcastle.com

Grace Darling Museum
Radcliffe Road
Bamburgh
NE69 7AB
Tel: 01668 214910
www.rnli.org.uk/gracedarling

Boat Trips
www.farneislandsboattrips.co.uk
www.farne-islands.com

Dunstanburgh Castle
The National Trust and English
Heritage
Craster
Alnwick
NE66 3TT
Tel: 01665 576231
www.nationaltrust.org.uk

The Ship Inn
Low Newton-by-the-Sea
Alnwick
NE66 3EL
Tel: 01665 576262
www.shipinnnewton.co.uk

The Olde Ship Hotel
Seahouses
NE68 7RD
Tel: 01665 720200
www.seahouses.co.uk

Swallow Fish Smokehouse
Fisherman's Kitchen
2 South Street
Seahouses
NE68 7RB
Tel: 01665 721052
www.swallowfish.co.uk

The Jolly Fisherman Inn
Haven Hill
Craster
Alnwick
NE66 3TR
Tel: 01665 576218

Robson & Sons
Craster
NE66 3TR
Tel: 01665 576223
www.kipper.co.uk

Mick Oxley Gallery
The Joiners Shop
17 Haven Hill
Craster
NE66 3TR
Tel: 01665 671082
www.mickoxley.com

46. Sea Change

OS Landranger Map Sheet 67,
Duns, Dunbar & Eyemouth
OS Explorer Map Sheet 346,
Berwick-upon-Tweed

St Abb's Head National Nature
Reserve
National Trust for Scotland
Northfield
Eyemouth
TD14 5QF
Tel : 0844 4932256
www.nts.org.uk

St Abbs and Eyemouth Voluntary
Marine Reserve
Rangers' Office
Northfield
St Abbs
TD14 5QF
Tel: 018907 71443
www.marine-reserve.co.uk

Coldingham Second-Hand
Bookshop
Coldingham
TD14 5TS
www.coldinghambookshop.com

St Vedas Hotel, Surf Shop and Beach
Café
Coldingham Sands

TD14 5PA
Tel: 01890 771679
www.stvedas.co.uk

Springbank Cottage
The Harbour
St Abbs
TD14 5PW
Tel: 01890 771477
www.springbankcottage.co.uk

Lough's Home Bakery
14 High Street
Eyemouth
TD14 5EU
Tel: 01890 750286

Crossing the Bar Bookshop
Market Place
Eyemouth
TD14 5HE
Tel: 01890 751997

Eyemouth Museum
Auld Kirk
Market Place
Eyemouth
TD14 5HE
Tel: 01890 750678
www.eyemouthmuseum.org.uk

World of Boats
Eyemouth Marine Centre
Harbour Road
Eyemouth
TD14 5SS
Tel: 01890 751020
www.worldofboats.org

47. Birdland

OS Landranger Map Sheets 66, Edinburgh and 67, Duns, Dunbar &
Eyemouth
OS Explorer Map Sheet 351, Dunbar and North Berwick

Boat Trips on Sula II with Chris Marr
and Pat Macaulay
See the board at the harbour for
sailings or phone
Tel: 01620 892838
www.sulaboattrips.co.uk

Seaholm B&B
Lorena Peressini
24 Melbourne Road
North Berwick
EH39 4LB
Tel: 01620 895150
www.seaholm.co.uk

The Scottish Seabird Centre
The Harbour
North Berwick
EH39 4SS
Tel: 01620 890202
www.seabird.org

Osteria Restaurant
71 High Street
North Berwick
EH39 4HG
Tel: 01620 890589
www.osteria-no1.co.uk

Tyninghame Smithy
Main Street
Tyninghame
Dunbar
EH42 1XL
Tel: 01620 860581

Lockett Bros. Wine and Whisky
Specialist
133 High Street
North Berwick
EH39 4HB
Tel: 01620 890799
www.lockettbros.co.uk

Tantallon Castle
East Lothian EH39 5PN
www.historic-scotland.gov.uk

48. The Magic Kingdom

OS Landranger Map Sheet 59,
St Andrews
OS Explorer Map Sheet 371, St
Andrews and East Fife

Crail Golfing Society (Balcomie
Course)
Balcomie Clubhouse
Crail
KY10 3XN
Tel: 01333 450686
www.crailgolfingsociety.co.uk

Crail Museum and Heritage Centre
62-64 Marketgate
Crail
KY10 3TL
Tel: 01333 450869
www.crailmuseum.org.uk

Crail Pottery
75 Nethergate
Crail
KY10 3TX
Tel: 01333 451212
www.crailpottery.com

Scottish Fisheries Museum
St Ayles
Harbourhead
Anstruther
KY10 3AB
Tel: 01333 310628
www.scotfishmuseum.org

Crail Harbour Gallery and Tearoom
Shoregate
Crail
KY10 3SU
Tel: 01333 451896
www.crailharbourgallery.co.uk

Pittenweem Arts Festival
www.pittenweemartsfestival.co.uk

St Fillan's Cave
Cove Wind
Pittenweem.
Key available from: Cocoa Tree Café
– see below

The Cocoa Tree Shop and Café
9 High St
Pittenweem
KY10 2LA
Tel: 01333 311495
www.thecocoatreeshop.com

Anstruther Fish Bar
42–44 Shore St
Anstruther
KY10 3AQ
Tel: 01333 310518
www.anstrutherfishbar.co.uk

Flemings Fish and Chips
4 Shore St
Anstruther
KY10 3EA
Tel: 01333 310106

The Dreel Tavern
16 High St West
Anstruther
KY10 3DL
Tel: 01333 310727

The Cellar
East Green
Anstruther
KY10 3AA
Tel: 01333 310378
www.cellaranstruther.co.uk

Pittenweem Fish and Chip Bar
5 High St
Pittenweem
KY10 2LA
Tel: 01333 311258

AJ Nicholson sweet shop and ice
cream
17 Mid Shore
Pittenweem
Tel: 01333 310812

Harbour Howff Community Café
6 Station Road
St Monans
Anstruther
KY10 2BJ
Tel: 01333 730901

Feather Your Nest
10 Station Road

St Monans
Anstruther
KY10 2BJ
Tel: 01333 730033

The Seafood Restaurant
16 West End
St Monans
Anstruther
KY10 2BX
Tel: 01333 730327
www.theseafoodrestaurant.com

Sangster's
51 High Street
Elie
KY9 1BZ
Tel: 01333 331001
www.sangsters.co.uk

Station Buffet Bar
29 High Street
Elie
Leven
KY9 1BZ
Tel: 01333 330972

The Ship Inn
The Toft
Elie
KY9 1DT
Tel: 01333 330246
www.ship-elie.com

The Golf Tavern
5 Links Road
Earlsferry
KY9 1AW
Tel: 01333 330610

Kingdom of Fife Millennium Cycle
Way
www.fifedirect.org.uk/fife-
cycleways

Fife Coastal Path
www.fifecoastalpath.co.uk

49. Making a Splash

OS Landranger Map Sheet 45,
Stonehaven and Banchory
OS Explorer Map Sheet 396,
Stonehaven, Inverbervie & Lau-
rencekirk

Stonehaven Open-Air Swimming
Pool
Queen Elizabeth Park
Stonehaven
AB39 2RD
Tel: 01569 762134
www.stonehavenopenairpool.co.uk

The Carron Art Deco Restaurant
Cameron Street
Stonehaven
AB39 2HS
Tel: 01569 760460
www.carron-restaurant.co.uk

Dunottar Castle
Dunecht
Westhill
AB32 7AW
Tel: 01330 860223
www.dunnottarcastle.co.uk

The Boat House Café
The Old Pier
Stonehaven
AB39 2JU
Tel: 01569 764666

Marine Hotel
9–10 Shore Head
Stonehaven
AB39 2JY
Tel: 01569 762155
www.marinehotelstonehaven.co.uk

The Ship Inn Restaurant
5 Shorehead
Stonehaven
AB39 2JY
Tel: 01569 762617
www.shipinnstonehaven.com

BayView B&B
Beachgate Lane
Stonehaven
AB39 2BD
Tel: 01569 766933
www.bayviewbandb.co.uk

50. Fishy Business

OS Landranger Map Sheet 29, Banff
and Huntly
OS Explorer Map Sheet 425, Huntly
and Cullen

Portsoy Salmon Bothy
Links Rd
Portsoy
AB45 2SS
Tel: 01261 842951
On the third Friday of every month
there is a live folk music show.
Bring your own refreshments.
www.salmonbothy.org.uk

Portsoy Ice Cream
24 Seafield Street
Portsoy
AB45 2QT
Tel: 01261 842279

Cullen Ice Cream Shop
Seafield Street
Cullen

Cullen Bay Hotel
Cullen
Moray
AB56 4XA
Tel: 01542 840432
www.cullenbayhotel.co.uk

Cullen Golf Club
The Links
Cullen
Moray
AB56 4WB
Tel: 01542 840685
www.cullengolfclub.co.uk

The Shore Inn
The Old Harbour
Church St
Portsoy
AB45 2QR
Tel: 01261 842831

Portsoy Caravan Park
The Links
Portsoy
AB45 2RQ
Tel: 01261 842695

Sandend Caravan Park
Portsoy
AB5 2UA
Tel: 01261 842660

Portsoy Marble Shop
Shorehead
Portsoy
AB45 2PB
Tel: 01261 842404

The Scottish Traditional Boat
Festival
The Salmon Bothy
Links Road
Portsoy
AB45 2SS
Tel: 01261 842951
www.stbf.bizland.com

Bookends Antiquarian & Second-
Hand Books
21 Seafield Street
Portsoy
AB45 2QT
Tel: 01261 842262

The Curiosity Shoppe
23 Seafield Street
Portsoy
AB45 2QT
Tel: 01261 843806
www.curiosityshoppe.plus.com

Soy Kilts
54 Seafield Street
Portsoy
AB45 2QT
Tel: 01261 843303
www.soykilts.co.uk

Findlater Castle
Grid Reference: NJ541672

51. On the Black Isle

OS Landranger Map Sheets 21,
Dornoch & Alness and 27, Nairn &
Forres
OS Explorer Map Sheet 432, Black
Isle

Cromarty Courthouse Museum
Church Street
Cromarty
IV11 8XA
Tel: 01381 600418
www.cromarty-courthouse.org.uk

WDCS Dolphin and Seal Centre
North Kessock
IV1 3UB
Tel: 01163 731866
www.wdcs.org

Fortrose and Rosemarkie Golf Club
Ness Road East
Fortrose
IV10 8SE
Tel: 01381 620529
www.fortrosegolfclub.co.uk

Rosemarkie Beach Café
Rosemarkie

The Emporium Bookshop
11–13 High Street
Cromarty
IV11 8UZ
Tel: 01381 600551
www.cromartyemporium.co.uk

Cromarty Pottery
Shore Street
Cromarty
IV11 8XI
Tel: 01381 600701
www.cromarty-pottery.com

Sutor Creek
21 Bank Street
Cromarty
IV11 8YE
Tel: 01381 600855
www.sutorcreek.co.uk

Crofters Bistro
11 Marine Terrace
Rosemarkie
IV10 8UL
Tel: 01381 620844
www.croftersbistro.co.uk

The Anderson Restaurant and Bar
Union St
Fortrose
IV10 8TD
Tel: 01381 620236
www.theanderson.co.uk

Black Isle Brewery
Munlochy
IV8 8NZ
Tel: 01463 811871
www.blackislebrewery.com

Glen Ord Distillery
Muir of Ord
IV6 7UJ
Tel: 01463 872004
www.discovering-distilleries.com
Because of maintenance require-
ments it's not always possible to
tour the distillery. Please call in ad
vance to avoid disappointment.

Hugh Miller Museum and
Birthplace Cottage
Church Street
Cromarty
IV11 8XA
Tel: 01381 600245
www.nts.org.uk

The Groam House Museum
High Street
Rosemarkie
IV10 8UF
Tel: 01381 620961
www.groamhouse.org.uk

Cromarty Arts Trust
Ardyne
Bank Street
Cromarty
IV11 8YE
Tel: 01381 600354
www.cromartyartstrust.org.uk

52. Royal and Ancient

OS Landranger Map Sheet 21,
Dornoch & Alness
OS Explorer Map Sheet 438,
Dornoch & Tain

Tain Through Time
Tower Street
Tain
IV19 1DY
Tel: 01862 894089
www.tainmuseum.org.uk

R. Macleod & Son
The Scottish Gun and Rifle Dealer
14 Lamington Street
Tain
IV19 1AA
Tel: 01862 892171
www.rmacleod.co.uk

Glasstorm Contemporary Glass
Studio
2 Chapel Street
Tain
IV19 1EL
Tel: 01862 893189
www.glasstorm.com

Tain Golf Club
Chapel Road
Tain
IV19 1JE
Tel: 01862 892314
www.tain-golfclub.co.uk

Tarbat Discovery Centre
Tarbatness Road
Portmahomack
Tain
IV20 1YA
Tel: 01862 871351
www.tarbat-discovery.co.uk

Tarbat Ness Lighthouse
Near Portmahomack
www.nlb.org.uk

Glenmorangie Distillery
Tain
IV19 1PZ
Tel: 01862 892477
www.glenmorangie.com

Balblair Scotch Whisky Distillery
Edderton
Tain
IV19 1LB
Tel: 01862 821273
www.balblair.com
Tours by appointment only.

Royal Dornoch Golf Club
Golf Road
Dornoch
IV25 3LW
Tel: 01862 810219
www.royaldornoch.com

Dornoch Cathedral
The Manse
Cnoc-an Lobht
Dornoch
IV25 3HN
Tel: 01862 810296
www.dornoch-cathedral.com

Country Interiors
The Square
Castle Street
Dornoch
IV25 3SD
Tel: 01862 811644

Jail Dornoch
The Square
Castle Street
Dornoch
IV25 3SD
Tel: 01862 810555
www.jail-dornoch.com

ANTA
Fearn
Tain
IV20 1XW
Tel: 01862 832477
www.anta.co.uk

The Oystercatcher
Main Street
Portmahomack
IV20 1YB
Tel: 01862 871560
www.the-oystercatcher.co.uk

Kyleview House B&B
Evelix Road
Dornoch
IV25 3HR
Tel: 01862 810999
www.kyleviewhouse.co.uk

Dornoch Castle Hotel
Castle Street
Dornoch
IV25 3SD
Tel: 01862 810216
www.dornochcastlehotel.com

List of Photographs

I ♥ MY BUS

Acknowledgements

Big thanks to Rick, Jill and Viv at The Seafood Restaurant for all your support over the years. To super Sheila, take a bow. To editors Davina and Louisa, designers David and Toby, Michael the map man and the team at Virgin, we are most grateful. To Ian, Lanie and Anthony, thanks for your help from the start.

To the terrific people we have encountered along the way and the lifetime friends we have made, thanks and see you soon.